'An enthralling hip hop coming-of-a[...] love. *Hip Hop & Hymns* is a raw & c[...] presents & histories – African, Australian & American – the harmonies & dissonances in what our nows & thens share & what they don't. Throughout, Mawunyo remains devotedly tethered to hip hop culture, music, faith & family, with hopes of arriving at a life in which she can ultimately "experience love without having to survive it". It's quite a trip.'

> – **A.D. Carson**, Assistant Professor of Hip Hop and
> the Global South at the University of Virginia,
> and award-winning hip hop artist

'A global read.'

> – **Rodney O**, KIIS FM co-founding radio host

'In the journey for a place to belong, Mawunyo shows us the way home . . . to ourselves.'

> – **Stan Grant**, award-winning journalist and bestselling
> author of *Talking to My Country*, *On Identity*,
> *Australia Day* and *With the Falling of the Dusk*

'A heart-pounding account of the realities confronting people of colour in the land of the fair go and beyond.'

> – **Janice Petersen**, journalist and news
> presenter at SBS World News

'A new voice that is uninhibited, distinctive and gripping – Mawunyo's memoir is full of love, joy, defiance and humour.'

> – **Richard Glover**, author of *The Land Before
> Avocado* and *Flesh Wounds*

'I was a young kid living in Brooklyn when DJ Marley Marl sat those speakers outside his family's apartment. Marley, using two turntables, started mixing "break beats" of popular songs with people like Kool Herc doing this other new thing called "rapping" over the beats and sometimes between them. It was like an artistic bomb hit New York City. A birth of a new musical genre. Hip Hop!

'It touched, entertained and educated us. It was spiritual, like the church hymns that filled my heart as a teenager. So it is fitting that these two have dominated the soundtrack of my life. This memoir, *Hip Hop & Hymns*, did the same three things: touched, entertained and educated me.

'Unsurprisingly, I first met Mawunyo on a hip hop boat party. The conversations that ensued about life, music and God were nourishment for my soul as well as my mind. Her ability to transfer that same feeling onto the page is amazing. Learning about Mawunyo's life helped me learn more about myself. I was transported in a way that, even if I would have made different decisions, I understood the motivations behind her actions.

'I don't think every writer can do that. As an avid book reader, I recognise that authors who have the ability to tell their story that way are few and far apart.

'Even though we disagree musically at times, we always come together in the end on the common ground that music is the key to life – it's used by God to convey his message.

'A lot of people would think hip hop is paradoxical to hymns, but they both have the same goal – to appeal to our very soul.

'Love her, debate her or hate her, you will all feel her.'

– **Tracy Williams**, Global Ambassador for
Charity Bounce, and former Harlem Globetrotter

MAWUNYO GBOGBO

Hip Hop & Hymns

A memoir of loving hard, falling apart
and fighting back, set to an unrivalled playlist

PENGUIN BOOKS

UK | USA | Canada | Ireland | Australia
India | New Zealand | South Africa | China

Penguin Books is part of the Penguin Random House group of companies
whose addresses can be found at global.penguinrandomhouse.com

Penguin
Random House
Australia

First published by Penguin Books in 2022

Aboriginal and Torres Strait Islander people are advised that this publication contains
the names of people who are now deceased.

*This book is a memoir. It reflects the author's present recollections of experiences over time.
In some instances, events have been compressed and dialogue has been re-created.
The names and identifying characteristics of some persons described in the book
have been changed to protect their privacy.*

Cover illustration by Joshua Yasserie
Cover design by Luke Causby/Blue Cork
Author photograph by Frederick McHenry
Internal design and typesetting by Midland Typesetters, Australia

Printed and bound in Australia by Griffin Press, part of Ovato, an accredited
ISO AS/NZS 14001 Environmental Management Systems printer

A catalogue record for this
book is available from the
NATIONAL LIBRARY OF AUSTRALIA   National Library of Australia

ISBN 978 1 76104 206 5

Australia
Council
for the Arts

Australian Government

This project has been assisted by the Commonwealth Government through the
Australia Council, its arts funding and advisory body.

penguin.com.au

MIX
Paper from
responsible sources
FSC® C009448

I would like to acknowledge the Traditional Custodians of the land on which this book was primarily written, the Cammeraygal people of the Eora nation, and pay my respects to Elders past and present. I would also like to extend that respect to all Aboriginal and Torres Strait Islander people. Sovereignty has never been ceded. It always was, and always will be, Aboriginal land.

For Dad. Me lɔ wo. And I love the way you love me.

Contents

A note from the author   xi

Prologue   Lay Ya Gunz Down   xiii

Part One

1   I Vow to Thee, My Country   3

2   All We Got Iz Us   23

3   Blessed Assurance   39

4   All That Thrills My Soul   43

5   Lily of the Valley   47

6   When I Get to Heaven   53

7   This Is My Father's World   69

Part Two

8   All Things Bright and Beautiful   75

9   Ice Ice Baby   85

10   Welcome to Heartbreak   91

11   Zealots   103

12   Rising Down   113

13   When the Morning Comes   127
14   Just Tah Let U Know   135
15   Choices   147
16   Music & Me   161
17   No Church in the Wild   167

Part Three

18   City of Gods   173
19   Element   195
20   Quiet Storm   213
21   Phone Home   219
22   Were You There   227
23   They Ask Me   235
24   Amazing Grace   245
25   A Mighty Fortress   253
26   January 26   257
27   Hood Scriptures   265

Part Four

28   Reunited   275
29   It Was a Good Day   281
30   Day by Day   289
31   O Perfect Love   293
32   Inspired by Love and Anger   309
33   Because He Lives   321
34   My Beliefs   327
35   Just As I Am   339

Resources   343
Acknowledgements   347
About the author   351

A note from the author

I didn't keep a journal during the most traumatic parts of my life because, let's face it, I didn't want to remember that shit. Some things, though, once lived through, are hard to forget. And though the pain may have passed with time, each experience has come with a lesson. This is my recollection of some of the events that have shaped me as a person.

I've debated whether to tell this story at all. After all, it doesn't cast me in the best light. But I'm sick of pretending to be someone I'm not. I'm sick of getting up every day, putting on my game face and living a guarded existence in which I'm not really me most of the time. I'm also tired of representing my race. And by that I mean being on my best behaviour because – as is often the case – I'm the only Black person some people will ever meet. I just want to be me.

It's not just the people I don't know well. The first thing my mother said to me when I told her I was writing my life was, 'Don't embarrass me.' But my objective is to tell my story honestly, without inhibitions.

This is also the story I wish I had available to me growing up in regional Australia, and I'm not alone in feeling that way. My Sydney hairdresser's twenty-year-old daughter was helping her mother braid my hair when I asked her if she reads much.

'No,' she said. 'Apart from textbooks that I have to read for uni, I haven't read a book since I was a kid.' There weren't a lot of mainstream books being published that appealed to her.

'What would you like to read about?' I asked.

She giggled and, excitingly for me, outlined many of the themes in this book. 'Romance, Black culture, societal issues pertaining to the Black race . . . and mental health.'

'Do you want to read about Black people in other parts of the diaspora or here in Australia?' I asked.

'Here,' was her reply.

This story is also a call to action. Because to be Black with heart is to rally against injustice. And it's in that spirit that I'm telling my story. So, here I am. Unapologetically Black, and unapologetically real. Because I'm tired of caring about what everybody thinks.

PROLOGUE

Lay 4a Gunz Down

If I only love once, at least I know I loved hard.

'He's a ratbag. You need to get rid of him.'

I'd dreamt about calling him mine. Wanted to be his girl. Now, both in our thirties, more than fifteen years after our first kiss as teenagers, we were officially an item – why would I give that up? He was my soulmate.

'I'm worried about you, Mawunyo. You could be in danger. He's just been shot, for crying out loud. You need to get him out of your life. The sooner, the better.'

I sat in my car on the phone to my friend Raquel. I had pulled over in the hospital car park after running a few errands but had the engine running to charge my phone.

'I've never been in love with anyone but him. Even after all these years, I'm still madly in love. I can't abandon him. I'm the only person who's come to visit. I'm not going to walk away when he needs me most. Besides, I'm more of an influence on him than he is on me. It's not like when we were teenagers.'

'It's not just about whether he's an influence on you. You have to think long term. You can't build a future with him. Imagine the type of influence he'll have on your kids.'

'He won't be an influence on our kids.'

'Of course he will be. He'll be their *father*. They'll mimic every-thing he does. They'll adore him just as much as you do.'

That rocked me. My first instinct is to do everything I can to protect my children, even if they don't exist, because they might exist in the future. The things Tyce had been through, the things he had done – these weren't the sorts of things I wanted for our unborn kids. But in that moment, I chose to push his previous behaviour aside; it was all in the past. I wasn't ready to let go of my love. My mother had called while I was on the phone to Raquel, so as soon as I hung up I called her back.

'Mawunyo.' Mum's tone was thick with concern. 'Are you okay? I've been so worried about you. I've been praying for you.'

'Don't you want to know if Tyce is okay? He's the one who got shot.'

'Mawunyo, he's fine. He doesn't need you. He's a convicted drug dealer who's had four children with two other women, and now he's come back to you when nobody else wants him. He doesn't care about you. If he did, he'd let you go.'

I was furious. I had already explained to Mum that he wasn't a convicted drug dealer. At least, I don't think he ever went to prison for that.

'He does care about me. He loves me more than you do right now.' I hung up.

I rejected her call a little later when she rang back but listened to the message she'd left, telling me she loves me no matter what: 'I just want you to be happy.' That meant a lot because there *was* something that made me happy, or at least someone: Tyce.

Tyce had been shot three days earlier by his friend Chase – who at the time of the shooting was presumably high. Tyce had walked in through Chase's side door, like he always did, but this time instead of being greeted with a fist bump he was met with a bullet, which had lodged itself in his left leg, alongside a vein. An inch closer to that vein and he could have ended up paralysed, or worse: dead. When Tyce expressed his firm disapproval at being shot, reacting the way anybody would if a good friend had shot them, Chase asked him if he wanted another one in the chest.

Tyce wasn't mad at Chase – he was off his head on drugs. Tyce had even asked me to pray for him.

I began walking towards the hospital. This was my fifth visit in three days. Tyce had already had surgery to remove the bullet and was doing well. I was staying at Uncle Bob's Yallarwah Place at John Hunter Hospital, a cottage reserved for the family members and partners of Aboriginal and Torres Strait Islander patients.

When I walked into Tyce's room, I found him sitting up in bed reading the Bible. You couldn't make this shit up! Here was a man trying to better himself. A man who, despite adversity, genuinely wanted to turn things around and be somebody. He had troubles all around him, but he was not defeated – an example of God's mercy if ever I had seen one. I had never been more in love.

He looked up at me and smiled. *That smile.* It always made my heart melt. And his chocolate complexion. Those dark, dark eyes.

'Let's get married,' he said. 'I don't understand why you don't see this as an opportunity. We're at a hospital. There's a chapel over there. There'll be a pastor on site.'

It wasn't the first time he'd expressed his desire to tie the knot, and I was all in. But in this setting? I drank in the white walls and white sheets, the beeping monitor, the sterile scent. I knew this wasn't a proposal – he was just being playful – but at the same time I contemplated what it would mean to marry him at the hospital chapel. I thought about how much I'd always wanted to be his wife, how I'd longed to carry his child. After spending so much time together while I was on long service leave over the past five months, I knew our future wouldn't be easy. We would face challenges most couples were shielded from. The kind of trauma my baby had been through, a cloud over our relationship. The hurt and pain I was carrying, a dagger in our joint prosperity. But we shared an undeniable love. We would have each other.

'You won't let me carry out just one little robbery so that I have enough money to marry you, so let's just do it right here, right now.'

He was joking, of course. He was always joking. Or was he? I smiled as he put his hand over mine. My sweetheart, my one and only, my poison.

PART ONE

CHAPTER 1

I Vow to Thee, My Country

A homeland so beautiful, it didn't deserve to be left behind.

Before I was born, some crucial events took place, the results of which would play out over the years in devastating detail, crushing the players involved and injuring the bystanders. I was one of the bystanders, and my wounds would take many years to heal.

Ghana's lush forests, broad beaches lapped by turquoise ocean and sparkling lagoons would form the backdrop of our family story, its natural beauty unable to camouflage the drama.

Mum is from a royal family in Ghana. When Queen Elizabeth II visited in 1961, English royalty was greeted by African royalty: Togbui Nyaho Tamakloe III. Mum's mother, my grandmother, was the youngest child of a chief, Togbui Nyaho Tamakloe I. He was a rich man who had lots of children, and adopted many more. These children were well educated and would go on to become doctors, lawyers and engineers, with many practising overseas. But it wasn't just his own children he educated – he was famous for donating a massive parcel of land where the Zion College of West Africa, a secondary school, was built in the coastal town of Keta in the Volta Region, and another in Anloga.

My grandmother, Grace Adzoyovi Amegamenui Tamakloe, was a beautiful woman. She was kind, generous and highly respected. She had a son with her first husband, and after he died, she married my grandfather. They were in a polygynous relationship; she was one of about eight wives.

Mum's dad, my grandfather, Abraham Kofi Amuzu Hotorwovi Amegadze, was a farmer who was gifted in healing people. When the sick came from afar to seek his help, he would pray to Almighty God in heaven, as well as the little gods in the form of statues on his property, and then use herbs to heal them.

Mum was very close to her father. She loved him so much, and he favoured her too. He was an industrious man, who was planting coconut trees one day when a man approached.

'You're old and you're planting these trees. Won't you die before you even get the chance to harvest them?'

'If I die, my children will harvest them,' my grandfather said. But not only did he live to harvest the coconut trees, he sent the coconuts abroad to London, where he sold them, the profits bringing him a handsome sum of money. He passed this lesson down to my mother – she should never think she was too old to do anything – and Mum would pass that same lesson on to me by example.

The fifth of December, 1958, began like any ordinary day for Mum, eleven years old, getting ready for school and sitting down to eat breakfast.

'I don't want you to go to school today,' her father told her. 'Stay at home with me.'

'But why, Pappa?' Mum looked up at her father as she ate her porridge.

'If you go to school today, when you come back, you will come and see me at Whuti.' The family cemetery was at Whuti.

'Oh please, I want to go. We'll get our exam results back today. I want to know how I went.'

'Okay, go,' my grandfather said, 'but you won't see me again when you return.'

Mum thought about her father all day at school, and while rushing home she ran into her brother and one of her cousins. 'Where are you going?' she called out. She could tell by their demeanour that something was wrong.

The two boys looked at her and then looked at each other.

'Oh, God . . . Pappa died? *Pappa died?*' Mum's heart was beating faster and faster.

'Yes,' her brother said, 'but don't tell anybody yet. He's a very important man. We are on our way to Anloga to make preparations for his funeral—'

Mum didn't hear the rest of the sentence. She threw her school bag and started howling. Her brother walked over, picked the bag out of the bushes and watched as his sister ran as fast as she could back to the house.

Mum saw her father's lifeless body tucked into his bed at home. 'No!' she screamed, tears streaming down her face. 'Oh, Pappa, wake up!' By then a group of people had gathered, conscious of the young child in the corner who continued to bawl. A man Mum barely knew snapped at her.

'You,' he said, pointing. 'Your father said don't go to school, because he'll die today. You went to school. How naughty can you be? We will put you in the same coffin as him and bury you too if you don't stop crying now!'

She looked up at the man, her eyes wide with fear.

Mum was overcome with grief and cried herself to sleep night after night after night in the wake of her father's death. She didn't own a diary, so she wrote on the wall in the bedroom she shared with her mother and siblings. *My father died on 5th December, 1958, ndokutsu.* She was unsure how to spell the word 'afternoon' in English.

Because she had lost her father so suddenly, Mum was always worried about her mother. My grandmother lent money to anyone who asked – usually fishermen, who would buy food to eat before going out to catch fish, but it got to the point where she would lend huge amounts of money to people who stopped paying it back, hurting her financially. She also couldn't understand how people could take advantage of her kindness and compassion, exchanging it for contempt.

When Grandma Grace ventured out to ask for the money back, she would return home disappointed and would get very sick. Mum was scared, not wanting to lose her mother as suddenly as she'd lost her father – so despite her mother telling her to go to secondary school, she chose not to. She wanted to work and do what she could for her mother.

One day, when Mum was seventeen years old, she was walking a fair way in the capital, Accra, looking for work, when a car screeched up beside her. A white man, or as Mum would refer to him, 'an Englishman', hung his head out the window and asked her where she was going. She told him and he offered her a lift.

The white man took a detour, via his own house, before dropping Mum off. It took her a while to work out what on earth this white man was doing as he reclined on his couch in front of her. She realises now, he was masturbating.

He would do something afterwards, however, that would change the course of Mum's life. Before they parted ways, he handed her 10 shillings. Mum used those 10 shillings to buy a Bible at the Methodist bookshop in Accra. There was nothing else she wanted more. Her spiritual journey continued in earnest that day.

♪♫

In another part of Ghana's Volta Region, my father, at eight years old, was the only surviving child of his parents, Lumor and Amekakporm. Two older sisters had died in infancy and a third girl, born after him, also died as a baby. Dad's father was a miller and his mother would grind corn into a paste, cooking akple to sell at market. Dad didn't live with his parents, who were in Mankrong Junction. He was being looked after by his grandmother – my great-grandmother – Mamaga, in the tiny village where he'd been born, Akplorfudzi.

Grandfather Lumor instilled in Dad early on that education was the key to getting ahead. But Dad didn't like school. He preferred to skip class and go fishing with his classmates. He wanted to be like his dad, who he thought was doing well for himself. But Grandfather Lumor hadn't had much of an education himself and didn't want his son to be a corn miller too. He wanted him to achieve so much more.

'If you don't want to go to school, you shouldn't have to go,' Mamaga told Dad, who had been busted truanting. 'I never went to school and I'm alright.'

'He will continue to go to school,' Dad's mum, who was visiting, said.

Dad jumped out of his chair and clung to his mother. 'I want to go to Mankrong Junction with you.'

'No.' His mother disentangled him from her dress.

Later, the trio walked down to the river, which flowed behind the house. Dad frowned as he watched his mother board a canoe and wave goodbye. Tears slid down his face as the canoe slipped away into the distance.

Dad continued to pester Mamaga until his mother's next visit, adamant that he wanted to leave the village and join his parents at Mankrong Junction.

'He's not happy here,' Mamaga told her daughter. 'He's been crying and abusing people. He's had enough of the village. He wants to be with you and Lumor.'

'You know it's not practical.' Grandma Amekakporm looked at her mother. 'The language is different. Lumor and I are always working, and he has been at the same school since elementary.'

Dad walked into the room. '*Ete*,' he said to his mother. 'Can I leave with you?'

'No. You're to stay here and that's final. The canoe will be leaving shortly. You can come and see me off.'

Soon afterwards, they walked down to the river. Dad jumped up and down, yelling, sobbing, saying he wanted to go too. His mother put her finger to his lips.

Dad watched as his mother's canoe left the shore and made

its way downstream. He tore himself away from Mamaga and ran, jumping fully dressed into the water. He tried desperately to reach the canoe. He didn't know how to swim and splashed his way through the water, arms flailing wildly, as the canoe pulled further and further away.

Dad didn't get very far before a group of bystanders who had witnessed the commotion jumped into the water and pulled him back to shore.

An old man restrained him while others from the village chastised his actions.

'"It takes a village to raise a child" is a true African proverb,' Dad would tell me much later. 'If you misbehave, anyone who knows your parents will discipline you, then they'll tell your parents, and your parents will thank them and discipline you in addition.'

Grandma Amekakporm saw what happened from the moving canoe and told her husband when she arrived back in Mankrong Junction what their son had done.

'Okay, the boy has grown up,' was his reply, and he decided then that Dad's time in the village was over. On his mother's next visit, Dad left with her to join his parents at Mankrong Junction, where he would at first struggle to learn the new language, before mastering several.

♪♫

Mum and Dad were just friends for some time after they first met. Things shifted when Dad's employer – the Electricity Commission of Ghana – sent him to Germany for a practical training attachment. He and Mum exchanged many letters and their relationship blossomed. He told her he wanted to settle down and start a family. He was in his early thirties and his parents were gently pestering him for grandchildren. But Mum was in two minds.

She had worked her way up from being a ward assistant to an enrolled nurse at Tema General Hospital in the Greater Accra Region, but her desire was to become a registered nurse. In order to do so, she would need to go away to study in Tamale, the capital of the Northern Region. The two would be away from each other for some time. In the end, Mum agreed to marry Dad, but insisted on going away to pursue her dream. As a symbol of their engagement, Mum asked Dad to give her some money so she could buy a ring in Accra – a humble gold band, devoid of diamonds.

Dad's mother died while he was in Germany, and he stayed with Mum when he returned to Ghana for the funeral. When his overseas training wrapped up, he was posted to Tarkwa, in Ghana's Western Region, as the officer in charge. It meant Mum and Dad were a daytrip away from each other.

The first time Dad visited Mum I was conceived in a hotel room in Tamale where Dad was staying. Mum was very sick when she was pregnant with me. She was diagnosed with hyperemesis gravidarum, a severe type of morning sickness, and even the sight of most foods would make her nauseous and vomit. Mum's sister, my Aunty Rita, was by Mum's side throughout her pregnancy.

When Mum's illness resulted in her being hospitalised, Dad paid her a visit.

'What's wrong?' Dad asked.

'Oh, God, I'm pregnant.'

'Why didn't you terminate the pregnancy?'

'*What?*' Mum couldn't believe what she was hearing. 'You told me you wanted to marry me, and I'm pregnant. And you want me to cause an abortion. *Why?*'

Dad's thinking was that Mum was only a year into her three-year degree. Her pregnancy would mean she couldn't continue. He *had* warned her not to blame him if anything happened.

Mum was five months pregnant when she went to visit Dad in Tarkwa with her niece, Lucy. They were at Dad's place when he delivered some news that would unsettle Mum and be a catalyst for years of heartache and distress to come.

'I have a baby son,' he said.

Mum thought he was joking. When he left the house to run an errand, Mum told Lucy just how humourless she thought the joke was.

'Listen, Aunty,' Lucy said. 'This is no joke. He said this to you – how can this be a joke?'

While Dad was away, Mum, still reeling from his words, got up and walked over to the chest of drawers in his lounge room. There were always letters sitting on top of the cabinet, which she had never before examined closely. But she wanted to see if she could find any evidence to support Dad's claim – or, she hoped, dispense with it as one of the worst jokes in history. Dad did joke around a lot. It was one of the things she liked about him, the way he could make her laugh.

Mum experienced a mix of emotions as she read a letter from one of Dad's cousins. In it, she discovered Grandfather Lumor didn't like her. He wanted Dad to marry 'the woman who had a boy for you' instead. Mum's interpretation of the letter was that Dad had been defiant, insisting on staying with his 'Anlo girl', Mum. *He must love me*, she thought. *He was facing pressure to stay away but chose not to.*

When Dad returned, he was apologetic as he filled in the blanks about his son, Selassie. Spelled differently, Selasi means *God has heard my pleading* in Ewe, my parents' native tongue.

Mum did the calculations and realised Selassie's mother must have been five months pregnant when Dad had come to see her and I was conceived.

'If you didn't want me, you should have told me,' she said. 'This is too much. You should have told me that you have someone already, but you came – I was in college and you came and did this to me when you knew you already had someone who was pregnant. If you didn't know, that would be different. But you knew. What you did is so cruel.'

'I'm sorry,' Dad said. And Mum, as hurt as she was but with the knowledge of what she'd learned in the letter, believed his apology to be sincere.

Mum didn't end up going back to her studies in Tamale. She returned to Tema instead because she was so sick. Her dream to become a registered nurse was put on hold.

Aunty Rita provided a shoulder to cry on and an ear to confide in during this period. Mum also leaned on Lucy and friend Aurelia, who'd bought some maternity dresses for her.

Mum's obstetrician wasn't there the day I was born at Tema General Hospital. Instead, one of Mum's colleagues, Dr Lawani, was on duty.

'If you haven't had this baby within an hour or two, we will have to take you in for a caesarean section,' Dr Lawani said.

Mum looked at him. They were close, having worked together, but she knew he had never performed a caesarean section before. When he left, the pain was so severe that the nurses started to prepare her for theatre.

'Your baby is suffering foetal distress,' Dr Lawani explained. 'Your baby's heart is racing. It's time to head to the operating theatre.'

Mum said a prayer. 'Lord Jesus, it's not Dr Lawani who is going to do this operation – you take the knife and do this.'

I was blue when I was born, from lack of oxygen, but soon recovered after being given a few lungfuls from the staff. Dr Lawani was so proud of delivering me – he bragged to all the nurses, who were calling me Baby Precious, or Baby P. for short.

One of the women who lived in Mum's building was shocked when she learned what Mum had decided to name me: Mawunyo. It means *God is good* in Ewe.

'When you were pregnant, you were always sick and sick and sick, and you have a baby and name her *Mawunyo*?'

But Mum, who never thought she would be able to put up with that much pain, felt that God had been merciful. She had delivered a healthy baby girl.

Dad had told Mum their baby was going to look exactly like him – that the only thing I would take from Mum would be her complexion, which was several shades lighter than his. When I came out looking exactly like Dad with Mum's complexion, Mum couldn't believe it. She started praying that all her other children would look like her. When Dad saw me for the first time he saw in me his dear mother, who he'd lost while in Germany.

Mum said she decided to forgive Dad for his wandering ways because she wanted me to have brothers and sisters, and my brother, Sedudzi – a name meaning *He reigns*, as in, *God is good and He reigns*, was born two years later.

Each time Dad visited Mum, he would go to see a friend of his, Ernest Watson, who was working in a control room nearby.

Ernest didn't want to live in Ghana anymore. He had applied to go to Papua New Guinea, saying, 'There are Black people there, we'll fit in,' but PNG didn't take migrants, and he was encouraged to try Australia. *Australia*. Now that's a place he hadn't thought of. Dad went along to the Australian embassy in Ghana with Ernest and another friend, Kemevor, followed by a trip to the library to read up on the country. *There were Black people in Australia too*, they read. They decided they wanted to migrate to Queensland, because the climate was similar to the one in Ghana. It was warm in Queensland: *Beautiful one day, perfect the next.*

All three applied and qualified. The White Australia policy had only come to an end a decade earlier, and Malcolm Fraser, who was pro-immigration, was prime minister.

Kemevor, an engineer, had also qualified for Canada and decided to go there instead. When Mum told Lucy that she was looking at moving her family to Australia, Lucy couldn't believe it. 'It's so far away!' she said. 'Look at a map!'

Mum visited the Australian embassy with Dad. A staff member there, happy to see them, boasted about how inexpensive it was to feed a family in Australia.

'Everything is really cheap,' he said. 'One chicken is three dollars! You should come to Australia and see. If God didn't want us to travel to each other's countries, he would have made us like a tree with roots in the ground so that everyone stays where they are born.' His words resonated with Mum.

Mum and Dad didn't have a proper wedding before they left. They said their 'I do's' in front of a wedding celebrant, Aunty Rita, and one of Dad's relatives, Uncle Gershon, and signed some papers to make it official.

♪♫

When I heard former prime minister Tony Abbott, an immigrant himself, say migrants needed to have jobs the day they arrived in Australia, I shook my head. Dad had flown from Ghana to Australia a year ahead of Mum, Sedudzi and me. He arrived on a Friday. By Monday he was on unemployment benefits. But three months later he was working and paying his taxes like everyone else. He was reliable, and he'd eventually retire without having taken so much as one sick day in more than twenty years.

When Dad's friend Harrison, also an African migrant, asked Dad to accompany him to the Bonds warehouse where he was applying for an advertised position as a machine operator, he suggested Dad apply for a job there as well.

'But that's not what I'm trained in.' Dad's training was in the electricity industry, including the eighteen months spent in Germany working on air circuit breakers.

'It doesn't matter. Just give it a go.'

Dad filled out the application, and the boss told them to call the next day to find out if they had been successful.

Dad was on the phone to Harrison the following day. After a while, he asked, 'How'd you go with that job?'

'Oh, don't mind them – they're racists,' Harrison said, having missed out on securing the position at Bonds. 'Don't bother ringing them. You won't get a job there either.'

When Dad hung up, he called the factory anyway, and rang Harrison back immediately afterwards. 'I've progressed to the next stage. They want to interview me.'

'What? *How?* What did you put on your application?'

'I just told them I had worked at the Electricity Commission in Ghana for five years, and about my training in Germany. I was very straightforward. No bullshit.'

Harrison had submitted a long, elaborate application, detailing every job he had ever had – six months here, twelve months there. He thought it made him look experienced, but to a potential employer he may have also looked unstable. (He later reapplied for a position at the factory and got it.)

So Dad's first job in Australia involved bleaching the material used to make undies and singlets for Bonds, based in Camperdown in Sydney's Inner West. Apparently it was a rite of passage for a lot of migrants. During his lunch breaks, Dad read the *Sydney Morning Herald*.

'What are you doing reading *that* paper?' Dad's Vietnamese co-worker laughed at him. 'You work in a factory. That paper is for people who work in offices. You should be reading the people's paper. You're taking up too much space on the table.' He wagged his finger. 'The *Daily Telegraph* is for people like you and me – not that big, big paper.'

When it came time for Mum, Sedudzi and me to leave Ghana,

Mum had to coax me onto the plane. I was determined to stay with my grandmother, who had accompanied us to the airport. She was dressed in Kente cloth that day; I was wearing a beautiful pink dress sewn especially for me by a local seamstress. While I was hanging back, wanting to stay in the Motherland, Sedudzi marched towards the plane and boldly waved goodbye to Ghana. On the plane, a white lady, also headed for Australia, excitedly wished us good luck when Mum told her we were migrating.

We lived in Ashfield, in the Inner West, when we first arrived in Sydney, then moved to the South West suburb of Campsie. We never did make it to the warmth of Queensland.

Dad, who himself had faced discipline as a child – not only from his parents, but also from elders in the community, as well as the cane at school – believed that if you spare the rod, you spoil the child, and it was Sedudzi who would sometimes cop a whack.

We were visiting Ernest Watson, who was also living in Sydney by then, when two-and-a-half-year-old Sedudzi had had enough. He turned on Dad.

'When I grow up and you become a small boy,' Sedudzi said, 'I'm going to smack you really hard. And when you start crying, I'm going to hit you again and tell you to shut up!'

For years my parents would laugh about this, but Sedudzi wasn't backing down then, and he sure as hell didn't see the humour in any of it. The fact that it was laughed off showed just how hopeless he felt his situation really was.

When Dad landed a job at Bayswater Power Station in the New South Wales Hunter Valley, he motioned for his Vietnamese co-worker at the factory to come over, showing him his employment offer. Dad would be earning twice as much in his new job than he was at Bonds. He couldn't help himself: 'You know that big, big paper I keep reading? I saw the job advertised in that.'

Dad had the choice of living in either Singleton or Muswellbrook. Unable to visit beforehand, he chose Muswellbrook because that's where one of his soon-to-be colleagues lived. 'If Muswellbrook is good enough for him, it's good enough for me,' Dad reasoned.

Dad's factory manager didn't want him to leave Sydney. 'Muswellbrook is a country town,' he said. 'There won't be as many people of different nationalities there as in Sydney. You might find it hard there.' But Dad was determined to make the move, and his boss told him there would always be a job for him should he return to Sydney.

Mum, Dad, Sedudzi and I, and our newest sibling, Sophia, born in Sydney, piled into our second-hand Datsun and sped north on the highway, on a 254-kilometre journey to our new town. Having never visited before, we drove straight through it. Dad only turned the car around after seeing a sign thanking him for visiting Muswellbrook.

As we drove back into town, Mum pointed out the window and gasped. She nudged Dad. 'Look.' She gestured towards a woman standing on the corner smoking a cigarette. 'That beautiful young woman is a prostitute.'

Dad smiled and shook his head. 'She's not a prostitute. Regular people smoke cigarettes on street corners in Australia.'

The main street was populated with the usual shops you'd find in a country town, just with different names: Serhan's, the men's clothing store; Pearly Shell, the fish and chips shop, which would become our Sunday haunt after church. Matthews Jewellers sat on the edge of Campbell's Corner.

It wasn't unusual to spot a kangaroo in town, making its way through the grasslands, with some of the tree-lined streets giving way to dirt roads yet to be tarred. My siblings and I would zigzag along the roads on our bikes with friends, falling off occasionally, our scraped knees covered in 'flesh-coloured' bandaids, which stuck out conspicuously against our chocolate-coloured skin.

There are more than 150 wineries in the Hunter Valley, but Muswellbrook isn't known for wineries. It had to make do with the 'Wine Estate', its houses sitting side by side along Shiraz Street, Chardonnay Street, Riesling Street, Merlot Street, Pinot Street, Claret Avenue, Chablis Close . . . And there was no shortage of local pubs.

Dad would soon learn that people in the wealthy neighbouring towns of Aberdeen and Scone looked down on Muswellbrook as a workers' town. One of Australia's richest families, the Packers, reportedly offloaded a 60-million-dollar stake in their property holdings near Scone in 2015. That kind of money evaded Muswellbrook – a quiet town, but for the whispers of gossiping town folk.

Muswellbrook itself was further divided into two areas. The one I grew up in was aspirational to moderately affluent, with sprawling houses – some with pools, others with trampolines. The goal of those who grew up there was to eventually get out of town, onwards to bigger and better things.

Then there was the other side of town – pockets of disadvantage, a sprinkling of housing commission buildings. There was one section of South Muswellbrook referred to by the locals who lived there as 'The Bronx', because it was considered dangerous.

One of the most notorious parts of Muswellbrook was Wollombi Road, a long, circular street known as a hotspot for drugs and home to a number of feuding families. It was an area afflicted by brawls, stabbings, car bombings, theft, property destruction and free-roaming pets. If you lived on that side of town you might have to contend with a sense of helplessness along with the crime. For you, Muswellbrook might well be a life sentence.

But, of course, there were people who called Muswellbrook home and prided themselves as locals – families who had been in the area for generations, and would be for generations more.

For me at the time, the worst thing about Muswellbrook, as I soon discovered, were the flies. Muswellbrook flies were like no other. The insects followed you around, buzzing in your ears, landing on your shoulders, or worse still, on the sanger you were about to down at a backyard barbie. Aerogard was the scent of summer, and the only way to escape these pests.

A subsidised three-bedroom brick house in Cousins Street would become our first home, courtesy of Dad's job at Bayswater Power Station. The rent ran around 40 dollars a week for employees, the company's way of encouraging staff to live locally.

It was clearly an upgrade, moving from a two-bedroom apartment in Campsie to a house in Muswellbrook, so Mum would get up early every morning to sweep the leaves from the front gutter and footpath. Dad had told her it was the thing to do. She was so dedicated to keeping a lovely home, inside and out, that she would wake up early every morning, ignoring the strange looks from the neighbours as she swept. It was freezing, hovering around zero most mornings in the autumn and winter. Mum was still not used to the change in climate and initially found it very difficult to adjust. Ghana had two main seasons: summer and the rainy season. She would step out at times in sandals, a dress with two t-shirts over the top and a Gotcha sweater.

After a period of daily sweeping, Mum heard a large whirring noise coming down the street. She watched as a truck glided past, large swirling brushes clearing the gutter. She laughs when she retells the story now, but she wasn't laughing at the time – her sweeping had been in vain. There were trucks for that in Muswellbrook, and, of course, she blames Dad for quite literally leading her up the garden path.

CHAPTER 2

All We Got Iz Us

One hand. Five fingers. That's how many other people looked like me. Only five who could possibly understand.

It was our first day at Muswellbrook preschool – five-year-old me and my brother, Sedudzi, now three. I assessed the scene.

Kids were bursting into tears as their parents said goodbye. These children were clearly distraught about being left at this new place. Our parents planned a quick getaway with baby Sophia. I wasn't even that upset, but I observed as one child after another pushed their cheeks out, drool forming around their pouting lips, tears coursing down their reddened faces. It made me feel like I was in some sort of danger.

Being more of a follower and not wanting to be the odd one out, I also burst into tears. Sedudzi, a natural leader, simply marched towards the preschool, head held high – the same way he'd marched out of Ghana.

Once we were inside, one of the preschool teachers tried to

give him a nickname because, to her, his name was just too difficult to pronounce.

'Can we call you Sam?' she said.

'No,' Sedudzi insisted. 'My name is *seh-doo-jee*,' he pronounced
clearly. *You better address me properly*, was his message. That
was my brother. Even at three he was someone who asserted
his rights, headstrong from the beginning. Relatives in Ghana
would tell him stories years later about how, even before we left,
he had some choice words for other children who'd rubbed him
the wrong way, insulting them in our native Ewe language, with
phrases such as *Miawo mo na soldier's mo na*. (Look at your
face, like soldier's face.)

We were attending the Presbyterian church in Muswellbrook,
where the congregation was as ancient as the music. But I felt an
immediate affinity to these old hymns. Even as a child, I adored
singing along to 'Thine Be the Glory': *'Thine be the glory, risen,
conquering Son, endless is the victory Thou o'er death hast won.'*
This was a triumphant hymn, professing that nothing could
stop Jesus – not even death. *'Let the church with gladness hymns
of triumph sing, for her Lord now liveth; death hath lost its sting.'*
When I stood, hymnal between my small hands, I could feel
every word and the melody of voices swelling around me. *'No
more we doubt Thee, glorious Prince of life! Life is naught without
Thee; aid us in our strife.'* It was a declaration of faith where faith
hadn't existed before, a call for assistance in this thing we call life,
a shout of praise, reverence. I sang these hymns resolutely, even

at such a young age. They were my gateway into Christianity, my entry point into faith.

At the front was a large organ, mostly shielded from view, except for a glimpse of fingers tapping away on the keys, bringing the grand injection of sound to a crescendo. There was no church choir – the congregation was just too old – but that meant we parishioners could confidently raise our own voices. Quite often an out-of-tune note would warble above the others, but almost as quickly it was drowned out by another amateur vocalist.

The Presbyterian church itself had a traditional layout, with wooden pews and stained-glass windows that looked just as brilliant inside as they did out – an image of the Virgin Mother Mary holding Baby Jesus in a kaleidoscope of faded colours. It stood tall among vibrant greenery – trees, shrubs and grasslands an attractive contrast to the reddish-brown building. There was a massive hill leading to another building where Sunday school was held. Beside that stood the manse – a large house where the pastor's family lived; years later it would be sold to the highest bidder, in favour of a more modern brick family home in town.

Once we'd belted out a few hymns, it would be off to Sunday school, where we would hear stories of the Bible's most charismatic characters. People like Noah, who obediently built his ark at God's command, and Daniel, who survived a lions' den. We were told that most of the women in the Bible didn't cloak themselves in glory, and Eve was the ultimate example. I listened as we were taught about her role in original sin. Personally, I couldn't understand how she could be tempted by an apple. Chocolate, maybe, but an *apple*?

On the days I did stay in church, I would nod off at times to the minister's calm, monotone delivery, only to be jolted awake again by the sound of the invisible organ.

On a hill far away stood an old rugged cross, the emblem of suffering and shame . . . Fully awake now, I'd join in, lifting my voice to the hymn, building to the chorus: *So I'll cherish the old rugged cross, till my trophies at last I lay down. I will cling to the old rugged cross, and exchange it some day for a crown.*

Outside of the pastor's young family, there were few kids for us to interact with at church, one of the reasons Mum suddenly pulled us out of the congregation.

While the church was a strong influence in my childhood, it wouldn't take long before the secular crept in and set up shop for the long haul, also in the form of music. One Saturday morning I was hanging out with Naomi Taylor, who lived just down the road, watching film clips on *Rage*, like we always did. Stevie Wonder sang about having a 'part-time lover', whatever that meant; we sang along to Madonna's 'Crazy for You' and watched the animated sketches come to life in A-ha's 'Take on Me'. Naomi was dancing around the room, pretending to hold a microphone, but stopped dramatically and began to instruct me on what she thought my parents got up to in their spare time.

'Your mum and dad *must* have had sex before they had you. In fact, they must have done it three times. One time each for you, your brother *and* your sister.'

I looked at Naomi, who was a couple years older than me. I would have been about five at the time. 'What's sex?'

Naomi explained that it involved kissing, touching, hugging, getting naked and jiggling a 'pee-pee' inside a 'wee-wee'. *My* parents wouldn't have done that! I had never seen my parents hold hands, let alone conspire to do all that other stuff behind closed doors.

I ran home to my mother.

'Mum! Did you and Dad have sex?' Mum looked at me with alarm. I waited patiently for her answer.

'No!' she declared.

Ha, I thought. I knew Naomi Taylor was wrong. That girl really had no idea. I went and told her firmly that while *her* parents might have had sex, *mine* certainly did not.

It was easy to believe my mother's claim. I can't remember them cuddling on the couch; never a hand on the shoulder or an embrace, never a kiss – not even on the cheek. *Me lɔ wo* – the words for 'I love you' in Ewe – were not words I'd heard them exchange.

My youngest brother's arrival completed our family: Mum, Dad, me, Sedudzi, Sophia and John. Sophia and John had Anglo names, not because they were born in Australia but because their names had been changed. Mum had given Sophia and John Ewe names at birth, after a friend from Ghana suggested *Nayra* and *Nuna*. When Mum decided she no longer liked this particular friend, she changed both their names by association at first and then officially through the Registry of Births, Deaths and Marriages.

Dad was the last one to come around. He insisted on calling them by their birth names long after they were known as Sophia and John to everyone around town. It must have been tiring after a while being the only person calling them by different names because, finally, one day he gave in. *Sophia*, he said softly to my little sister. When she responded, that was it. Her name was Sophia.

♪♫

Muswellbrook at Christmas time was a town bejewelled with bright lights trailing across homes and illuminating yards. It was an event to drive around town, checking out the decorations and displays. Some yards were adorned with divinity symbols, while others were populated with a variety of Santa Clauses, or a floodlit Rudolph the Red-Nosed Reindeer.

On Christmas Day, when I was about six, I ripped open my carefully wrapped gift, feeling a pinch of excitement as I stripped away the layers of colourful Christmas paper.

My neighbour, Renee Reid, had opened her gift first, as our mothers watched on expectantly. When I saw her gift – a Cabbage Patch Kid named Myra – I couldn't wait to see what mine would be. Myra had long, beautiful blonde hair tied in pigtails and bright blue eyes. She looked exactly like Renee, who was beaming. My parcel was the same shape – maybe Santa had bought a doll that looked exactly like me!

I tore off the last bit of wrapping, and tears welled up in my eyes.

'I don't like it,' I said. I looked at the doll. It was also a Cabbage Patch Kid, but mine was a boy. *A boy!* He had white skin with freckles and short, light-brown hair. The eyes painted onto the doll were a muddy brown, several shades lighter than mine. The doll didn't look anything like me! It didn't even look like Renee's doll, which would have at least been some sort of consolation.

My Cabbage Patch Kid's birth certificate revealed his name:

Rollo. He even had a stupid name. I instantly disliked him. 'I don't want it.' I pouted.

Mum and Mrs Reid looked at me. I could see the disappointment on their faces.

'Well,' Mum said, 'if you don't want the doll, put it back underneath the Christmas tree and Santa will come and get it while you're asleep.'

'Will Santa bring me another doll?' I asked.

Mum gave me a noncommittal look. 'Maybe,' she said. That didn't sound too promising. I put Rollo back underneath the Christmas tree.

I went to bed that night thinking about Rollo. My feelings of resentment gave way to something else: I started to feel a little uneasy about abandoning him. I began to squirm, feeling a sense of guilt. I panicked at the idea of Santa taking him away. What if he didn't bring back another doll and I was left with nothing? Where would Santa take Rollo? Would he go to another child, or would his fate be much worse than that? Was there an open grave for unwanted dolls that Rollo would be chucked into? A place where there were no rainbows, where there was no laughter, not even air. What if he couldn't breathe?

I hadn't given him a chance.

I jolted up and out of bed and ran over to the Christmas tree in a bid to beat Santa and rescue Rollo. I found him exactly where I'd left him. I took Rollo to the room I shared with my sister and snuggled down with him for the night. It wasn't long before I was fond of Rollo.

Rollo, an acquired taste. Rollo, my companion. Rollo, my favourite doll.

Throughout my childhood, I was never given any dolls that looked like me, which was unfortunate, because there *were* Black Cabbage Patch Kids in the 1980s – just maybe not in Muswellbrook. One of the blonde girls up the road had a Black doll. Where on earth her mother got it from I don't know. The doll used to sit uncomfortably on her hip, loved but clearly out of place in that family. Later, my younger sister was blessed with Denise, a Black doll that she loved. I had to make do with Rollo and the series of white dolls and Barbies that came after him. I grew to love Rollo so much, but I wonder what it would have been like if I'd been given a doll that looked like me.

♪♫

I remember being shocked the day I stumbled across Sophia as a three-year-old kissing one of the boys from our neighbourhood behind the couch in our living room.

'Oh, that was no big deal,' Sophia insisted years later. 'We were just doing what kids do. I don't consider that my first kiss – we were three!'

While Sophia was kissing at three and considered that normal, I was far more conservative when it came to male affection.

I was very young as I watched on, mesmerised, while Lorenzo Mancini played the guitar sitting on his torso, eliciting the most majestic sounds. We were both in primary school. Singing Bon Jovi's 'Bad Medicine', he strummed away on those chords, and strum, strum, strummed his way into my heart. This was my first crush.

Lorenzo was three years older than me and in the coolest

of bands. I barely noticed the other members around him as they performed in the library at Muswellbrook Public School, known as Roger Street. It was Lorenzo's shoulder-length hair, his confidence and composure, the fact he was a little bit older, the way he dressed – it was all very alluring. *Bad Medicine . . .* Lorenzo's brother was in my year, but it was Lorenzo who set my heart on fire. I stared and stared until the performance was over. As I was walking away, the distinct yellow spine of a book caught my attention. I picked it up. It was one of my favourites – Nancy Drew. I flicked the cover over to see which adventure Nancy would be going on in this novel. *An underground passage . . . a secret staircase . . . her father, a prisoner in a tunnel . . .*

'Hello.' There was someone behind me. Could it be? *Lorenzo?* I panicked. Turning slowly, I glimpsed past Lorenzo's muso hair and into his smile, aimed directly at me. I dropped the book and ran. I enjoyed admiring him from afar, but acting on my crush? Oh no, no, no. But I'd fill my sister in on my crushes.

As she grew older, Sophia – beautiful Sophia – was becoming a legendary bookworm. She'd spend most of her afternoons at the library with Dad. She loved to read, still does, and would devour book after book after book. She's an introvert, despite always being the most stunning person in the room. Sophia and I shared a room. I loved having a little sister. I would tell her everything that was going on with me, not realising until later that she wasn't doing the same.

'Maybe I don't tell you anything because you tell me too much,' she said.

I stopped spilling my guts after that.

♪♫

On 12 December 1987, my beautiful, much-loved grandmother died. The day we left Ghana proved to be the last day we would see her alive. Mum was devastated.

'You're going back?' Mum's friend Dr Jeremiah asked. He was a local GP, a white doctor who had lived in Tanzania, which served as a foundation for the bond his family shared with ours. They hosted us every Christmas at their place, where we'd play board games, and they cooked up a storm. That day he was wearing long socks, which sat just beneath his knees, and shorts that sat just above.

'No, I'm not going,' Mum said in tears. 'I don't have the money.'

'How much do you need?'

'Two thousand dollars.' Mum had some money saved but was short of two grand.

'You're going.' He hugged her. 'Me and my family will help you go.' They ended up giving her an interest-free loan so she could fly to Ghana for the memorial service, a year after my grandmother had been buried.

While Mum was back in Ghana, she retrieved her transfer certificate in nursing, which meant she could start working in Australia. She got a job at Muswellbrook Hospital as an enrolled nurse.

When Mum got her driver's licence, she would sit in the car in the driveway for a little longer than necessary whenever she arrived home from work. Sometimes I'd peer out at her, wondering what she was thinking and how she must have wanted to take a breather before the chaos of four children descended on her. She may have just been listening to the radio, rounding out a song on Rhema FM, the Christian station, or listening to the end of a news report on ABC Radio Upper Hunter. I would stand there and wonder, but never interrupt, because I didn't know what I'd be interrupting.

Her work uniform back then was a light-blue dress with white trim around the sleeves. Mum would rock that uniform beautifully, with such style, such pride. She loved nursing and caring for patients. What she didn't love was dealing with a certain wardsman, who did things like rubbing her arm with a dirty tissue to see if the Black would rub off. If there was one career I was convinced I would never pursue, based on Mum's description of her workplace, it was nursing.

'I have to wipe people's bums and clean up vomit,' she would say, summing up her day's activities on the regular. None of it sounded fun.

'Do you think you'll be a nurse someday?' she asked me.

'No way.'

'Why? It's such a good job.'

'You don't make it sound like one.'

'That's because I'm an enrolled nurse. If I was a registered nurse, I would get to serve my patients holistically. I've always wanted to be a registered nurse. But all things work for good for those who love Jesus. Never say die till the bones are rotten. One day I'll be an RN.'

There's nobody on earth with faith stronger than my mother's. Not once during my childhood or adolescence did I ever see her waver. There was one time, as I lay in a hospital bed as an adult, when I overheard Mum question God for the first time – His motives, His existence – but even then her conclusion was swift: God is real. God loves us. God is for us. Her steadfast devotion swiftly replaced whatever doubt had been festering. It was God alone who would get us through that moment, and any other adversity to come. There is no Mum without God; she is His child.

She thinks carefully and prayerfully before doing or saying anything, seeking guidance and counsel. And oh does she love to bring her Saviour up in conversation. It's idiosyncratic, the way she can turn a conversation about anything – work, leisure, life's hardships – into an expression of divine love.

There is rarely a sentence out of my mother's mouth in which she doesn't acknowledge or reference God – or rebuke the Devil – in some way. She loves to quote Bible verses. *All things work together for good for those who love God. I will not die, but live to declare the goodness of the Lord. Jesus said ask anything, and it will be given to you. Call to Me, and I will answer and show you great and unsearchable things you know nothing about.*

But then, and this never made sense to me, she didn't insist on things like saying grace before a meal – sometimes we did, more often we didn't.

Mum rarely read *The Lamp*, the magazine of the NSW Nurses and Midwives' Association, but the magazines would pile up. Dad, who read everything, would go through them instead, and sometimes relay the contents to Mum. The one book she insisted on reading was the Bible. If the best book ever written was available to her, why waste time on others? While Mum was what

people might call a 'Bible basher', Dad was quietly religious –
a believer who didn't flaunt it.

Before bed each night, Mum would gather us to pray. She
would usually open and close the prayers. Each prayer would
start with *Dear Father*, followed by a shopping list of things she
wanted for us all: good health, good marks, abundant blessings,
and that God *destroy our enemies*. Then we would pray in order
of birth. I would pray, then Sedudzi, then Sophia, then John, then
back to Mum. Dad mostly didn't join us. Then we would end by
saying the Lord's Prayer in unison.

Quite often my prayers weren't answered. Knowing this,
I would sometimes refrain from praying for things I really
wanted, or I would bet in my head that the prayer I was saying
was not going to come true – and then I'd metaphorically throw
my hands in the air and think, *See – my prayers never come true.*
Of course they weren't going to with that type of approach, with
that little faith. I pray very differently now.

♪♫

We had a new car, a Toyota, parked at the top of our driveway. All
of a sudden, my dad noticed that the car was moving.

John, who was tiny, had managed to jump into the driver's seat
and release the handbrake. His little feet couldn't reach the accel-
erator, but he steered the vehicle as it slowly moved backwards
into the street.

Dad ran as fast as he could to catch up with the car. When he
reached it, he pulled the brake and then turned to John. 'You did
very well steering the car. Well done,' he said.

Sedudzi, who had run up behind Dad, turned to Mum. He couldn't believe Dad's reaction. 'If that had been me, I would have got in so much trouble.' Despite this, Sedudzi held no resentment towards John. On the contrary, he insisted that John got the chance to do the things he had missed out on because Mum and Dad had put their foot down. One of those things was boxing – John would go on to be well known around town as an amateur boxer. While Sedudzi took it to heart when Mum told him not to go to other people's places because they'd get sick of him, he stepped in when Mum tried to tell John the same thing. 'Let him go. You wouldn't let me visit people, and now I'm in my room all by myself. Let John visit his friends.'

And so, John would go on to socialise and make many friends.

Sedudzi has always been one to barrack for the underdog. In later years, he decided to sponsor a child in Africa.

'I chose the ugliest kid I could find,' he said.

'Why?' I asked.

'Because everyone always goes for the cute kids. The ugly ones need help too. It's not fair that they miss out on help just because they're not genetically blessed.'

His words were in jest, but he had a point there. Sedudzi always took his compassion and generosity a step further than most.

The Commonwealth Bank had a way of capturing customers early, and that was through the Dollarmites Club. Children under the age of twelve would put away two dollars a week and watch their savings grow. One of the things about getting our Dollar-mites accounts was that we had to create our own signatures. I drew up a variety of different options and settled on the rather ordinary scrawl that I'm stuck with today – if I'd known I would still be using it, I would have come up with something far more elaborate and imaginative. There was nothing special about my signature – except to Sedudzi. When he copied me by coming up with an almost identical signature, I couldn't understand it and expressed my displeasure. A signature is a signature – your unique imprint in the world of formal documents. *Why would you copy somebody else's signature?* Maybe I should have been flattered, but I was incredulous.

'That looks exactly like mine.'

'Yeah.' He smiled.

'Why would you copy my signature?'

Sedudzi shrugged his shoulders. 'It's no big deal. It's just a signature.'

'It is a big deal. A signature is meant to be unique.'

I might have been overreacting at the time, raking him over the coals for doing something younger siblings always do – copy their older siblings – but the thousand cracks in our relationship were quickly growing into a chasm.

CHAPTER 3

Blessed Assurance

*The thing that makes you unique is the thing
that will make you.*

I was growing up in the Hunter Valley and yet, for many years, I never had a sip of wine. Not even in church, where the blood of Jesus was actually grape juice.

It was a blue-collar, heavy-drinking kind of place – there were about seven pubs in town – far more than a town with a population of only 11,000 needed. Among the pubs stood just as many churches. The Baptist church was our new church home and was perched on a corner up the road from the Prince of Wales Tavern. It was a 1970s light-brown brick building that looked like a house; in fact, a section of it had actually been donated, trucked in from out of town. The hall was filled with plastic chairs lined up in rows from front to back for the congregation.

After the church choir wrapped up and the lyrics to the modern songs faded from the wall, where they'd been projected, the congregation would laugh at the doctor delivering the weekly announcements, punctuated with dad-jokes. 'In church news today, a glimpse into the future. And by the future, I mean 11 am today. We'll be christening a new baby. Because christening an old one wouldn't make much sense.'

The church was made up of young families from around town. There were couples with two children. Couples with three. Some, like my parents, with four. There were single people as well, but they would often meet their future spouses at church, and have children as well. These children, including myself at the time, would be present for the worship songs, the offering and the announcements, and then we would be sent off to Sunday school. The Sunday school building next door was known simply as '77', as it stood at 77 Sydney Street. As I sauntered towards it one morning, Sally Smith, another of the Sunday school kids, blocked my way.

'Did you know . . .' she began, the expression on her face serious, 'that you're never going to be white?'

'Huh?'

'Well, I asked my parents how much longer you'd have to stay in Australia before you turned white. They said you'll always be Black. That you'll never, *ever* turn white.'

I looked at her, a little wary. 'What made you think I would turn white?'

'I just thought that's what happened.' Sally shrugged, nudging past me to make her way into the building.

At the door, she threw a final pitying look over her shoulder and skipped inside.

I took a moment to think about what she'd said before following her in. The thought of turning white had never occurred to me. I had never, *ever* wanted to be white. There had been incidents where I'd been teased because my hair was different to everyone else's. Mum had taken to styling it in a number of different ways. One of the ways she styled it led to one kid in particular pulling at it constantly while referring to it as a 'spiderweb'.

He lived just up the road, and we used to hang out outside of school, but once we were on the school bus he would pull my hair. *Spiderweb, spiderweb, spiderweb.* Sedudzi tried to defend me, but it got so bad one day that I got off the bus at a friend's house. Mum panicked when the bus pulled up outside our house and I wasn't on it. My hair was the first obvious sign to me that I was different from my peers. Even so, I was comfortable in my Blackness. And now, I was relieved that turning white was not in my future.

♪♫

'Are you going to be like Trisha Goddard?' My teacher smiled at me. We were standing just outside the demountables at recess as she looked down at me expectantly. I was about eight years old.

Until then it had never occurred to me that I could follow in the footsteps of the first Black anchorwoman on Australian television and host of the *7.30 Report* on the ABC. Mum and I had discussed her hair. I asked her why Trisha had long, curly hair, while mine had an afro texture.

'She's wearing a wiglet,' Mum said.

'What's a wiglet? I want a wiglet!'

My teacher made me realise I could aspire to having more than just hair extensions.

'You could be like her, you know,' she said. 'You could be on TV too.'

I thought about it and liked the idea. I was going to be a journalist. It was something that thoroughly suited me. I used to ask a lot of questions – I was asking so many questions all the time that one of my friends, Amber Jones, told me that a mutual friend of ours was really sick of all my questions.

'Like what? What questions?'

'I don't know – she just said you ask a lot of questions.'

In addition to my natural curiosity, I had an early passion for writing. At school, one of our teachers, Ms Clark, got us to write our own children's books. It was hands down my favourite assignment. I took great care in coming up with a title and choosing the characters – my main character was a bunny called Benny Bunny. I developed a plot – it was Benny Bunny's day off, a clean slate for the adventures that ensued – and illustrated my story, cutting and pasting real fabric onto the pages to clothe my characters. Completing the assignment, seeing what I could write and illustrate, was electrifying. Storytelling became a passion, but it's telling true stories, about real people and real issues, that gives me the biggest thrill.

CHAPTER 4

All That Thrills
My Soul

*Having role models is great, but I guess
I just need to remember they're human too.*

I sat on the edge of my seat.

'BANG!' The gun went off. It was the 1988 Seoul Olympics men's 100-metre final.

I leapt out of my seat in unison with the sprinters on the television set. My fists clenched together, I cheered on the American star Carl Lewis, believing if I was loud enough it might get him over the line in first place. I watched on in anticipation, my eyes glued to the action.

The race was over within seconds – 9.79 seconds to be exact. But Carl Lewis wasn't the winner. Instead, it was the Canadian, Ben Johnson. It was a massive upset.

My shoulders slumped. I was disappointed, but rather than stew over the result, I walked over to my mother.

'I'm going to marry Carl Lewis,' I said.

Mum, who was more of a fan of commentator Bruce McAvaney than any of the athletes, laughed and shook her head. 'He's a lot older than you, Mawunyo,' she said, as if age was the only impediment to our nuptials. Nine-year-old me didn't care that he'd just lost the race of a lifetime. I wanted to cheer him up.

Three days later, Carl Lewis was proven the winner after all when he was awarded the gold medal and the world record after Ben Johnson was disqualified for testing positive to steroids.

Florence Griffith Joyner was another of my favourite sprinters. Her fingernails, which were so long they'd curl over, were always painted in an array of colours. It couldn't have been easy to make those '80s track outfits look so stylish, but she did just that. The one-legged tights, the belts she wore, the day-glo colours – she always looked stunning. I wanted to be just like her.

I could identify with Carl Lewis. I could identify with Flo-Jo. They shared the same kinky hair, the same smooth dark complexion. I was one of them. They were just like me.

Not long afterwards, I channelled my track heroes when I competed at the school sports carnival. I tied my jumper around my waist, stood in position at the starting line for the 100-metre sprint and *ran*. I came out the winner. I repeated this feat in the 200-metre race, and I also placed first in long jump, becoming the local Junior Girl Athletics Champion. I'll never forget the look on the face of my main competitor Kelly Winter's mother: *sour*. Her daughter was the hot favourite to win the title, but I had come out of nowhere to beat her.

Mum and I would sometimes talk about what country I would represent if I was in the Olympic Games: Ghana or Australia.

'Can't I represent both?' I asked.

'No.' Mum laughed. 'You can only represent one country at the Olympics. You'd have to choose.'

The concept of having to choose between Ghana and Australia was all too much for me. Ghana was where I was born. It was where the bulk of my extended family still lived.

When I think about it now, had I reached the dizzying heights of Olympic-level competition, of course I'd race for Australia. My dual identities were important to me though. I was as much from Australia as I was from Ghana. Even now, people ask me where I'm from all the time based on how I look. I tend to mess with them. I know what they're asking, but my answer is always Muswellbrook – that's where I'm from, even though I know they want to know where I'm *from from*. An African Australian friend said to me, 'You know the reason they're asking that, right? They want to know where we're from so they can decide how to treat us.' And she's right, of course. The one time I replied to that question with a straight answer – Ghana – the old man who had asked said, 'Well, that's better than Nigeria or Sudan!'

A TV commercial came on while we were watching the Olympics. The voiceover stated, 'Keep Australia beautiful. It's the only one we've got.'

'But we've got Ghana too!' I said, Mum looking over at me in amusement.

Another commercial, another jingle: *Aussie kids are Weet-Bix kids.* I considered myself an Aussie kid. But Weet-Bix? Weet-Bix was not my favourite cereal. It was so bland. Did this mean I couldn't really call myself an Aussie kid?

I placed my dinner on my lap and sat in front of the TV to watch *The Cosby Show. I wonder what Vanessa and Rudy will get up to today*, I thought to myself. I lifted the fork to my mouth.

'You're not supposed to eat that with a fork.' Dad laughed at me. I shrugged my shoulders and persisted. My parents used their fingers to eat okro soup and akple, but this wasn't even real akple – it was semolina. You couldn't get akple in Muswellbrook.

I laughed at the look on Dr Huxtable's face as he told his daughter Vanessa she couldn't attend a slumber party. His wife, Clair Huxtable, walked into the room. My laughter grew louder as I watched her give Vanessa one of her hilarious death stares. She was an attorney, and very elegant. The Huxtables were an exemplary TV family.

They were Black, intelligent and successful – not to mention gifted with a great sense of humour. I, too, was all of these things. I took another bite from my makeshift akple. I was Black and proud. I was special and highly favoured – just like the people I watched on TV. They looked like me, and as a kid growing up in a country town where few other people did, to be aligned with greatness on television meant that a kind of greatness rubbed off on me.

CHAPTER 5

Lily of the Valley

Teachers teach. And so too the layperson.

On Sundays, I'd sit in the middle of our eight-seater Toyota Tarago on the way to church, while the other three were squashed in the back.

We were now back at the local Presbyterian church, where there was a new young family pastoring the flock.

While the Baptist church was all about modern worship songs, the Presbyterian church continued to rock out to hymns like 'Mine Eyes Have Seen the Glory of the Coming of the Lord', 'Immortal, Invisible' and 'Great Is Thy Faithfulness'. I was, once again, in my element. It wasn't one of those hand-raising, demonstrative, dynamic churches, but I found a lot of comfort in familiar hymns. Their melodies enveloped me in that old-school charm, while the lyrics told the story of a forgiving and merciful Lord. *Crown Him with many crowns, the Lamb upon His throne. Hark!*

How the heav'nly anthem drowns, all music but its own. Awake, my soul, and sing of Him who died for thee, and hail Him as thy matchless King, through all eternity.

Mum and I argued every now and then, and I was doubly cranky with her one Sunday morning after she disciplined me for putting a Sweet Valley High book on top of one of her many Bibles. 'Nothing should sit on top of the Bible,' she scolded, making a point to pick up one of Jessica and Elizabeth Wakefield's adventures and toss it aside so that the Holy Word could take pride of place on the table.

When we got to Sunday school, our teacher put a question to us. 'Now, I want you to write down on a piece of paper who you think is the kindest person you know or have heard of.'

Well, there was no question in my mind that that person was my mother. Mum was the kindest person in the world, as far as I was concerned. She was selfless, someone who never bought anything new for herself – certainly not the latest fashions – and she always looks after others first. But I was fuming at her for tossing my Sweet Valley High novel aside.

I heard my name being called. 'Who did you choose and why?'

'Mother Teresa,' I said. 'She's always helped those in need.'

The teacher went around the room until it was my brother's turn to answer the question.

'Who did you pick, Sedudzi?'

'Mum,' he said. 'She is the kindest person I know. She's always been there for us and would do anything to help us out.'

'Wow, you must have a very special mum.'

Damn it, I thought. Why hadn't I swallowed my pride and said

Mum too? Imagine how special our Sunday school teacher would have thought our mum was if *both* of us had given that answer. It was on the tip of my tongue, but no . . . I went for Mother Teresa. A woman I had never met, would never meet and knew very little about. Nobody else had named their mother as the kindest person they knew.

My mother is strong. Gentle but tough. A true steward of God, who's set an example of faith unmatched by anybody I've ever come across. And that includes Mother Teresa.

But, like every human being, she's complex. And one of her favourite pastimes was highlighting my father's flaws, and pointing out how she could have done so much better.

'You know, I could have ended up with a really nice man, someone who was a doctor, a lawyer or an engineer. There were plenty of men who really wanted me, but I ended up with your father. But all things work for good for those who love God. No weapon formed against me will prosper. Still, I regret being so shy that I didn't talk to these other men. I could have lived a good life. I could have been happy.'

'But then you wouldn't have me. Do you realise that? You wouldn't have me, Sedudzi, Sophia or John if you hadn't ended up with Dad.'

'I would have had you with someone else.'

'I really don't think it works that way, Mum,' I said, pulling the fridge door open and looking inside to see the exact same contents that were there half an hour earlier.

'Oh, I saw your friend at the shops,' Mum said.

'Which friend?'

'I don't remember her name.'

49

'Did she have blonde hair, red hair, brown hair? Did she have blue eyes?'

'I don't know.'

'What do you mean you don't know?'

'Everyone has the same colour hair and eyes in Ghana – it's not something I've ever had to pay attention to.'

Oh, yeah, I thought. 'So how do you identify people then?'

'I don't know – whether they're tall or short, or skinny or fat . . .'

'Well, was she tall or short? Was she skinny or fat?' I asked.

We never did get to the bottom of who she saw that day at the shops.

♪♫

I let each sweet layer of chocolate melt on my tongue as I gobbled down the treat, unaware I had just unleased World War Three. Mum had given us all some chocolate when she returned from the shops. What I didn't realise was she knew exactly how much was left, and she felt the need to take on the role of chocolate guardian.

'Who took some more chocolate?'

I put on a poker face. Mum, determined to get to the bottom of it, gathered all of us into a circle. She asked us again. The denials came thick and fast. In addition to being a boxer, John would later, inadvertently, become a champion 1500-metre runner after getting up early every morning to train, in a bid to lose weight. But at that point he was still a chubby kid. He had a pained expression on his face. I looked at him as Mum's attention was directed his way. It looked as if he was going to get the blame for eating the chocolate.

Still, I said nothing.

Mum brought out her Bible. 'Mawunyo, can you read from Luke eight, verse seventeen.'

I took the Bible from her. 'For nothing is hidden that will not be made manifest, nor is anything secret that will not be known and come to light.' I was terrified.

'I'm going to put this in the centre of the circle and spin it,' she said, holding a thermometer. 'It's going to land on whoever ate the chocolate, so you better tell me now.'

The thermometer landed on John. She tried to catch him out. 'John, did you eat the chocolate?'

'No,' he said. Truthful. Solemn. Unfairly tarred.

'Sedudzi, did you eat the chocolate?'

'No, Mum.'

'Sophia?'

'No.'

'Mawunyo?'

'Yes,' I said quietly.

Mum, surprised but triumphant, paused, looking at me quizzically, as if to say, *Why didn't you own up to it from the beginning? You were going to let your brother take the blame?* I felt so ashamed.

'I want you all to know how important it is for you to tell me the truth. I will always defend you in anything you do. But I need to know that you're telling me the truth, so I know that I'm not defending a lie. It's so important for you to be honest with me.'

51

I hung my head in shame. It was a lesson for the ages, a compelling plea from my mother, whose own honesty was sacrosanct. It would take me some time, though, to learn that the thrill of getting away with something wasn't worth the guilt of having done wrong.

CHAPTER 6

When I Get to Heaven

These days, I stand up to bullies.
These days I use my voice.

It was 1990. Bobby and Frank were, sadly, no longer an item on *Home and Away*. On the other side of the world, the Chicago Bulls had been dominating the NBA since Michael Jordan was drafted in the mid-'80s, and just about every kid in Muswellbrook had a jersey, despite the fact that most would never experience a day in the stands at an NBA game. It was also the year Nelson Mandela was released from a South African prison after twenty-seven years and six months on the inside. As he was exiting prison, I was walking into my own prison of sorts: Year Five at Roger Street. Back then, there was no fence surrounding the school like there is today, but many of the buildings remain the same – an unwonted mix of brick and painted steel.

I had been chosen for the composite class based on merit. The high-ranking Year Five students were placed alongside the not-so-bright Year Sixers. Apparently, this way, both groups would be challenged, sitting side-by-side in the same classroom.

'Don't get too comfortable,' Mr Miller said. 'You won't be in those seats for long.' I shuffled my feet underneath the Laminex desk. 'I want you all to write your names on a piece of paper after I've read out the roll. I'm going to draw your seating arrangements out of a hat.'

The class groaned collectively. 'Keep it down, you guys. I'll be having none of that,' Mr Miller said.

I listened intently as he read out the names in front of him. I could always tell when a teacher was about to call out my name because there would be a pause – an indication they'd come across a variety of letters unusually linked together, like a set of Scrabble tiles pulled randomly from the bag. I wouldn't let the pause go on for too long, because that would be embarrassing for the both of us – particularly me – as it guaranteed my name would come out of the teacher's mouth a mangled mess.

I immediately took the opportunity to jump in this time too. I said my name out loud, pronouncing it the way I wanted him to – and not how it appeared phonetically on the page. He smiled and repeated after me.

I actually taught people to mispronounce my name for years, because I found it so difficult to say myself. I sat down one day and invented a variant. At the time – I was five or six years old, *MAH-nyoh BOH-BOH* sounded silly to my young ears because it rhymed. *I can't have a name that rhymes!* I thought. So, I told everyone to call me MARN-you. I managed to convince an entire town that MARN-you was spelt M-A-W-U-N-Y-O. And then a town became everyone I met thereafter. I didn't start pronouncing my name more authentically until after I turned forty.

We all popped our names on a piece of paper as instructed, strolling up to the front of the classroom to place it inside a hat. We waited as the delegation got underway. Mr Miller told me I would be sitting next to Elliot Robertson, who was in the year above me. I knew his sister Wendy, who was in my year. Curiously, Wendy said things to me all the time, like, 'My dad thinks you're so nice. Even when he's sitting on the toilet, he'll go on about how nice you are.' I don't recall ever meeting her father.

I looked at Elliot and smiled.

'Hey, nigger,' he said. His manner and tone were so soft that I was taken off guard.

'What are you looking at, you Black bitch?' Again, that soft, delicate tone, his face almost expressionless.

I turned my head away from him and caught the teacher having a go at a student for being too loud. 'You ignorant little boy,' he said. I would learn that 'ignorant' was Mr Miller's favourite word. He used it a lot to describe students who were playing up.

When I heard the bell at the end of class, I walked straight up to Mr Miller's desk. The Batlow apple that had been sitting there that morning was gone. Mr Miller had a penchant for apples, I discovered – but only if they were red. 'Excuse me . . . can I please sit somewhere else in class?'

'No,' he said without hesitating. 'The seating arrangements will remain this way until the end of term. Why do you want to move anyway?'

I didn't know how to respond. If I told him what Elliot had said, it was unlikely the racist taunts would suddenly cease.

Things were likely to get worse, I reasoned. Plus, Mr Miller sounded as if he'd already made up his mind, no matter what came out of my mouth next. Although, *the guy you've got me sitting next to is a racist little shit* might have got his attention. I looked at Mr Miller expectantly, willing him to read my mind.

'Yeah, I thought so,' he continued. 'There isn't a good reason.' This man was clearly no mind-reader. 'You'll get used to sitting at that desk. Who knows? By the time I get you to change seats you might be begging me to leave you there.'

'I doubt it,' I said under my breath. My classmate was unlikely to go from being a deep-seated racist to being alert and opposed to racial prejudice and discrimination overnight.

'What was that?' Mr Miller asked.

'Oh, nothing.' As I walked out of the classroom, I braced myself for what was to come. I wasn't looking forward to school the next day.

'Hey, Dad, can you go faster?' I asked later that afternoon as we were headed home from the library. I could see Mr Miller out the window, going for a jog. He could almost keep up with the car. Dad threw a look over his shoulder and continued at a *Driving Miss Daisy* pace.

When we got home, I leafed through my dictionary. 'Ignorant' wasn't a synonym for rude, as I had thought. In fact, it described Mr Miller when it came to the situation I found myself in at school at that moment.

I began to get bored with my homework so turned my attention to the *Encyclopaedia Britannica* that was sitting on my desk and started flicking through it. My parents had bought a complete set of the encyclopedias and would update them with the latest yearbook every twelve months.

I landed on a page with a photograph of Whitney Houston. My mouth fell open. This passage was about physical attractiveness. Whitney Houston was pictured there as an illustration of beauty. Sure, her music was all over the charts. Her voice was phenomenal. But the encyclopedia definition of attractive was illustrated by *Whitney*? Weren't encyclopedia's written by white people? I was under the impression that the commonly accepted notion of beauty was reserved for those with blonde hair and blue eyes. Elliot 'you're a nigger' Robertson certainly thought so. Sally 'you'll never be white' Smith gave off those vibes too. It was okay to have a tan – in fact, society even encouraged it – just so long as you weren't Black. But there it was, in print. Whitney Houston was the ideal of attractiveness. These academics had given her the stamp of approval, and they had to be a whole lot smarter than Elliot Robertson or Sally Smith.

I ran over to my mother and showed her. Then, still smiling, I put the encyclopedia back on the shelf. Whitney Houston was Black like me. I, too, was beautiful. *Black is beautiful.* The phrase had implanted itself inside my mind and consciousness, long before I understood where it'd come from, who was saying it and why they were saying it. It empowered me. *Black is Beautiful.*

When Muhammad Ali died, TV networks replayed interviews he had done, and there was one with Michael Parkinson that resonated with me deeply. Muhammad Ali was questioning why Jesus was white with blond hair and blue eyes. I had wondered the same thing growing up – Mum, being so religious, had a picture of white Jesus in our house. She hadn't got around to putting it on the wall, but she did have it sitting on the floor against the wall, like our family photos. White Jesus was one of the reasons it took me so long to really believe, because to me it just didn't make sense, as it hadn't made sense to Muhammad Ali. Why were all good and pure things white, while anything evil and impure was associated with black? It was one of quite a few things that didn't make sense in Christianity. Some of the stories seemed far-fetched. Why did Mary have to be a virgin? How did Daniel survive that lions' den? How did David manage to overcome Goliath? How come snakes could talk? How could God speak directly to Moses, through a burning bush no less, when He speaks to us in much more subtle ways?

When I learned that the images of white Jesus were fanciful at best, things started to click into place. I still had questions, but at least this was one answer that sat well with me. No matter what anybody said, being Black was something to be proud of.

Black is beautiful.

'Hey, nigger.'

I resisted the urge to look over at Elliot.

'Don't you reckon, nigger . . .'

'I want you to work with the person next to you on this next exercise . . .'

'It's about time you went home and scrubbed the Black off ya? That's right. Go home and have a shower.'

'You've got fifteen minutes to complete it . . .'

'Look at me when I'm talking to ya, nigger . . .'

He prodded me with his vicious words in a tone so placid that he could easily have been talking about the weather.

My immediate problem was Mr Miller's expectation that we work together on the class exercise. I had no intention of puzzling over a bunch of decimals and fractions with Elliot.

'Now, here's one sheet between two.' I held my hand out as Mr Miller came by with the equations.

'Niggers are stupid,' Elliot said. 'You ain't nothin' but a stupid little nigger.'

♪♫

At recess, eleven-year-old Michael Thomas was clearly upset about being dumped by his girlfriend, Samantha Lee.

'I really want her back,' he said. 'There must be a way I can convince her to take me back.'

'What is it you like about her so much?' I was curious.

'She's funny and smart, and soooo pretty. I don't know anyone else who looks like her. She's perfect.' He stepped it up a notch, going into victim mode. 'It's not fair. I don't understand why she dropped me. Do you reckon you can talk to her for me?'

'She's not interested in you anymore,' I said. 'You're right about nobody else looking like her. She's the only Asian girl I can think of in our year.'

His eyes narrowed as he stared at me, clearly confused. Then they began to widen. 'Is she . . . Asian?'

It was my turn to look at him, confused. 'Uh, yeah. Her mum is white, but her dad is Chinese. Her last name is *Lee*.'

'Ohhhh.' His face was a picture of disgust, then relief. 'Well, I'm glad she dropped me then.' He was suddenly over Samantha Lee.

I stood there, not knowing whether to laugh or cry. If that was his reaction to finding out the girl he desperately wanted back was Asian, I wondered what his reaction might have been if she had a little Black in her.

♪♫

Elliot hadn't eased up for a single day. I tried again, on the verge of tears, to convince Mr Miller to let me move.

'I've already told you, the answer is no.'

At least he didn't call me an *ignorant little girl*. I continued to put up with Elliot's daily abuse and felt battered and bruised by the time the ordeal was over, when our seating arrangements finally changed towards the end of term.

It's possible I didn't stick up for myself because I hadn't worked out the best way to do so. I was methodical in most things, an overthinker – I would have considered the cons of speaking up. Somehow, I must have thought that whatever Elliot might do to me for telling on him would be worse than the racist bullying itself. I also gather that I didn't involve my parents because, to my Year-Five mind, what could they do to make things better? Would they even take a break from fighting to get involved? Of course, I tell myself now that that's silly. My parents would have turned up to the school and that racist dickhead would have been silenced. I don't know why I didn't just speak up. What I *do* know is something inside of me shifted that year: I was different. But Elliot had failed to convince me that this difference was something to be ashamed of. There was beauty in this difference.

When I was too young to know any better, I stopped talking to my little brother, Sedudzi. He had a way of pushing my buttons, upsetting me, so one day I decided I was going to ignore him.

Eventually he gave up trying to get my attention. I may have also been influenced by kids at school who thought it was perfectly normal for brothers and sisters to not get along – in fact, to them it was weird if you *did* get along. The thing with our family, though, that I should have realised back then, is we didn't have anyone else. There was no one else in that town who knew what it was like to be us. So sticking together should have been of utmost importance to me. The white kids at school had cousins – what they called 'first cousins', 'second cousins', 'third cousins' – all in their vicinity. We had none of that. We were isolated from our relatives.

The only connection I had with my extended family was through the letters I used to write to my Aunty Rita and one of Dad's relatives, whom I called Uncle Gershon, always anticipating the day we might reunite.

My parents weren't very good at explaining things or helping us navigate this difference. They raised us as Aussies. We would abandon Ewe – the language Sedudzi and I could speak when we arrived in Australia. I understand the spoken language, having grown up hearing my parents use phrases like *Dedi te wunye* (I'm so tired), *Edor wuim* (I'm so hungry), *Ago* (Move out of the way for me to pass). Sometimes, I would translate things literally.

'*Eduokuiwo dum,*' Dad said once.

'I'm not eating myself!' I replied.

Dad and Mum both cracked up. I got the literal translation right, but the phrase actually means, 'You're annoyed for nothing.'

Mum and Dad didn't want us to be behind at school, so they spoke English to us at home – something they regret doing now because my siblings and I can't find the words to express ourselves in Ewe.

We were outsiders who after a while blended in so much that my sister can't recount an incident of racism she experienced in Muswellbrook. She puts it down to the fact she had older siblings, so by the time she was in school, the Gbogbo family were part of the fabric of the town. She was accepted because we'd paved the way.

As Sedudzi and I were drifting further and further apart, Sedudzi, Sophia and John were becoming closer and closer. When I did start talking to Sedudzi again, it was too little, too late.

Our family was visiting a Nigerian family who lived in Doonside, in Sydney's west. The kids played and the adults did whatever adults do. We were watching *Mad Max*.

Across the room, away from the television, I heard the angry words of one of the children directed towards my brother, who had grabbed a toy from the boy's hands. 'I'll tell your sister for snatching!' He aimed his finger in my direction to punctuate that he expected Sedudzi to have some sort of fear of me, born of reverence and respect, because African culture dictates that you respect your elders.

'Hahahahaha,' came the raucous laughter. 'He said he'll tell my sister for snatching. What's *she* going to do?' Tears spilled out of the corners of his eyes as he laughed and laughed and laughed. Sophia and John laughed along with him. They didn't subscribe to any type of sibling hierarchy. In fact, I was constantly telling Sedudzi to show respect.

'Respect is earned,' he'd reply. 'You've done nothing to earn my respect.'

The kid, realising he'd lost that battle, turned his attention back to the movie. 'Now Mad Max is mad!' he exclaimed with a giggle. I was left to digest the humbling moment.

I was twelve years old when *The Simpsons* first started airing on TV screens in Australia. Sedudzi, Sophia and John loved *The Simpsons*. Me – not so much. They would walk around the house speaking in Simpsons quotes. Sometimes it was Homer's catchcry, 'Doh!' At other times, 'You don't win friends with salad,' or 'You'll have to speak up. I'm wearing a towel.' But by far Sedudzi's favourite phrase was 'Greetings, friend,' the words from Homer's autodialler. Even now, when he sees me, the first words out of his mouth are quite often 'Greetings, friend.'

I was never a fan of *The Simpsons*. I felt like I was too old to watch cartoons. At twelve, I was blithely unaware that adults were the main consumers of the show, and the satire was quite sophisticated. My lack of interest, though, meant that I couldn't speak my siblings' adopted language; I didn't have the same reference points. When they dropped a Simpsons quote mid-conversation, it would go over my head. That meant I didn't understand them. And they certainly didn't understand me.

Around this time, also on television, also imported from the United States, were the LA riots. A Black man, Rodney King, had been beaten savagely by police. The images, caught on camera, were beamed right across the world and into our living room in the Hunter Valley. What I saw on TV was a clear-cut case of police brutality, but not according to the American justice system. Three officers involved in the beating were acquitted by a jury, who could not decide on a verdict for the fourth officer. The riots ensued. Blocks were set on fire, bricks thrown through shop windows. There were Marines in Humvees driving through Compton. I felt the injustice of the verdict from the safety of my sleepy town, across the ocean, not knowing then that, almost three decades later, my diasporic brothers and sisters would be no safer Stateside.

What I admired then, and continue to admire in Black people now, however, is the fight within us. Black Americans in particular are constantly fighting for themselves and each other. 'No Justice, No Peace' was the chant at Black Lives Matter protests after George Floyd was murdered by a police officer in 2020. I, like so many people around the world, was enraged by what I saw captured on film. The protests that followed gave me hope that change may come.

That fight, that willingness to be of service to your community, is something to be valued and revered. It's that fight that is at the root of my admiration and respect for Black America. An Indigenous friend told me recently that part of the reason Aboriginal and Torres Strait Islander people struggle to be heard in the way African Americans are has a lot to do with numbers. Indigenous Australians, who have historically been massacred, and even subject to government policies designed to breed the Black out of them, make up just 3.3 per cent of the Australian population, while African Americans are 13 per cent of the US population. It's not that the will to fight isn't here locally, and there will be a day when we're all forced to listen.

Mum wanted to buy a house and heard through the local grapevine that the Electricity Commission was selling some of its properties. When she approached Dad, he asked her where the money was to buy the house. Determined as ever, Mum refused to take no for an answer. She gathered up all her savings and met with the bank, borrowing enough money for a deposit on a house in Claret Avenue in the Wine Estate.

But money was a source of tension in our household, and sometimes Mum and Dad just didn't seem to enjoy sharing the same space. There was a lack of trust. Mum was convinced Dad was hiding stuff from her, given he'd hidden a whole child. As a consequence, when a letter arrived from Ghana she would try to intercept it, so she would know what was going on. Dad, of course, didn't like her going through his personal things. He even had a photo of his son Selassie in a diary at home, and underneath it he had written something in German, so that Mum wouldn't understand it.

Mum wouldn't dare confide in anyone outside the family about what was going on for fear it would get back to Dad. She confided in me, and I in turn would go and confront Dad, admonishing him for being mean to Mum.

'You'll see,' Dad would reply. 'You'll see.'

I could hear the raised voices, the insults being hurled about the room. Mum didn't think Dad was doing enough for the family she'd given him – how dare he secretly send money to another one. At least be open about it. Mum didn't hide the fact she sent money to family back home. She's since moved on and wants us kids to have a relationship with our brother, Selassie, but back then things got rather heated. When Sophia found a letter addressed to Dad from Selassie's mum, not knowing the chain reaction it would set off, she handed it to him. Mum, who hadn't been able to get to the letter first, wasn't happy, but later seized it.

'You won't dip your hand into your pocket for a single little thing,' Mum said. 'When I want to do something – buy a house, send the kids to a nice school – there's no money. But you'll send money back to Ghana for the family you care about. Your mind is always there. You don't care about me suffering here with you.'

Dad's voice began to rise also. 'Give that to me.'

'No.' Mum was holding the letter to ransom.

'Give it to me.'

'No.'

Back and forth they went; me, gasping, calling out for them to stop. Unheard, I whimpered. My chest heaved.

My parents were constantly fighting now. Quite often, Dad would shut down and not say much at all, seething as Mum yelled at him. But the fact he didn't challenge her validated her words in my eyes, even if they weren't on point.

Fight, fight, fight, fight, fight. That's what they did. That's how they lived. That's what I'd see.

We knew things were getting tight when at Christmas one year, Mum thought it would be a good idea to wrap up tennis balls as gifts because she didn't have enough money to buy us anything else. It was too much for my brother John, who wept. It wasn't that he'd received the worst gift a kid his age could get, wrapped in deceptively alluring packaging, but that he had to contend with the fact his friend who lived across the road had been showered with an array of cool gifts that he was parading around the neighbourhood.

'What did you get, John?' his friend asked him.

John avoided the question. *Tennis balls. Tennis balls. No racquets to even go with them – too expensive. Just tennis balls.* John did his best to avoid his friend for as long as possible that day, a difficult task when you live so close by.

CHAPTER 7

This Is My Father's World

If you love someone and they don't know it,
could there be a better way to love?

Mum always had something to say to me about Dad. 'Your father tells me *my father* had so many wives, but *my father* didn't hide that from anybody . . .' It went on and on and on. There was even one time when we were in the kitchen, Mum talking to Dad while he was making toast, when Mum, gesticulating wildly, accidentally knocked his toast, already peanut buttered, onto the floor. With Dad's back turned, Mum looked at me as if to say, *Don't say a word*. She picked up the toast, put it back on the plate and continued talking, giving me a sly smile.

My relationship with my father was complicated. There was a point in my childhood where I wanted to change my name to Albertina because his name is Albert. But there also came a time when I was convinced he hated me. There were the 'You'll see' comments, delivered sullenly, Dad upset that his daughter would challenge him. Where was the respect for my elders?

Dad was often quite negative. While Mum is all: 'I can do all things through Christ who strengthens me,' Dad is a realist: 'Man proposes, God disposes.' He never hesitates to point out the obstacles.

If Dad told me something I did was 'alright', my head would swell to the size of a watermelon. If it was 'alright' to Dad then it must be truly extraordinary. He had no problems telling me when he didn't like something. He was never one to waste time sugar-coating his words to avoid hurting my feelings.

He was confusing to me because I've always been aware he does have a sense of humour. When *Crocodile Dundee* came out in 1986, Dad would develop a go-to catchphrase. We were sitting watching the movie when Paul Hogan's character delivered a line that caught Dad's attention – even more than the *That's not a knife* line that most people quote.

Sue Charlton asked Mick Dundee what he thought of a meal they were tucking into. 'You can live on it, but it tastes like shit,' he replied.

Dad burst out laughing: *Hahahahahaha.* From then on, every time we went out to eat, that's how he would respond to any questions about his meal.

'Hey, Dad, how's your meal?'

'It tastes like shit,' Dad would reply, pausing for dramatic effect, 'but you can live on it.' His face almost concealed his wry smile.

He's the most straight-laced person I've ever met, does everything by the book, follows all the rules, even speaks formally for the most part – *Hello, Good morning* – but he loves to have a laugh.

I desperately wanted confirmation that he loved me, but deep down I believed he didn't. That's why I'll never forget the day the door-to-door salesman came by.

'I'll get it,' I called out as I walked to the door. I held it slightly ajar and peered out at the stranger on the other side. He was carrying a large bag, the contents a mystery.

'Well, hello there.' His voice was husky. 'Are your parents home?'

'Dad?' I summoned and waited as he cast his Wilbur Smith novel aside and approached.

The salesman grasped my father's hand with both of his and shook it firmly, introducing himself. 'And you are?'

'Albert,' Dad said in his no-nonsense tone.

'May I come in, Albert?'

Dad stepped aside as the salesman strode into the house as if it were his own.

He followed my father into the family room, walking past Dad's record player, which had long since broken, silencing the tunes of Caribbean artists Jimmy Cliff, Bob Marley and Boney M, whose records were still housed in the glass compartment beneath the player.

The salesman placed his bag down and began to unpack.

'Have you ever owned a vacuum cleaner like this one?' he asked. Mum and Dad shook their heads in unison. 'Well, I'm going to show you how one of these beauties can save you time and money.'

The salesman reached into his bag and pulled out a carpet sample, which he placed onto our tiles. He then pulled out a mini hand-held vacuum cleaner and threw a small container of dirt onto the carpet.

'Now watch this,' he said.

ZHROOM! The dirt disappeared in a matter of seconds.

'Let's try this with liquid.' Once again, he zapped up the mess.

'Did you know,' he said, 'there are about a million dust particles living in the cleanest of carpets? They pose a danger to your health.' He turned to my father. 'Albert, do you love your family?'

Well, I knew the answer to *that* question. I looked at Dad, bracing myself for what would come next. Dad looked at the salesman solemnly and paused.

'Yes,' he said.

What? I thought. *Did I miss something? Since when? That is news to me. But of course! You're just saying that so you don't look bad in front of the salesman.*

'Well, it's important for you to protect your family against the organisms that lurk in our environment . . .'

Dad didn't buy the vacuum cleaner that day, but that didn't mean a great deal. He was too frugal to even buy the newspapers – he'd pop over to the library every day for his dose of news and current affairs. We never saw the salesman again, but it got me thinking: Did he or didn't he love me? And if I couldn't find love where I wanted it most, what lengths would I go to find it myself?

PART TWO

CHAPTER 8

All Things Bright and Beautiful

Muswellbrook.
Where so many of the good girls ain't that good.

Year Ten. Muswellbrook High School. 1995.

I placed my hand on a piece of paper and traced around it. I wrote my name above the outline, with my nickname – Marnz – underneath it in brackets for good measure.

'Once you've done that, leave the paper with the outline of your hand on the table,' the teacher said. 'Now it's time to let your classmates know what you think of them. Nice comments only. I want you to roam the room and select a word or two to describe your peers. Pop your thoughts on their hand. Let them know you appreciate them.'

I made my way around the table, popping comments on each of the hands I came across. When I arrived at Tyce Carrington's hand, I paused. *Tyce. What to say about Tyce?*

Like me, Tyce was Black and living in Muswellbrook – his

father is a Dunghutti man and his mother a Gomeroi woman. Tyce was just so damn sexy, but I couldn't write that on his hand, could I? I liked them tall and thin, just like him. His complexion was chocolate. When he wasn't in school uniform, as a general rule, Tyce's clothing rarely bore the stamp of a brand name. He mostly dressed like he didn't give a damn, but that took nothing away from his looks. If anything, it added to his persona of cool indifference. He wore a cap most of the time, like the rest of his crew – the homeboys. Beneath the lid were the most alluring eyes I'd ever seen. I would stare into those deep, dark eyes for days, if I was ever blessed with the opportunity. The way he walked – I didn't have the language for it then, but I'd now describe it as a swagger. The way he talked – he always delivered his punchlines off the cuff yet right on cue.

Tyce was really intelligent, but school wasn't his thing. He used to play up in class and give the teachers a hard time, but then he would answer a question that demonstrated the true breadth of his knowledge. I was fascinated by how bright he was. Whether it was English, Maths or Science, Tyce knew the answers.

More often than not, he would exploit a situation to inject his brand of humour. His jokes were usually very funny, but occasionally they were at the expense of others. My perception of him had changed over time – I hadn't always liked him. He was a smartarse, plain and simple, and when we first met in Year Seven, that cheekiness wasn't something I immediately hooked onto as a positive. It was something that grew on me, his quick wit a characteristic I'd come to embrace and admire.

I thought about what I could write on his hand that would stand out. He would already be well aware of how much he made people laugh. I wanted him to know that I'd noticed how smart he was. And it wouldn't hurt if I could, in a roundabout way, let him know just how much I appreciated that face of his.

Smart and cute, I scrawled, and wrapped up the exercise.

'Hey, Marnz.' It was Tyce. My heart somersaulted. There was something about the way he initially said my nickname that would have bugged me if it wasn't him saying it. It sounded more like 'Munz'. I had a feeling that that's what he thought it was in the beginning. But I didn't care what he called me, as long as my name remained on his lips and my hips on his mind. He was smiling. We had all picked up our paper hands and were taking in the comments our classmates had written. People had littered numerous comments on mine: *nice and friendly; love your hair; nice; choice hair; cool; intelligent; friendly; fun to be around; sense of humour; cool hairdo.*

'Guess what I wrote?' Tyce said. I looked closely and shrugged. I didn't know his writing. He pointed. There, along the edge of my palm, just underneath my thumb, were the words *nice buns*. I looked up. He was grinning. I shook my head, grinning too. The Sir Mix-a-Lot song 'Baby Got Back' entered my head, a rap ode to every healthy curve and contour on a woman. I'd picked up from popular Australian culture in the '90s that skinny was best, and if you were going to have a booty, it'd better be as compact as Kylie Minogue's. But 'Baby Got Back' challenged all that, and it further stressed to me that my Black was beautiful. Although Sir Mix-a-Lot did say how alluring a slim waist was, he wanted it paired with a booty so big, round and bountiful as to be eminently noticeable and boldly shown off, celebrated. I wasn't much concerned with how unapologetically sexual the song was – it was an anthem.

'Do you know what I wrote on your hand?' I asked.

'Nope,' he said. I pointed at my attempt to sum up everything I thought of him. *Smart and cute.* He looked down at my words, then awkwardly up at me. He was too Black to blush, but I swear I saw a rose swirl sweep across his cheeks. His gaze lingered. And then he was gone.

♪♫

In my Year Ten Science class I sat next to Stacey Hoxton and Wendy Robertson.

Stacey Hoxton was the most popular girl in our grade, a bronzed athletic brunette with grey-blue eyes and a lopsided smile that made her look like she was smirking most of the time. Wendy Robertson, Elliot's younger sister, was a scatterbrained but friendly girl, blissfully unaware her brother had tortured me in primary school. She had a long blonde perm and a short, stocky frame. The two were best friends, even though to me their relationship felt more like a convenient business transaction.

My classmates and I used to write letters to each other – the '90s equivalent of texting or sliding into someone's DMs. Curiously, Stacey had written me a letter the previous year after I'd been around to her house to hang out, saying I was her second-best friend and Wendy was sort of number one. 'I'm fading away from her,' she wrote. 'She's not as funny as she was when I first met her.'

I found this statement extraordinary. Stacey and I weren't friends. I mean, I'd have loved to have claimed I was second-best friends with the most popular girl in our year, but the fact of the matter was, I was considered a square. Then there was Wendy, who was known as a 'Commodore slut' because she had a fondness for guys who drove Commodores. A harsh label with a dash of truth. She wore her school dress as short as humanly possible – the opposite of square.

Stacey and Wendy were the girls who had made braces cool in Year Nine. Everybody, myself included, had wanted braces because they had them. Unfortunately, I didn't need them. I'd look on with envy as they adorned their silver tracks with coloured bands, their mouths of glistening metal a fashion statement at Muswellbrook High – their early version of grills.

'I'm so fat,' Stacey wailed. 'Look at my tummy.' She pulled her school uniform tight against her washboard abs. She was teenage-toned. Her physique, optimum. Wendy copied Stacey, only to reveal . . . nada. 'Yeah, me too,' she said.

I looked at them in disbelief. 'That's nothing,' I said. 'Look at mine.' I pulled the same move, except I let my stomach expand to the size of a fully inflated helium balloon.

'*Bahahahahahaha.*' Stacey almost choked on her own laughter. Yeah – I had real issues. The thing was, though, I wasn't fat – far from it. I was tall, with a somewhat hourglass figure. My stomach had never been flat; instead, it was reminiscent of the starving children with distended tummies in World Vision ads. It was easy to hide, especially since I'd hit puberty. My breasts were annoyingly large, but they helped me conceal my stomach, which I would suck in on the occasions I wanted to make it look *really* flat.

When I got home, I put on Denise Austin's *Super Stomachs* workout video and diligently followed the routines. I did this every day for five months – *five months*. But nope. It just didn't work. My sweet tooth, of course, didn't help.

I was certainly attractive. I was being told that quite often. My hair was braided past my shoulders – a new look for me. The only thing was, I had to wear it half up to hide the fact that it wasn't finished – a family friend had begun braiding it for me while I was out of town, and we'd run out of time. To the untrained eye, you couldn't tell. And there were a lot of untrained eyes in Muswellbrook.

The nice kids drew comparisons to Janet Jackson. The mean ones called me Whoopi Goldberg. Everyone loved my new hairdo. The girl who braided it for me – Jennifer Sterling – was the coolest person I'd ever met. She and Mum became friends while Mum was at Newcastle University, studying to fulfil her dream of becoming a registered nurse.

Jennifer was also Ghanaian. I loved the way she dressed – usually jeans with a cool top – and she braided her hair too. Instead of saying 'choice', like my classmates would when they thought something was cool, she would say things like 'Kool-Aid'. Mum and Jennifer had spotted each other in a mass lecture, where students studying medicine, medical science and nursing converged. There weren't many Black people at Newcastle Uni, and Jennifer was certainly the first Black person Mum had met on campus who was also from Ghana. I stayed with Jennifer while doing work experience at NBN Television. My desire to become a journalist wasn't just something I flirted with in primary school and then forgot about – I had been working towards it ever since.

My first media 'job' was designing the layout in the PCYC magazine in Muswellbrook. I then went on to write for *The Voice* in 1994, a student newspaper published in the *Scone Advocate* and the *Muswellbrook Chronicle*. Joining *The Voice* became a story itself, with me pictured with five other student reporters – the new recruits responsible for planning content for the paper and selling advertising space.

When I got down to business, I penned local interest stories: *There is often a claim by the youth of the Upper Hunter that there is nowhere to go and nothing to do.* Voice *Reporter* **Mawunyo Gbogbo** *has discovered two venues with activities that disprove these claims.* I wrote about Blue Light discos and how they were set to undergo a change – there were going to be videos and giveaways, as well as costume nights. I broke news from their events: *There was a great uproar when male model Nic Testoni appeared on stage, and an even greater one when he took his shirt off and threw it into the audience.* Always there to report on the action, that was me.

I wrote about how the PCYC was undergoing renovations and fast becoming 'the place to be' for young kids and teenagers. The headline: 'Lack of Venues Disproved'. The irony was that I would have been one of the first people putting my hand up to say there was nothing to do in town, but here I was finding examples to debunk those claims.

I also did internships at the *Muswellbrook Chronicle* and *Hunter Valley News*, and I had a regular work experience gig at ABC Radio in Muswellbrook. The rural reporter and breakfast presenter, Mike Pritchard, had taken me under his wing. It was just him and a news reporter in the office then. I got to read the weather and community notices on air and went out on the road with the journalists. Mike was always so encouraging. I learned early how to craft a good script for radio, which is quite different from writing for a newspaper and even TV. In a TV report, the pictures also tell the story. With radio, sound is everything – birds chirping, a knock on a door, a phone ringing – it all adds to the storytelling. I'd also learned to be conversational in my scripting, drawing in the audience by outlining why the story might matter to them. I was taught the KISS method: Keep It Simple, Stupid.

Writing had become an essential part of my life, and I was branching out. I'd gone from writing poetry when I was a kid to writing songs. My lyricism was another way to express myself, and putting music to my rhymes felt like a natural progression.

I got along well with the girls in the popular crowd; I just wasn't *one* of them. I desperately wanted to be, but I didn't have the courage to even attempt to switch groups.

The girls at my school fit into a number of cliques, each with an equivalent male posse. My group – the 'squares' – included Kimberley Lawson, a good girl with a penchant for a bad boy. She had light-brown hair with blonde highlights, blue eyes and a cute shape, plump in all the right places. There was the policeman's daughter and amateur model, Fonda Jackson. Fonda was like me: desperate to break free from the good-girl mould. She was softly spoken but knew too much. People confided in her because she didn't blab a whole lot, but she let a few slip every now and then.

In Hollywood high-school movies, the groups are clearly defined, the boundaries firm – the classic nerds-versus-jocks set-up, the outsiders and the in-crowd. In order for a nerd to make the leap into the popular group, they're required to undergo a dramatic change – most often in physical appearance. In my version of life, things didn't fit as neatly into a box as that. The boundaries were more blurred; there was nuance. There was definitely a popular group. But even though my group was treated like squares, we could be elevated at certain times, brought into the fold. We weren't all goody-goodies – at least not in the way you'd be led to believe.

Although the popular group was by far the largest, not everyone was on the same level. Stacey Hoxton and Wendy Robertson were, of course, at the top of the tree. People like Miranda Johnson and Jane Watson didn't really hang out with Stacey and Wendy, but they were also popular, just one rung down on the ladder.

Miranda had long strawberry blonde hair that she mostly wore tied back. She was pretty and gentle, and wore lots of jewellery, including a bracelet she'd designed herself from shells she'd found at a beach in Newcastle. Jane Watson had short white-blonde hair, an athletic frame and freckles. She was really sporty and took on everything from handball to tennis.

Those in the tough group included Cynthia Woodford, who was so tough no one dared tease her. April Clarkson was a gorgeous, quiet sweetheart, but you'd be a fool to mistake her for being soft. The girls in that group had mostly gone to primary school in South Muswellbrook, the rougher side of town. If there was a fight in the quadrangle, you could almost guarantee that one of these girls would be involved.

Tyce was known as a bad boy. He would later tell me how he was first arrested because he'd broken into the police boys' club in a bid to get warm while roaming the streets with a friend.

When Fonda told me she believed some Indigenous youth deserved to be locked up because of the way they resisted arrest, putting people like her dad in danger, I was appalled. Cops shouldn't be locking up children. Period.

Tyce didn't always make the best case for himself, though. He shunned the rules. He was the leader of the toughest group in my grade, and he didn't let anybody push him around. He had dated most of the popular girls, including Stacey *and* Wendy. I always wondered what Elliot would have thought of his sister dating someone who is Black.

CHAPTER 9

Ice Ice Baby

Indeed, charm attracts.
But it's also a distraction.

Our Year Ten school visit to Canberra wasn't my first. My parents were friends with a Ghanaian family who lived there, and on an earlier visit I'd been to the cinema for the very first time – to see *Point Break*. It was a '90s classic: the escapism, the quotable lines, the visual quality, and by that I mean Patrick Swayze and Keanu Reeves, who were really hot in it.

The school trip lasted a week and we stayed in cabins. Cypress Hill's 'Insane in the Brain' was being blasted from the cabin next door, and I tried to match the volume by cranking up Warren G and Nate Dogg's 'Regulate' from the *Above the Rim* soundtrack – a hotter track by far.

Soundtracks were huge in the '90s, and I had *Above the Rim* on repeat. I don't remember anything about the movie, except that it was about basketball, but I knew the soundtrack by heart.

It starts out innocuously enough with a track by R'n'B group SWV (Sisters With Voices). I was listening to it on cassette tape, so it meant a lot of fast-forwarding to get to my favourite tracks, like 'Big Pimpin'' by Tha Dogg Pound and 'Didn't Mean to Turn You On' by 2nd II None, and rewinding to listen to them again. Hip hop had its hooks in me – I was both appalled and drawn in. As much as I loved 'Big Pimpin'' and the artists behind it, the song hit me where it hurts. From Daz's opening lines where he drives around, drunk and high, looking for a 'hoe' to fuck, before going home to his partner and newborn, to Nate Dogg appealing to the masses not to blame him for his 'hit it and quit it' behaviour – it's clear he can't help himself. A chorus of female voices in the know leads into Snoop Dogg laughing as he confirms his disdain for 'bitches' and 'hoes'.

As a sixteen-year-old, I couldn't differentiate between bitches, hoes and women. They were all the same thing. In fact, 'bitches and hoes' to me was just a euphemism for women – all women, even girls, even me. If 'Big Pimpin'' didn't do enough to reinforce that women weren't good for much else but fucking, 'Didn't Mean to Turn You On' sealed the deal. The disrespect was incredible: rappers KK and Gangsta D marvel over the fact they didn't have to work that hard to get a bitch to give it up.

I was starting to listen to hip hop more and more. I had the *Dangerous Minds* soundtrack on CD. 'True O.G.' by Mr. Dalvin and Static was my skip-to-and-replay track on that one, with its pace, production, beats and laid-back drawl.

Naughty by Nature had piqued my interest off the back of their success with the hits 'Hip Hop Hooray' and 'O.P.P', but *Poverty's Paradise* proved to be a departure from the material they were famous for. It was a gritty ode to the streets – streets very different to Claret Avenue and the rest of the Wine Estate in Muswellbrook – but it didn't have to be *my* reality to draw me in. The album won a Grammy in 1996 for what was a new category that year: Best Rap Album. Rap had well and truly entered mainstream culture. The production was chill – if you'd danced around like crazy listening to 'Hip Hop Hooray', *Poverty's Paradise* felt like the type of album you'd sit back and smoke weed to. And I was definitely smoking weed then, and listening to almost as much Bob Marley as hip hop.

We did everything during our trip to Canberra, from rock climbing to bumping into each other at Go Karts Go to ice-skating. Tyce, who'd hit the ice before I had even done up my skate laces, made it look so easy. He glided gracefully around the rink, spinning, jumping, putting his full athleticism on display. He was so good at sport. And boy did he look good on that ice.

It can't be that difficult, I thought, and jumped enthusiastically into the rink. *Whoosh*. I slipped on the ice and fell hard. Getting back up, I held onto the railing, slowly shuffling my way around the outside of the rink. I caught another glimpse of Tyce, gliding towards me with his friend, Lance Dempsey, in tow.

'You alright, Marnz? Wanna hand?' He reached out towards me.

'Thanks.' I put my arm through his and looked up at him sheepishly. 'It's my first time.'

'Yeah, me too.'

'*What?*' I was incredulous.

'Hey, Lance, grab her other arm. Marnz, let's go for a spin.' Lance did as he was told, and the two of them led me around the rink, slowly at first. I began to enjoy myself as we completed the circuit, Tyce instructing me on the best way to hold myself up and connect to the ice.

'Wanna go around again?' he asked.

'Yeah, sure.' The longer I could be this close to him, the more my day improved.

After the ice-skating, Tyce and I stood outside Telecom Tower, talking. I felt a hand grab my hair, bunch my braids together and push them into my face.

'Ouch!' I was not impressed. It was Jim Broderick, one of the more annoying boys from school.

'Ay,' Tyce snapped. He faced up to our classmate. 'Leave her the fuck alone. Don't *ever* touch her again.' He looked ready to slap Jim down.

'Yeah, okay. Steady,' Jim said as he backed away.

'Thanks for that,' I said as we walked into a souvenir shop together.

'That's alright, Marnz. No respect, that one. I won't let anybody mess with you.'

Tyce spotted a bunch of badges with the Aboriginal flag emblazoned across the front of them and stopped. 'Ay,' he said to the man behind the counter, pointing to the badges. 'What percentage of profits go to Blackfullas?'

The shop guy looked at him, mystified. 'I don't know, mate.'

'Yeah, zero per cent would be my guess,' Tyce said, shaking his head. We continued looking at the Canberra trinkets.

As we headed out of the shop, Tyce leaned over and grabbed an Aboriginal flag badge and walked out of the store.

Beside the badges were a number of silver charms in various

shapes. I picked up one in the shape of a fish. I felt the adrenaline rush through my body as I dropped it into my palm, closing my fingers into a fist.

I don't know what possessed me to nick that fish charm, but it was the first thing I'd ever shoplifted. It seemed Tyce had an influence on me without even trying.

It was close to the end of Year Ten and it had been a while since I'd seen Tyce at school. The last place I was expecting to see him was on stage at the Muswellbrook amateur modelling parade my friend Fonda Jackson was taking part in. He belonged up there, as hot as he was, but I would have thought he'd be the type to have a go at a dude for strolling down a runway, rather than be on one himself. As I would learn over the years, there was a lot to his personality. He had an artistic side – he knew how to paint, he dabbled in music (like every Black guy I knew, at some point in his life he was a rapper) – and as with everything he did, he was good at it. Modelling was just an extension of all the things he was capable of mastering.

The music was at high volume – 'Return of the Mack' by Mark Morrison, 'How Bizarre' by OMC, 'Fly' by Sugar Ray, and the one that really set the audience off, 'Stayin' Alive' by the Bee Gees, which was the song Tyce walked down the runway to. Damn, he looked good. That walk, that cool swagger. I had an excuse to let my gaze linger on his lean frame. He looked into the crowd, smiled, and I couldn't help but smile along with him. He lit up the room.

Amateur model after amateur model took to the stage, show-casing the clothes for the local shop Mundarra Garments. There was a bit of a hippie aesthetic, and the outfits included tie-dyed pink-and-white tank tops, and Fonda looking gorgeous in a short blue silk skirt with pink flowers scattered across it.

'You were great up there,' I said to Tyce once the show was over.

'Thanks, Marnz. You really should have been up there too.'

'I've done a little bit of modelling this year, actually, just not on a runway.' The photojournalist at the local newspaper where I'd been doing work experience had taken me on as his muse for a portfolio he'd been assembling. 'Where have you been? Haven't seen you in school for a while.'

'I dropped out. Working with Dad at the National Parks and Wildlife Service.'

'That sounds pretty awesome,' I said. 'Do you like it?'

'Yeah, it's alright.'

'Do you miss school?' Fonda asked.

Tyce started laughing. 'About as much as I'd miss a heart attack.' His gaze lingered on Fonda. 'Nah, I don't miss it.' Then his eyes were on me. 'All I miss is some of the people I don't get to see as often.'

CHAPTER 10

Welcome to Heartbreak

With hindsight, I see what happened there.
In the moment, I was in the moment.

I had always hated shopping, so I didn't have many clothes. This lack of choice made picking an outfit for Miranda Johnson's end-of-Year-Ten party relatively simple. I stood in front of the mirror and examined the cream-coloured jeans I had squeezed into. I had paired the jeans with a sleeveless midriff with horizontal stripes in yellow, orange and a greenish khaki.

Flicking my plaits over my shoulder, I smiled at my reflection: *cute*. I felt really pretty.

There had been an open invitation to the entire year. I'm sure I wouldn't have been invited otherwise – I didn't get invited to many parties. None of my friends were even planning to make the effort to show up, but I didn't care. I wasn't going to miss this party for the world. My friends preferred a day out of town at the movies or clothes shopping at Muswellbrook's poor excuse for a mall. They threw parties, too, but they were often dry events.

Dad agreed to drop me off at Miranda's acreage, which was a fair way out of town.

'Can I call you if I'm not having much fun?'

'What? No. I'll be asleep. You said you were staying the night. I'll pick you up in the morning.' Little did Dad know that this new habit of dropping me off at parties and refusing to pick me up late at night meant I could run amok without supervision. I wasn't at that point yet – but I was about to be.

'Whose party is it?'

'A girl from school. Miranda Johnson. Everyone will be there.'

'Will Fonda be there?'

'No.'

'How about Kimberley?'

'No.'

'So, who's everyone?'

'Everyone *else*, Dad.' I rolled my eyes.

Dad was playing the role of the primary carer while Mum was studying part-time and still working full-time. Sometimes Sedudzi would tease Mum by singing the chorus to Tupac's 'Part Time Mutha' to her.

'I am not a part-time mother!' Mum would insist. 'I am a full-time mother!'

Often for dinner, Dad would serve up rice and barbecue chicken, prepared for us by the chefs at Woolworths. He also always seemed to be ironing; it's an image that sticks in my mind from that period. He'd get through a stack of clothes in one session – a hangover from Ghana, when he never knew when the power might shut off for a period of time without warning.

♪♫

I walked up to my classmates when I arrived at the party and mingled, downing one or two drinks while we talked about nothing in particular. We were all underage, but underage drinking in Muswellbrook was the norm and punctuated most get-togethers – everything from Passion Pop and West Coast Cooler to your garden-variety goon. Before you were eighteen, it was a bit of a sport to sneak into popular hotels, like the Prince or Eatons. With no cinema or beach in town, there was not much else to do. Miranda's mother stopped short of serving us drinks, but she had no qualms about supplying them.

Jane Watson looked me up and down. 'You're wearing white pants to a party?'

'They're not white, they're cream,' I said.

The expression on her face wasn't unkind, but if my complexion was the same colour as my jeans, I would have been blushing a deep shade of crimson at that moment. Boy, were there some perks to being Black. I stood there wondering why I hadn't picked my *other* outfit though. I changed the topic.

Mid-sentence, I noticed Tyce walking towards us. I gazed over at him.

'Hey, Marnz,' he said. I smiled and returned the greeting. 'You wanna go for a walk?' I shrugged a *why not* as he steered me away from the rest of the group. We'd spent plenty of time together over the years, and I always felt comfortable around him, whether we were in the company of others or not. We walked to the top of the hill to a secluded part of the acreage, surrounded by trees, and sat down. We had managed to get so far away from everyone else that we couldn't even hear the throb of the music.

'So, you came out tonight,' he said. 'I don't see you at many of these parties.'

'Yeah, I don't get out much.'

'Why's that?'

'I don't know. I'm pretty shy.'

'What do you have to be shy about?'

'I don't know.'

'You've got nothing to be shy about.'

It wasn't long before Tyce had me breaking down in laughter. Just as I stopped, he had me laughing again.

He reached over to touch my hair. I summoned up my courage.

'You know, Tyce.' I smiled. 'I've never kissed anybody before.' I paused, unable to decipher the look on his face. 'I'm sweet sixteen and never been kissed.' Tyce continued to study my face intently as I went on. 'I'd like you to be my first.' I could tell he wanted me, which is the only reason I had the guts to kick things along a little.

'Sweet sixteen and never been touched,' Tyce said as he moved his hand down to the side of my face. He leaned over and planted his lips on mine. I tried to respond as best I could, but I felt like we were out of sync. Tyce began to kiss my neck but jumped off me when we heard a rustle in the bushes.

'Where can we find a place where we'll be completely alone?' he said. I pointed ahead, towards another small clearing, and he walked briskly in that direction. We were back on the ground again within minutes, kissing. He pushed his hand up my shirt and undid my bra. I felt a little self-conscious. *Isn't this a bit much for a first kiss?* Then he started kissing one breast and rubbing the other. His hand moved down to my crotch.

'Do you trust me?' he said.

'Yes.'

'Can I put it in there? Just for a feel?' I looked at his erection, which I'd just been fondling. 'Okay.' *It's not as if we're actually going to do it*, I thought. He hovered above the entry to my vagina, but then he began to release the full weight of his body into mine.

'No!' I pushed him away with all my strength. I didn't know I had that much power in my arms. He sat back and looked at me, bewildered. My mind was running faster than Carl Lewis in the 100-metre sprint. What on earth just happened? I didn't want my first kiss to turn into *sex*. I wanted to be in a relationship when that happened. I started to put my clothes back on.

'I'm glad you were my first,' I said, referring to our kiss.

'That's cool, Marnz.' At the time, I thought his response was casual, cold and insensitive. 'I would have liked to have been your first . . . you know, as well.'

I shrugged, my face downcast. *That would be nice*, I thought, *but not tonight*.

'Did it hurt?'

'No.'

'That means that you're ready . . . You're just not ready *right now*.'

'It hurt a bit,' I said quickly. I didn't consider myself ready.

'We probably shouldn't walk back down there together.'

'You go first,' I said. I watched as he walked away, not believing what had just happened. I was happy that I had finally kissed someone, and even happier that it was Tyce. All the other kids used to pash and dash at the Blue Light discos. It was quite the scene: teenagers would rock up in tartan vests and Tencel jeans, some of the girls opting for bodysuits, the guys wearing Stüssy or Hot Tuna hats that barely covered their uppercuts. Others positioned their hats to accentuate their rat's tails. But I had missed out on my chance to kiss someone there.

I was very aware that I was well behind my classmates, and it was something that bothered me. At that moment, I was glad my first kiss was reserved for someone who was worth it, but I was also perplexed. I hoped I hadn't misread the little signals I thought Tyce had been giving me – the glances, the flirtations, the moments between us that felt like a *wink wink*. I prayed that the feelings I had for him were mutual.

I eventually made my way back to the party. I felt like everyone was staring at me. I had dirt on my jeans and grass in my hair.

'So, did you root him?' one of the girls asked as I walked towards her. I looked at her, aghast.

'No, I didn't!' I said. *Not that it's any of your business*, I thought.

One of Tyce's best friends, Malcolm Harvey, sidled up to us. 'She's telling the truth,' he said. 'I already asked him. He said he tried.'

I couldn't believe what I was hearing. Malcolm then pulled me aside. 'So, did you root him?'

'*What?* No!'

'Yeah, I believe you. You'd have blood running down your legs if you did. Don't tell anyone else you didn't fuck him,' he instructed. 'Keep your mouth shut.' He walked away, leaving me heartbroken by his words, and pissed off at Tyce.

What was everyone going on about anyway? I hadn't given it a lot of thought but before we hooked up I had assumed Tyce was a virgin, like me. But his experienced manner with me had me convinced now that he wasn't.

I wandered off and joined a group of people huddled together, pulling a few cones. I had a smoke and a little more to drink. For a moment, I was chatting with the long-haired and not particularly engaging Stuart Damon. He was in the unpopular clique. I ducked when he suddenly leaned in towards me.

'I've already kissed someone tonight,' I said.

'So what? Everybody's doing it.'

'Yeah, well, not me.' I walked off.

My thoughts were with Tyce. Although our little rendezvous in the bush meant everything to me, it obviously meant nothing to him. I walked up and told him about Stuart's advances, just to see what type of reaction I would get. He didn't look very impressed but said little. I avoided Tyce after that and walked into the house.

About an hour later the party started to wind down. Miranda's mother set up a number of mattresses in the lounge room and people settled in for the night. Tyce jumped onto a mattress and called out to me from across the room. 'Hey, Marnz. How 'bout we crash in here and have some fun in the sun when it comes up?'

I was stunned. There were about fifty other people in the room, but he didn't care. I joined him on the mattress. We kissed until our faces went numb, touching each other intimately under the sheets through the night. The only song I could remember playing was TLC's 'Waterfalls' – a song about chasing after things that will only harm you in the end – and for a while, every time I heard that song it reminded me of him.

'Fuck, the sun's up,' Tyce said hours later when the two of us opened our eyes.

'My thoughts exactly,' I replied, yawning.

We ignored each other in the morning. At one point I saw him on the other side of the room wearing his cap as he sat silently with his homies, gazing over in my direction. He suddenly lifted his leg dramatically and let one rip.

Oh my God, I thought. I had actually read an article just a few days earlier in *Girlfriend*. It was about how you know you're in love when a guy breaks wind and you actually think it's cute. *Am I in love?* Either way, when Dad picked me up in the morning, there was something different about the girl he drove home. The experience I'd just had forced me to grow up a little. I wasn't a little girl anymore, far from it.

♪♫

I had never been teased so much in my life. 'Mawunyo Carrington' was what they were all calling me at school on Monday. Funny thing is, I didn't really mind. Everybody knew about Tyce and me. And what they didn't know, they just made up.

When our Drama teacher left the room, the class decided to play 'truth or dare'. One of the girls spun an empty bottle, and it eventually landed on me.

'Truth or dare?' she said, pausing for dramatic effect. 'How far did you go with Tyce?'

'What's the dare?' I asked.

'If you refuse to answer the question, you have to kiss Terrence Tilman.'

'Can I kiss him on the cheek?' I asked.

'Sure,' she said. I got up and walked over to Terrence and planted one on his pimply cheek.

In line with my square status, I was a good student and teachers liked me. English was the subject I embraced the most – I expressed myself through language and would often take what I'd learned in class and write stories in my own time, unrelated to the assignments I'd been given. I decided to present some of these stories to my English teacher as a gift. She wrote me a letter:

Dear Mawunyo, I want to thank you most sincerely for the beautiful present you gave me. To me nothing is as special as sharing your writing with someone, and I appreciate this more than I can say. My children are complaining as they tell me, 'Mum, whatever we give you for Christmas will not please you as much as that gift from your student' – and they're correct!

Fonda teased me about the fact I had created my own dictionary, as she put it. In addition to writing poetry and short stories, I was reading a lot, and whenever I came across a new word I'd write it down and then try to use it in conversation.

'I was watching the news last night ... the reporter displayed quite a bit of cerebral rigour in outlining the inadequacies of moribund democracies.'

'*What?*' Fonda rolled her eyes.

At Peer Support training, we were told how as student leaders we would need to help the Year Nine students by encouraging them to speak up about their ideas. As part of the training, we carried out a similar exercise to the one where we had to write nice things about our classmates within the outline of a hand, except this time there was no hand. We wrote on a sheet of paper, then folded our comments over so the next person could write underneath. At the top of my sheet: *Carrington Kiddies soon,* and on it went. *Marnz Carrington, you're my idol; She's a legend; Marnz, how's Tyce?!!! Choice mate; Mrs Carrington – legend (Go Janet Jackson); Very funny; Great smile.* And this, from the teacher. *Great, great work, you will be a terrific P.S. leader.*

Imaginations were running wild over what had happened between me and Tyce, including the imagination of number-one popular girl Stacey Hoxton. I had just walked through the exit at the Muswellbrook pool after our class had been there for a swim. Stacey, who had been walking in front of me with a group of people, suddenly spun on her heel and approached.

'Did you have sex with Tyce?'

'No,' I said.

She rejoined her group. 'She didn't sleep with him, everybody,' she said at the top of her lungs.

While everyone at school was obsessed with the nature of our relationship, it appeared Tyce wasn't. Days later, he still hadn't called me on the landline. I hadn't seen or spoken to him since we got together, given he wasn't at school anymore. Sure, I hadn't given him my number, but we were the only Gbogbo family in the Muswellbrook phone book (and probably in the whole of Australia). If he cared enough, all he had to do was look me up.

But I took great comfort in my horoscope that week:

VIRGO (August 23–September 22) **Love:** The situation with that guy in your life will change quickly following a phone call, letter or card. If you are single, a chatty or smart guy will attract you. **Friendships:** You'll feel much closer to a friend or more involved in their life. Friendships become more powerful around November 12 to 14. **Life:** There'll be a lot of action surrounding a family member, house or flat, and there are plenty of changes on the way.

My horoscopes were always so accurate! We were moving house – my parents had just built a new one. My mother had asked for the floor plan to the house next door and had built an identical one on a different street. I had been feeling a lot closer to my best friend – her birthday being in November. *And Tyce is going to call*, I thought to myself.

It took a week for me to come to terms with the fact that he wasn't going to call. I was devastated, heartbroken. He didn't care about me. All he wanted was sex. He knew he was the only guy I had ever been with. Shouldn't that make me special? Why was he being so damn insensitive? And how could the stars have got it so wrong? I quit reading my horoscopes after that.

I knew I liked Tyce a lot. At that stage I didn't realise just how much – but I knew that he was special to me. *I guess those feelings will be unrequited*, I thought, *and there's nothing I can do about it.*

I wondered how long it might take to get over him.

CHAPTER 11

Zealots

Ask. Don't assume. Then you'll know.

Sedudzi's first two cassette tapes were more traditional pop: Michael Jackson's *Dangerous* and Bobby Brown's *Dance! . . . Ya Know It!* But at that point in the game he was becoming a student of rap, having purchased his first two CDs, one of which was Ice-T's *Home Invasion*, which had an intro that got Sedudzi's attention as a fourteen-year-old. Ice-T might be better known now as a cop on *Law & Order: SVU*, but these were the days when he was a seminal gangsta rapper. (Of course, Ice-T wasn't just making hip hop. Sedudzi also bought *Body Count*, the 1992 self-titled album by Ice-T's metal band, which I soaked up as well.)

In the intro to *Home Invasion*, he lists one foul word after another, saying that if you find these expletives offensive, you need to switch off immediately – the content is not for you. It 100 per cent makes you want to keep listening. The highly controversial and disturbing album cover artwork features, among other things, a white kid steeped in Black culture – a medallion of Africa around his neck, a book on Malcolm X by his side. It was a recognition that Black culture had invaded suburban homes, and the message was clear: you might not like it, but your kids do.

As a teenager, this wasn't lost on me, but when I look at the cover now, I think to myself that the white kid could just as easily have been a Black kid growing up in a country town in Australia, feasting on a culture she believed to be hers, but still only observing it from a distance.

The album intro drew me in too. Here was a man saying 'Fuck you' to the establishment. Under the 'Parental Advisory, Explicit Lyrics' flag, he was going to say whatever he wanted to say. While society sought to disempower him, he shrugged that off and asserted his rights to rap about everything he'd seen and lived through. Your ears prick up as a teen, you take notice.

The other album Sedudzi bought that day was *All Eyez on Me* by Tupac Shakur. He told me later he did a double-take when he saw the album because up until then he'd only known Tupac as the guy in the movie *Poetic Justice,* a romantic drama starring Janet Jackson as Justice, a poet. I'd had it playing over and over again in our house growing up. Revered poet, author and civil-rights activist Maya Angelou wrote the poems featured in the movie.

Tupac is still Sedudzi's favourite artist to this day. Sedudzi loved how real and raw he was. He was both conscious and gangsta, rapping about subjects that highlighted social issues affecting the Black community, like on the track 'I Wonder If Heaven Got a Ghetto', and then throwing down a hot party track like 'California Love', featuring Dr. Dre. Sedudzi then went and bought up Tupac's entire back catalogue.

Sedudzi's next purchase was Nas's *It Was Written,* then Ice Cube's debut solo album *AmeriKKKa's Most Wanted,* which led to all of NWA's records.

I soaked up all of this music.

But what ran parallel to this for Sedudzi was the conscious rappers – rappers with a political slant, writing about stuff you might find in the news, about history, about social and racial injustice, about hope. Arrested Development's 'People Everyday' and 'Mr. Wendal' were big then, so he purchased *3 Years, 5 Months and 2 Days in the Life of . . .* I wasn't into the conscious rap. For the most part, I left that alone, which is unfortunate because it was mostly about Black empowerment and had rich references to the African continent.

It all came down to the beat for me, and the all-important question: did it sound good? If so, it got my full attention. Later, I'd take in the lyrics – the more risqué the better. The more they involved bitches, hoes, drug use and conspicuous consumption, the more my senses would light up, until I was hooked. Gangsta rap and party rap sounded good. The synthesised beats, the clever sampling of hit songs, present and past. Despite being a budding lyricist, to me the beats, the instrumental, the melody – these were the most important elements to a song. By the time I was hooked on the flavour of a track, it was too late – I already liked that shit. I was way beyond the point where the misogyny, the violence, the gritty themes might have turned me off.

Sedudzi's rap collection had been steadily growing and I'd been listening to the albums he'd purchased over time: Public

Enemy, Onyx, Dr. Dre, Eazy-E, Biggie, Tupac, Wu-Tang Clan, Jay-Z . . . My personal favourite at the time, which I'd dubbed from someone else's copy in town, was Snoop Doggy Dogg. I loved his voice – the easy drawl is one of the most recognisable in rap music. I reckon he'd sound good rapping the telephone book. Yet despite the relaxed sound, what he's rapping about isn't relaxed in any way. His debut album *Doggystyle* makes it clear that he really doesn't like bitches and hoes, but he has no problem giving them the only thing they're good for: sex. It's strangely easy to romanticise it all – the promiscuous lifestyle, smoking weed, ongoing beefs with other rappers, other gangs, the brotherhood.

And aside from the beats and the lyrics, there was another reason I loved these rappers' music so much: it was one of my few connections in Muswellbrook to Black people.

I would walk into the music store and make a beeline for the Hip Hop and R'n'B section. Sedudzi obviously had a monopoly on the male rap artists, so I started buying the CDs of female rappers, my appetite whet by the Lady of Rage's 'Afro Puffs' track on the *Above the Rim* soundtrack and her guest features on *Doggystyle*; and Queen Latifah's *Nature of a Sista'* and *Black Reign*, which I copped early. Apart from Salt-N-Pepa, female rappers got very little airplay on Australian music programs like *Rage* and *Video Hits*, so I would often have to judge whether particular female artists were rappers just by how they looked on the album covers.

On one visit, I picked up an album by a group called Y?N-Vee. *Parental Advisory Explicit Lyrics* label? *Tick.* The four women certainly looked like rappers – baggy pants, underwear on display, crop tops. *Tick.* I flicked the cover over – the track list included titles like 'Stra8 Hustler', 'Real G' and 'Gangsta's Prayer'. *Tick.*

This album was going to make it home with me. Turned out, Y?N-Vee was a mix of R'n'B and rap.

Sometimes I got it very wrong. The group Total, for example, looked like rappers on the cover of their album, standing in front of a flashy car, dressed in black silk blazers, and their album featured other big-name rappers like Da Brat, the Notorious B.I.G. and Puff Daddy, who was also the executive producer on the album. But they were strictly R'n'B and soul. Still not a bad album, though, so that's okay. Adina Howard of 'Freak Like Me' fame – not a rapper. Often buying one album would lead me to others, because rappers love to collaborate, and each female rapper was usually backed by a male rapper – for Yo-Yo, it was Ice Cube; for Suga-T, it was her brother E-40 – a legend then, and a legend now. E-40's ability to introduce Bay Area slang to a wider audience is unrivalled and his delivery, hot.

Before I knew it, I had quite the collection myself: Queen Latifah, Da Brat, Foxy Brown, the Conscious Daughters, Suga-T, the Lady of Rage, Nikki D, MC Lyte, Yo-Yo, Mia X, Ghetto Twiinz, Missy Elliott, Gangsta Boo, Bahamadia, Salt-N-Pepa and, my personal favourite, Lil' Kim, plus a whole lot more. Lil' Kim wasn't afraid to say it how she saw it, her voice distinct and authoritative. And she unapologetically owned her sexuality, she meant business. Her cadence and flow, always on point.

Each artist rapped about different issues and themes, their reality as they saw it. Queen Latifah, for example, was about as conscious as I got. Her song 'U.N.I.T.Y.' decried the use of the words *bitch* and *hoe*. The refrain and verses called out men for using these words to denigrate women, and it also called out women who used the words to describe themselves.

Lil' Kim and Missy Elliott, on the other hand, delighted in calling themselves bitches. On Missy's album *Da Real World*, Missy and Kim explain in skits between tracks why they believe the word suits them – a strong word to fit their strong personalities. To me back then, the word *bitch* had become synonymous with all women, so this didn't faze me.

I loved everything about Missy's style, the fact that she rapped *and* sang, and that *Supa Dupa Fly* and *Da Real World* were albums you didn't need to skip any tracks on – a rarity for me, as I'm a skipper from way back. There was something wildly innovative about the way Missy approached each song – the rapid-fire repetitions, the alliterative flow of nonsensical sounds and the creation of words that were never bound for a dictionary. They were upbeat party albums, the high-energy Timbaland-produced beats bouncing off the gyprock walls in my room.

I created a mixtape of my favourite tracks by female rappers, dubbing the album I'd created *Female Vocalism*, after a Conscious Daughters song. Sedudzi used to tease me about that. 'Ha, *Female Vocalism*,' he'd laugh. To him, they just weren't as hot as the guys. They didn't have the same clout; they didn't have the same command in the industry and therefore the airwaves and music videos.

Sometimes I'd play 'U.N.I.T.Y.' at high volume, Queen Latifah's words a call for respect – the type of respect I wanted from my siblings – but that would only make them laugh even harder.

Tyce continued to dominate my thoughts. It wasn't long before I heard through the local grapevine that he had hooked up with one of the St Josephs girls at a party. Victoria Richards had big breasts like me. I figured he must be going through a stage where he liked big boobs. So, he was just attracted to my physique – a physique I was apparently intent on destroying through my rapidly growing junk food habit.

A few months later, I read in the paper that a sixteen-year-old 'ringleader' had been arrested for assaulting and attempting to rob a pizza delivery boy. He faced further charges for resisting arrest and assaulting police, having spat at an officer. Already feeling down that day, I cried when a friend of mine confirmed it was Tyce.

I ran into him shortly afterwards, stubble encasing his face, tatty clothing, a mini rat's tail escaping the back of his hat.

'Hi, Marnz.'

'Hi,' I said. 'I hear you're in a bit of trouble.'

'I'm in a lot of trouble. I'm always in trouble.' His tone was laconic, almost jubilant. 'See you in six months.'

I wasn't sure exactly what he meant by that. Was he going to be locked up for six months? It had been six months since I'd last seen him – is that what he was talking about? No, surely he wasn't that sentimental. Either way, he was gone.

I was in a good mood and ready to impress when my mother and I turned up for my interview at Joeys. Mum was desperate for me to attend the Catholic school in Years Eleven and Twelve.

The school's deputy asked me a series of questions – What subjects was I interested in? Was I involved in any extracurricular activities? What did I want to do after I left school? – which I answered enthusiastically. It was towards the end of the interview that he hit me with what should have been a deal-breaker.

'Now, you do realise you'll have to remove your braids?'

I inhaled sharply. My face fell.

'You see, if we let you wear your hair like that, we'll have to let everybody do it.'

Really? Because it was *so* likely the blonde girls at school would start rocking braids? We were not the same. I must have been their first Black student for this to even be an issue. Later, I would think, *Here's an idea: just let the entitled brats embarrass themselves in braids so they can realise years later how ridiculous they looked in their yearbook photos, punishment for their hubris.*

'Oh, that's no problem,' my mother said quickly, brushing her hand against my leg.

I couldn't believe they were going to make me take my braids out. I was so used to them. I felt attractive in braids. And for a teenage girl, that's everything. They had become a part of me. They were considered natural for a girl of African descent. They kept my hair neat. They helped secure existing locs – even aiding in their growth – without the use of harsh chemicals and daily brushing. Now, I would have to go back to my nappy, unruly hair. I knew it would make a big difference in the way I felt about myself, and I was right. If I had my time again, I would have turned up to school in a massive afro that got bigger by the day, a 'fuck you' to the man who would become the principal.

(Years later, after I'd left, Sophia started attending the school, and she wrote the principal a letter: *49 Reasons Why I Should Be Allowed to Wear Braids.* He relented and Sophia, who had grown into a stunning young woman, rocked the style at school. The other girls weren't allowed – one actually tried and had to take them out.)

When I told Fonda I was going to have to lose my braids, sobbing in my sadness and fury, she sat beside me, not knowing what to do or say, offering sympathy. She was upset for me.

At least my popularity status had improved at Joeys. I already knew most of the girls before arriving for my first day at school. I had gone to preschool and primary school with Amber Jones, the most popular girl in my grade, and we'd remained good friends. Amber was one of those rare popular girls: she was beautiful *and* kind. She treated everyone with respect, and people loved her for it. She'd say hello to you with a kiss on the cheek and never forgot a birthday.

On occasions, I would go walking with Lisa Leonard, who was South Asian, and Victoria Richards, the girl with the big boobs who I'd heard had pashed Tyce. Tyce never came between us because that's the way it is in a small town. You might have exclusive rights to someone if you're in a relationship with them, but if you're not, they're fair game. Victoria was a sweetheart with a dimpled smile that could make anyone feel at ease. I went home from one of those walks, however, feeling quite depressed. I couldn't believe the way some people took sex for granted, while I felt like the Holy Virgin Mary. I started questioning what was wrong with me. Lisa and Victoria had been telling me sex stories. I knew Lisa had slept around, but for some reason I had the idea in my head that Victoria was a virgin too. *Bam!*

Wrong there. They asked me what kinds of things I'd been up to, and I felt so inadequate admitting I was a virgin. Tyce was the only guy I had ever been with and the only one I wanted to be with.

After a while there were other guys, and given my experience with Tyce I always moved way too quickly when I hooked up with someone. But I had yet to go all the way. This had nothing to do with Christianity. It wasn't something that had been drummed into me by my mother – you must remain a virgin till you're married. Mum had given me 'the talk', and as far as I could gather, having sex before marriage might have been frowned upon in the Bible, but it was just what people did. I, for example, was a product of two people who weren't married when I was conceived.

At that moment, I didn't see my virginity as a precious gift from God, one I shouldn't have felt rushed to give away to anybody, because it was something I could never get back. What I did feel, unfortunately, was shame that I was so far behind my peers. They were experienced, I wasn't. My innocence should have been a source of pride. Instead, it was a source of embarrassment.

CHAPTER 12

Rising Down

Self-destruction should really be referred to as selfish-destruction,
because it often affects more than just one person.

My eyes settled on a sweater, noting there were a few of them on the rack. Examining the tags, I picked up the one in my size, and then grabbed two others in different sizes. I slipped one of them off the hanger so it looked like I only had two items. I hid the jumper I wanted in the middle.

'Can I try these on please?' I asked the saleswoman, adrenaline pumping through my chest.

'How many have you got there? Two?' she asked, glancing at the hangers.

I nodded and she handed me a ticket.

Once I was in the change room, I stuffed the jumper that was the correct size straight into my bag, my heart beating faster and faster. I waited a few moments and then walked out of the change room, returning the other two jumpers to the saleswoman, telling her they didn't fit.

My breathing began to slow a little as I walked out of the shop. But I still felt winded, as if I had just run a marathon. My mind started to rehearse a variety of outcomes. The saleswoman had been counting stock when I'd walked in. There was a good chance she was well aware of how many jumpers had been on the rack. It was possible she might even see me wearing the jumper around town – Muswellbrook was not very big, and I kinda stood out. But at that moment, the jumper was tucked safely into my bag. I had got away with it. Again. I was shoplifting for nothing more than the adrenaline rush. Because it was bad. Because I knew I shouldn't be doing it. That was my motivation.

My mother thought stealing was worse than prostitution. Every time someone did something wrong, her response would be, 'Well, it's not as if they *stole* something from someone . . .' She would have been shocked and appalled if she found out her daughter's pastime – the same daughter who accompanied her to church every Sunday and belted out hymns next to her. She would never have suspected that I was doing the unthinkable.

It's common knowledge that Black people, most of whom have no intention of taking anything from anybody, are often unfairly suspected of being thieves, followed around stores and treated like vermin by actual vermin. I was playing into a stereotype, a teenage me confirming prejudices and racist tropes. My white friends were just as likely to shoplift, but the fact that I was Black meant the guilt I felt over what I was doing quadrupled. I was not only doing the wrong thing, I was tainting my race.

I worked so many different part-time jobs as a teenager – I'd go from one to another. Muswellbrook employers were happy to put their trust in me. When I got a job at a newsagency, I threw this trust back in the face of my boss, a man who was so lovely and kind. I still feel guilty about it today. I'd be alone on shift most days and seized the opportunity to nick a few boxes of cigarettes. I was a social smoker then, but I didn't need entire boxes of cigarettes, so I'd give the bulk of them to Fonda's brother, exchanging them for weed. It was a dog act, betraying the trust of an employer, and eventually the guilt was too much for me to bear.

I got up one day and gathered the things I had flogged, with the intention of burning them. I drove out to South Muswellbrook and dumped the goods in a bin at the park. Bringing fire into the mix suddenly seemed like an unsafe move, so instead I walked away, vowing never to steal again. Stealing had been something I'd witnessed Tyce doing as an act of protest. For me, it was about the adrenaline high, no drugs necessary. But the feeling afterwards, that I'd done the wrong thing by someone who'd placed trust in me, wasn't worth that initial rush. Eventually, I couldn't stand to even be at the scene of the crime. I quit my job at the newsagency and turned over a new leaf.

I cried when, much later, on my first shift at McDonald's, 50 dollars went missing from my till. I was innocent, but it felt like I was being shown up for my past transgressions.

'I guess I made a lot of customers happy today,' I said to my boss as I wiped away my tears.

'It was probably just one customer you made happy,' he said. 'It's more likely you handed an extra note to one person. Don't worry, I'm not going to sack you,' he reassured me, telling me to just be a little more careful next time. Another kind boss, except this one, I'd do right by.

♪♫

Although I had made it into the popular group through sheer luck of association, I still didn't feel as if I really belonged. Regardless, I was being invited to a lot of parties. And when somebody from either one of the high schools I'd been to threw a party, I would know about it, and most of the time I would go.

It was 11 pm by the time I arrived at Christopher Maxwell's party. Being teenagers living in the country, our key source of entertainment, other than each other, was drugs and alcohol. So, one of the first things I did when I got there was huddle behind a large tent set up in the backyard for a session with a few friends.

I was feeling pretty laid back and was dressed casually. My hair was chemically straightened, using hair relaxer that Black people now appropriately call Creamy Crack, because of how toxic it is. Given I was banned from wearing braids at Joeys, I had taken to throwing my hair up in a bun most of the time. There wasn't exactly a plethora of hairstylists in Muswellbrook familiar with afro hair. In fact, there were zero.

'Hey, Marnz,'

'What?'

'Wanna suck me off?'

I narrowed my eyes at Malcolm Harvey and Ted Wolf.

'Do me, then do him.'

'Yeah, you wish,' I said. 'Fuck off.' Teenage boys could be such filthy, dirty creatures, and these two should have known better.

I wanted to get as far away from them as I could and was about to leave when I was introduced to two guys I had never met before. One of them handed me a beer.

'I'm Ben, but people call me Dots.'

I looked at the splattering of freckles across his face and figured that's how he got his nickname. I loved his freckles. They held a certain charm, a certain character. They were appealing and so was he. He had an *I don't give a fuck* look in his eyes. I could tell he was a bad boy, as authentic as they come, and I was into bad boys then. Tyce was a bad boy. And with Dots, I sensed that element of danger. As a seventeen-year-old I found what he had on offer alluring. I wanted to get the attention of the guy whose attention was hard to get – I wanted to be the girl who would break down that wall of indifference.

While all the other girls were bitches and hoes to Snoop Dogg, he had his boo – his Queen, the one who would have his baby, a woman on a pedestal that no one else could reach. No side bitches, no hoes. I wanted to be Tyce's boo. And if I couldn't, well, this guy seemed interesting.

Dots and I chatted as Coolio's 'Gangsta's Paradise' blended into Blackstreet's new track 'No Diggity'.

His friend had had enough of the party. 'Let's get outta here.'

'Nah,' Dots said, his eyes on me. 'There's still a bit of action here. Let's hang around for a bit.'

'C'mon. I wanna go.' His mate was persistent.

Dots turned to face me. 'What are you doin'?'

'I don't know,' I said.

Dots turned to his friend. 'Why don't you go? I'll meet you at the Prince later.'

Not long afterwards, Dots and I left the party together. We ended up in the bushes behind some blond-brown brick town-houses in a cul-de-sac, and he started kissing me.

Maybe he wasn't even going to suggest sex, but after half an hour we had done everything else.

'I don't want to do it without a condom,' I said. Somehow, in my naive seventeen-year-old mind, I thought our little dalliance would end there. That he would shrug his shoulders and that would be it.

'I've got some at my place,' he said. 'I live just around the corner.'

Shit, I thought, as I pulled my clothes back into place. But okay. Maybe it was about time I lost my virginity. Ultimately, I'd been proud of myself for making it to seventeen with it intact, and although I'd had no stories to share on those walks with Victoria and Lisa, I'd developed an uneasy truce with myself that I was going to wait until I was ready. Maybe that was now.

We got up and started the long trek to his place. He kept saying he thought he lived closer, but we went a hell of a long way. While we walked, we talked.

It turned out Dots was Ben Clarkson – his younger sister, April, was in the same grade as me. I had gone to school with her at Muswellbrook High.

'My little sis is pregnant,' he told me.

'Wow. How did your parents react?'

'Aw, they're cool with it. My olds are really laid back. We're a tight fam. I'm real protective of my sister.' He pulled me closer. 'Are you warm enough, babe?'

I nodded.

'I want you to walk on this side,' he said, jostling me away from the road and towards the grass.

'Why?'

'I want to protect you from the cars, babe.' He was so gentle and caring, and he made me feel at ease.

Dots told me he was not long out of jail, and how he always ended up brawling when he hung out at the Prince.

'Are you a boxer?' I asked. He had the physique of one.

'I used to do a bit of boxing,' he said. 'It's the kinda sport where you have to learn to keep your cool so your opponent doesn't get the better of you.'

'What type of music do you listen to?'

'Ah, you know, I like a bit of rap, a bit of hip hop.'

'Oh yeah? Who are your favourite artists?' He had my attention.

'I listen to a lil' Public Enemy, the Beastie Boys, NWA, Ice-T, Ice Cube . . .'

Since music was a big deal to me, I was impressed when he said he was a fan of rap. And he'd mentioned some classic artists, but he had me at hip hop.

'I really thought I lived closer,' he said. 'It takes you half an hour to walk home when you're pissed and five minutes when you ain't.'

I stood still for a moment. 'Are you drunk?'

'Nah,' he replied quickly. 'Not really, I'm just feelin' alright.'

Finally, but all too quickly, he turned to me. 'Here's my house.'

It dawned on me why we had walked all that way. I was suddenly really scared. He sensed it.

'Are you okay?' he said. His tone conveyed such concern, such care – there was only one answer to that question.

I nodded. We went inside.

Dots dumped a dish of marijuana on the table and grabbed a bottle of cordial from the fridge, neglecting to make the warm cuppa he'd been talking about on our way to his house. While he was in the kitchen, I browsed through the CDs on display.

We couldn't get comfortable as we made out on the couch, so he went into his bedroom and came back out hauling a mattress, which he dumped onto the lounge room floor. His muscly body made it appear feather-light. He positioned it in front of the TV, which he switched on. *Rage* played in the background, the Spice Girls dancing across the screen.

He kissed me passionately, but in my fear I wasn't very responsive.

'You don't have to do anything if you don't want to.'

I was so relieved. I felt obliged to have sex with him since he had taken me all the way back to his place . . . for a condom. I felt a little more confident about getting undressed, figuring we would just muck around, like we did in the bushes, like I had with other guys.

'Is it your first time?'

'Yes.'

'I'm the best person to lead you through it the first time. Nobody else. You're my baby.' He kissed me. 'I'm your baby.'

I thought about Tyce in that moment. I wanted *him* to be my baby. But maybe it was about time I gave up on Tyce. I turned my attention back to Dots.

'I'm scared,' I told him.

He continued to explore. 'I love you.'

'No, you don't. Don't say that.'

He laughed. I thought about getting up and walking out of the house. There was no way he could love me – we'd only just met. Why did he feel the need to say that? He continued to kiss me, caress me.

'Don't forget to put on a rubber.'

'I'm wearing one.'

'No, you're not.'

He laughed again. 'I ain't got nothin'.'

'I don't want to get pregnant,' I said, pretending that was the only thing I was concerned about.

'I've got ways to take care of that.'

In that moment, I realised that I could never get an abortion. Dots relented and put a condom on.

'I haven't used one of these in a long time,' he said. I let him inside my body. It was incredible but painful. He kept telling me to relax, but I couldn't. I did wonder whether we were *actually* having sex, and even asked him afterwards, just to make sure.

'Did we do it?' My eyes were wide as I gazed into his.

'Yes,' he replied.

Afterwards, I lay next to him, his strong arms around me. I felt protected. In spite of myself, I did feel loved.

He suggested we go to his room, where two pornographic posters took prime position on the wall above his bed. I felt intimidated by the bodies of these naked women, which I believed at the time were so much better than mine.

By the time the sun had risen, I felt so comfortable, warm and safe, waking up in his arms, but I cringed when he squeezed at my love handles. I look back now at the body I was uncomfortable in then and think of just how much it suited me and how lucky I was to look the way I did.

We did it again in the morning, this time without a condom. I had given away my virginity without even a relationship to justify it. My virginity meant more to me when I no longer had it.

For a while, I was in complete denial. I tried to convince myself that, clinically, I could still be a virgin.

I didn't bleed, and I always thought I would bleed the first time. But maybe somebody else had broken my hymen just by playing around. Maybe I didn't have a hymen – one in every two thousand girls doesn't. I desperately wanted to hold on to the belief that I was still a virgin, even though deep down I knew I wasn't. Why? The bastard never called me.

I saw Dots down the main street roughly six months later. He was wearing a pair of dark sunglasses. I wanted to punch him in the face – *smack-bang*, right on the fucking nose. I pictured his glasses smashing to pieces.

'Hi,' I said. 'You didn't call me.' Yeah – me stating the obvious. He looked at the ground. And then it was as if he couldn't get away from me fast enough.

'Anyway, it's nice to see you,' I said, and meant it.

A few weeks later I ran into his sister, April, at the pub.

'Ben really liked you,' she said. I didn't even know she knew about us. 'He wanted to call you. The only reason he didn't is 'cos Tyce still likes you.'

What?! I didn't even know Tyce *liked* me, let alone *still* liked me. What was Tyce doing getting involved? He'd had his chance. And now, when I was trying to move on . . . I was very upset. There was more to the story, but not knowing it at the time, I drowned my sorrows in hip hop and listened to a steady diet of Snoop Dogg and Dr. Dre, rapping that 'bitches ain't shit'. *Tell me about it*. I played my bootlegged cassette of *Doggystyle* over and over again. I loved almost every song on it, except for one I absolutely couldn't stand: 'Ain't No Fun (If the Homies Can't Have None)'. Although I would fast-forward it on most occasions, I had heard it enough times to know the lyrics well. They'd had a major effect on me, especially when Nate Dogg got in on the act, singing about how there wasn't a woman alive he could love. There was no wining and dining in this version of reality, no romance on this track, no respect in the mouths of these rappers. For a woman to expect that type of treatment – oh, she must be a gold-digger. Women were only good for one thing, and that was fucking. Once you'd had enough of her, you passed her on to your boys – let them get in on the action.

That type of track confirmed to me that men only ever wanted sex and didn't really care about women, except for maybe their mothers. The problem was I *loved* hip hop. Boyz II Men just didn't do it for me. When they sang about making love to a woman just the way she wanted to be made love to . . . I just didn't believe it. It didn't ring true to me. But I believed Snoop Dogg when he rapped about hoochies, about taking what was thrown at him and moving on to the next one. I really wish I had found Boyz II Men more alluring. I probably should have appreciated the white linen suits and the roses. I really wish that clean-cut, lovey-dovey stuff was more my speed. But it wasn't, not when my life was telling a different story.

My collection of female rappers provided some comfort. I felt like Lil' Kim's songs at least gave me a voice. My personal favourite was 'Big Momma Thang'. In this song, I heard a woman who was at first hesitant to give these men what they wanted, and then thought, *Fuck it. Let's go.* I heard a woman who embraced her femininity and used it to her advantage. Someone who got hers, because a guy was certainly going to get his.

I was obviously having a few problems and wasn't happy at Joeys, so I saw a school counsellor. I told her about the few experiences I'd had with guys. There were the ones I *hadn't* slept with who didn't call me. There was the one I *had* slept with who didn't call me. I asked her whether guys had feelings. I was convinced they didn't, given my own experiences and the messages that were engrained in hip hop.

'Do guys care about girls?' I asked.

'What do you mean?'

'Do boys have real feelings? Like we do . . . Or is it normal for them to have sex with girls they don't really care about or even like?'

'I don't know. I'll have to ask my husband. I'll tell you what he says at our next session.'

She reported back that her husband had said yes – not only was it possible for a guy to have no emotional attachment to the girl he was having sex with, but that's how it was in the majority of cases. Guys didn't have the same types of feelings girls did. Guys really didn't give a shit. What I wish somebody had told me then was some guys just weren't worth my time, but there was going to be someone out there who was. *And girl, pick some better stuff to listen to – or at least don't take what you're listening to so literally.* But at the time, I decided I wasn't going to care either. If guys could bury their feelings and sex was just sex to them, then I wasn't going to catch feelings either, and sex would be just sex to me. Somehow, years later, it worked. I became cold-blooded when it came to knocking boots. I switched off my feelings.

The drama didn't end before a pregnancy scare, eliminated when I got my period. But I noticed some clotting. When I told my mother, she mused about how blood clots could be a sign of losing a baby. 'But you've never had sex, so that couldn't be the case.'

I looked at her, alarmed.

'You have had sex?' The look on her face was one of pure disappointment. 'Mawunyo! *Who?*' My mind was still on the fact that I could have miscarried. Of course that wasn't the case, but that conversation stuck with me.

While Mum lamented the fact that her little girl was no longer her *innocent* little girl, I – who had lost that innocence the moment Tyce touched me – could feel her pain and the tragedy of that moment, because I too was filled with remorse.

CHAPTER 13

When the Morning Comes

Another near miss.
But maybe that wasn't a mistake, Miss.

'I don't want you to go to that party,' Mum said.

'But my friend has been planning her eighteenth for almost a year. I already told her I'm going.'

'Well, you'll have to tell her you're no longer going. I don't want you to go.'

'Why?'

'Because I said so. You went out last night,' she said, referring to a party Lisa Leonard had thrown. 'I don't want you going out again tonight. I'm your mother. The Bible says honour your mother and father. It doesn't matter if you think what I'm telling you is stupid. Even if I tell you stupid things, you have to listen, because I'm your mother.'

I rolled my eyes. I had every intention of going to the party. I had only seen Jayne a few times since leaving Muswellbrook

High, and each time I saw her she'd mentioned her eighteenth. She was super excited and had been planning it for a long time. I didn't want to disappoint her, despite what my mother had said, and so I went to the party. I had finished my homework, done some study after work and even tidied my room. I didn't see why I shouldn't be allowed to go.

Despite all that planning, I was bored on arrival, so I got one of my friend's mothers to drop me back home. I walked through the door around 8.20 pm. Mum was asleep in the study. Everyone else was watching TV. Eventually, I went to bed.

Mum came into my bedroom between one and two in the morning.

'Get up and get out of the house!' she said. 'If you're not going to listen to me, I don't want you staying here.'

At first, I resisted – she couldn't be for real. She'd tried to throw me out once before, when she caught me smoking in my room, so, as tired as I was, I stayed put. Mum left but came storming back a few minutes later, asking what I was still doing there.

'Go, go, go! Take what you want and go!'

At that point I realised she *was* for real. Too tired to protest or fight back, I got dressed and grabbed a little bag. I didn't pack much – no clothes – because I didn't have any plans. I had almost walked the full length of our street when I realised I didn't have my Bible with me. Mum has this thing about taking the Bible with you wherever you go.

'Make sure you take your little Bible,' she would say, referring to the pocket-sized New Testament. We had so many of them scattered around the house. I thought about this and felt it was sufficient enough reason to head back. Mum approached me after I'd grabbed a Bible and was on my way back out.

'Give me the key,' she demanded.

It was clear she didn't want me coming back in. I thought of where I might go, and what I might do, my tiredness overtaking any sadness or fear.

I walked past Lisa's house and saw the light on in her brother's room. I thought about going over, but decided not to. Victoria's bedroom light was on too – but no.

I thought about going to Fonda's house and started walking in that direction, but then took a detour down another street instead. There was no need to burden Fonda with this. There were a surprising number of people out and about in Muswellbrook at 3 am. Peter Anderson, one of the guys from Muswellbrook High, skated up to me. It had been a while since I'd seen him, and I told him what had happened. I hadn't yet processed everything, and relayed the night's events with a shrug of the shoulders and a touch of remorse.

I headed to the train station; by then it had started to rain. I waited for the 6.18 am train to Newcastle, hopped on it and spent the day shopping. I figured there'd be more to do in Newy than if I hung out on the streets of Muswellbrook. It hadn't sunk in yet that I could potentially be homeless. When my Walkman broke, I headed to Brashs and listened to a few CDs on the new listening bays they'd installed. I thought of the days when I used to guess whether certain artists were rappers by looking at the cover – no need to do that anymore. I bought a diary and a pair of earrings, and thought about going home that evening, but figured Mum would still need some time to cool off.

While I was at the outdoor mall in Newcastle, one of those street-corner evangelists handed me a booklet. It was aptly entitled 'Going Home', and I slipped it into my bag with my New Testament.

I slept at Newcastle University that night – in the games room, lying on one of the couches. I knew my way around after staying with Jennifer Sterling when I was doing work experience in Year Ten. I tried directory assistance but couldn't find her new address. It was freezing, and I had a restless night.

I thought Mum, who was still a nursing student at Newcastle Uni, might be on campus the next day, so instead of catching the train back to Muswellbrook come morning, I hung around, hoping to run into her on campus. Maybe I could convince her to take me back. I went to both libraries but didn't see her, so I did some research for Drama.

I was really unsure about going home. Mum had made it clear she didn't want me there, but I couldn't imagine an alternative. Would I end up on the streets? Would I have to drop out of school? If I was going to get anywhere in life, I would need an education – that had been drummed into me. So I made the decision that I was going to catch the train back to Muswellbrook that night and ask for Mum's forgiveness. After all, she usually forgives me quickly.

I was walking home from the station when Kelly Winter's mother hooned up beside me. Fonda and Kelly were in the car. Kelly stuck her head out the window and told me to get in.

'What's going on?' I asked.

'Your mum is *so* worried about you,' Fonda said.

'She threw me out,' I said in disbelief, and by then I was in tears.

'Sometimes parents say things on the spur of the moment, but they don't really mean it,' Mrs Winter said.

I still couldn't be sure. I was the only person who'd heard Mum that night. Mrs Jones and Amber had been doing laps looking for me as well after hearing that I'd been 'spotted'.

When I got home, Mum gave me a hug – for what felt like the first time ever. Our family didn't do hugs. I had tried to hug her in the past, but she always pushed me away. We didn't talk about our feelings and we didn't do hugs. I found it really weird when Amber and the other Joeys girls would kiss each other on the cheek to say hello. I'd often avoid their puckered lips and hold my arms out for a hug, because at least that felt a little less odd.

I thought Mum was acting because everyone was still there. When they left, however, she completely broke down. I'd never seen my mother so devoid of strength. She started crying.

'I didn't mean what I said,' she repeated, asking herself *Why?* over and over again. 'I reported you as a missing person to the police. You were missing for forty-one hours. *Forty-one hours!*' She hugged me again.

'Do you know what we used to call you when you were born? Baby P. That was short for Baby Precious,' she said. It was the first time I'd heard this story. 'The whole family was really upset that you were missing.' I thought about Dad, Sedudzi, Sophia and John.

Mum must have really caused a racket given the impact my 'disappearance' had on my friends. Fonda told me they all went back to her place because they couldn't think of anything else at school. They were all crying, and they hugged Peter Anderson to death when he told them he'd been talking to me. He'd been one of the last people I'd seen in Muswellbrook before heading to Newcastle.

One of the girls from school told me later that I had too many friends to do that kind of thing. Everyone thought I was some sort of runaway. But it wasn't my choice to leave that night.

What this scenario did do was create a shift in my relationship with Mum. It made me realise how much she really did care about me, and it changed the way we related to one another. She started telling me she loves me, and made sure I knew that she cared. And hugs were now on the table.

♪♫

As a teenager, music was one of the few things that made sense to me. But then again, it didn't make much sense at all. My mother would constantly look at my CD collection and shake her head. 'How much is one CD?'

'Thirty dollars,' I would say, neglecting to tell her I'd pay more if it was an import, and most of my CDs were imports. CDs were what I spent my money on from my various casual jobs around town – more than on clothes, more than on shoes and definitely more than on make-up, which I couldn't get in my shade in Muswellbrook anyway. I didn't care about those other things. I was all about my music.

'All those CDs would add up to more than a thousand dollars. What a waste of money. Do you know what you could buy with a thousand dollars?'

But I wasn't just buying music when I bought a new CD. I was buying an *experience*. I can remember driving to Newcastle to buy

Macy Gray's *On How Life Is* when it first came out and playing it at high volume, blinking away tears as I listened to the first track, 'Why Didn't You Call Me'. I could relate to those lyrics blasting through my speakers – pining away for a guy who failed to call when you thought he might. Although my experience was different, the sentiment was the same.

When Tyce finally called our landline – about a year late – I was still excited. It had been ages since I'd last seen him, and he told me he would be coming to visit tomorrow. I thought about introducing him to my parents, hanging out at our house and catching up.

He called the next day and confirmed that he and his friend (whom he hadn't previously mentioned) were about to leave, and that I should go looking for them if they ended up lost. I waited and waited, and then recruited my nearby friend Amanda Carey for the search, because they did, indeed, end up lost.

We hailed down one of our schoolmates who had a car, and he took us around Muswellbrook. We finally found them wandering around, looking dejected. They had already been to my house, and Tyce seemed a little peeved.

'Your dad didn't look too happy to see us,' he said. 'I'm never going to that place again.' (Dad later told me Tyce had been trying to be polite – it seemed Dad didn't quite buy the act.)

Tyce introduced me to his friend – a Pacific Islander guy he'd met in jail. 'I heard you ran away,' Tyce said. 'I also hear you've been going out a fair bit and partying.'

I looked at him pointedly. I knew exactly what he was referring to when he mentioned partying, or rather *who*: Dots. And as for running away . . .

HIP HOP & HYMNS

'Don't believe everything you hear,' I said.

'I worry about you a lot, Marnz,' Tyce said.

When they were gone, Amanda turned to me.

'Man, I felt so uncomfortable just then,' she said.

'Why? 'Cos they're both jailbirds?'

'No,' she said. 'Because I was the only white person.'

I scoffed. *Imagine how Tyce and I usually feel in this town of ours.*

CHAPTER 14

Just Tah Let U Know

Read widely. Study independently.
School just gives you the basics.

I was so immersed in African American culture that I grew up thinking my ancestors were slaves. I was flicking through my favourite hip hop magazine, *The Source*, when I stumbled across an article on the Lady of Rage. In it, I discovered that Rage had performed the same poem I had chosen for my HSC Drama performance – 'The Negro Mother' by Langston Hughes. My performance included these lines:

Children, I come back today / To tell you a story of the long dark way / That I had to climb, that I had to know / In order that the race might live and grow. / Look at my face – dark as the night – Yet shining like the sun with love's true light. / I am the child they stole from the sand / Three hundred years ago in Africa's land. / I am the dark girl who

135

crossed the wide sea / Carrying in my body the seed of the free. / I am the woman who worked in the field / Bringing the cotton and the corn to yield. / I am the one who labored as a slave. / Beaten and mistreated for the work that I gave. / Children sold away from me, husband sold, too. / No safety, no love, no respect was I due. / Three hundred years in the deepest South: / But God put a song and a prayer in my mouth. / God put a dream like steel in my soul. / Now, through my children, I'm reaching the goal.

I was intrigued to find out more about the Lady of Rage's performance, so I called the United States and managed to get a hold of the journalist who wrote the story – P. Frank Williams. He was a contributor to *The Source* at the time.

'The P is for positive,' he told me.

After discussing the Lady of Rage and trying to glean as much useful information as I could for my performance, I asked Frank where he was from.

'Oakland, California,' he said.

'No, I mean before that.'

'I was born and raised in Oakland.'

I persisted. 'Where are your parents from? And grandparents?'

'I guess my family is originally from the South,' he said. 'Louisiana and Texas.'

I remember thinking at the time, *Why won't you tell me whereabouts in* Africa *you're from?*

Once, on a trip to Sydney, I met an African-American man who pointed out that, due to slavery, he didn't know where in Africa his ancestors came from.

'Your ancestors weren't slaves,' he told me. 'You say you're from Ghana. You know where you're from. Due to three hundred years of slavery, I don't know. That's the difference between you and me. African Americans have lost that link with the past. We had our language and culture stripped from us.'

So African Americans didn't know where in Africa they originated from. That explained P. Frank Williams's response – he simply didn't know. My world began to unravel. It was the first time I realised that there was a difference between me and the Black Americans I'd admired so much my entire life, that there was more than just geography separating us: my ancestors weren't slaves. My admiration stemmed from the fact that these people looked exactly like me, and there was so much power in their revolt against an impossibly painful legacy, and now I was finding out that I didn't share this legacy. That I was, again, *different.* I was already different from everyone else around me, and now I was different from them too?

My very sense of identity was now in question. I was shocked, then I felt devastated. I thought back to when I was younger, and a poem I had written. It had a line about my ancestry, which I had linked to slavery. My mother had shaken her head when I read it to her: 'Your ancestors weren't slaves.'

I looked at her, thinking *she* was the one who was wrong. I never twigged when it came to names – my parents had friends from Ghana called Ernest Watson and Jennifer Sterling. It turned out I *did* have more in common with the kids in the World Vision ads than I did with Carl Lewis. Or Flo Jo. Or Whitney Houston . . . Or the Cosby kids. The World Vision kids were African and lived on the continent. I was African, born of the continent. *Fuck.*

If my identity puzzle was jumbled before, it was now missing a few crucial pieces. And I had no idea where to find them.

♪♫

I used to sometimes wonder whether Dad was my real father. Except it's obvious that he is – I look just like him.

I wanted to know my dad loved me, because, deep down, I looked up to him. I considered him a very intelligent man. He was my 'dictionary of knowledge'. If I wasn't sure of something – historical, political, scientific, or anything to do with current events – all I had to do was ask my father. Most of the time he would know the answer. He's a news junkie, but prefers his books to be fiction. Quite often his eyes would be fixed on the pages of a novel, with names like Jeffrey Archer or Wilbur Smith emblazoned across the front. By far his favourite TV show is the British political satire *Yes Minister*.

Dad rarely shared his good sense of humour with me back then. He is a quiet man, but physically he is a dominating figure – tall with a filled-out frame. He had made a few unsuccessful attempts to lose weight and was once a member of GutBusters.

'I just want to lose five kilos,' he would sometimes say to me, a comment that never failed to make me smile on the inside. (Let's just say it wouldn't hurt if he lost more than five.)

I'll never forget those brown shorts he used to wear back in the day. The colour was identical to his complexion, and from a distance he looked like he was walking around naked in public.

When he was younger, Dad only wore glasses to read, but they have since become a permanent fixture above his nose. He gave up using hair dye after a while in favour of ageing gracefully, but for many years he would dye his greys black.

While Mum is always late, Dad is extremely punctual. You could set a clock against any number of his regular activities.

And he wasn't always forthcoming when I asked about the details of his life.

I'd often ask him what his role was at work, but he refused to tell me.

'What do you do at work, Dad?'

'I'm a technical officer.'

'Yeah, but what do you actually *do*?'

'I work as a technical officer.'

I found it very frustrating. In later years, he explained that his job involved handling contracts, administration and maintenance in the electrical section and later the coal plant section at Bayswater.

And while Mum would tell us *who* to vote for, Dad wouldn't tell me who got his vote in local, state or federal elections.

'It's a secret ballot,' he'd say.

My sister once told me that when she was going out to do the grocery shopping, Dad impressed on her something he felt was of utmost importance: 'Make sure you get *cage* eggs.' Sophia laughed as she told me this, as if to say, *Darling Dad, going against the grain.*

To Dad, it probably seemed ridiculous to pay for overpriced eggs due to the guilt of the Western world – people who are several steps removed from animal husbandry, appeasing their consciences with images of chickens flapping about in boundless space, right before they reach the slaughterhouse. *Why would you pay more for that?*

I got a taste of what my father's reaction might be the day he gives me away when I participated in the Debutante Ball in Year Eleven. The girl was supposed to ask the boy to be her partner, but a good friend of mine – Barry, who was half Filipino, half white – asked me. He was the shortest guy in our year and I was the tallest girl. We were hopeless at doing the waltz. Our Deb teacher was constantly scolding us and mispronouncing my name in the process.

'Mawani and Barry, pay attention!' But the two of us would keep stepping on each other's toes.

On the night of the ball I got all dressed up in a white dress, which resembled a wedding gown. Barry and I were the first to walk onto the basketball court and be 'introduced to society'. Later, Barry and I waltzed on the dance floor, giving it our best effort. Dad was there in the audience, but he refused to join me for the father–daughter waltz.

Sometime later, I confided in my friend Mike Brennan that my father didn't like me.

'He does,' Brenno told me. 'Your father *loves* you.'

'How can you say that? How on earth would you know?'

'Listen, when you walked out at the Deb he started crying. My old man had never seen him cry before. He didn't know what to do. Nobody knew how to react.'

My brother John gave me a pointed look. 'I'm a fortune teller,' he joked.

'Okay then, what am I going to get in my HSC?' I asked.

'I reckon you'll get . . . seventy-nine per cent.'

I explained that a mark of seventy-nine per cent would mean I had fallen short of gaining entry into the course I wanted to study at university.

'Well, study harder and I'll tell you your fortune again later,' he said.

Turned out my brother was no clairvoyant, and the study I did for my HSC didn't pay off. I failed miserably. I never did recover from accidentally skipping a page in my Maths exam. I had flipped the page right before the bell rang and realised there was still an entire section to go. And I'm sure picking Drama as an elective didn't help either.

The members of my family crowded into my bedroom when I got my results back.

'Let's pray,' Mum said before I opened the envelope. 'Dear Father, thank You for Your love and mercy. You say when two or three are gathered in Your name, You are in their midst. Lord, we gather here today to pray that You give Mawunyo the marks she needs to set her on the path to success. Help her to get into the course she wants to get into at uni and for her future to be bright. In Jesus's mighty name. Amen.'

I opened up the envelope containing my marks. A groan wrapped in a disappointed sigh rose from my throat as I read my overall mark to my family.

I needed a TER in the high nineties if I was going to pursue my childhood dream of studying journalism. What had begun as a light-bulb moment in primary school, where I realised I could have more than Trisha Goddard's hair – I could have her career – had evolved into a love of anything and everything journalistic. My forays into work experience had been exhilarating, and my passion for the craft grew with every line I wrote, each answer I uncovered and the people I came across in the process. At forty-five-point-whatever, my marks fell well short of what was required for a degree in journalism.

'Half price,' John said – a catchphrase my family soon adopted when referring to my marks.

Not long afterwards, a relative who was visiting from Sydney, knowing my disappointment, gave me some advice I would never forget. He picked up a piece of paper and drew a straight line. 'If you can't get there like this,' he said, 'you can always get there like this.' He drew another line, but this one had a number of curves on its way to the same destination.

I decided he was right. I was going to fight long and hard to get into journalism at Charles Sturt University, which was considered one of Australia's best communication and journalism schools. Graduates were referred to as the Mitchell Mafia, their voices appearing on the airwaves, their faces on television screens and their names in newspaper by-lines across the country. I was determined to join the Mitchell Mafia.

I started the engine and made my way over to the Bi-Lo in South Muswellbrook on a mission to buy some junk food. I'd scored my licence on my second attempt at the test and was taking Mum's car, a white Ford Laser hatchback, for a spin.

I might have fallen for Tyce – our first kiss and string of near misses – and I'd had other crushes over the years, but there was another love close to my heart: lollies.

I was obsessed with my weight, but I couldn't stop eating junk. It was the legal drug addiction I just couldn't shake.

I was quite motivated when it came to working out at the gym. The problem was, after slogging it out in an aerobics class, I would go home and indulge in my poor eating habits.

I had a particular weakness for white chocolate. John once joked that you could sprinkle white chocolate on anything and I would eat it. I was also a big fan of caramel. Creamy éclairs combined the two and were a favourite, and for some reason the Woolworths on my side of town didn't stock them. I figured my tastes were different from most people's because the sweets that I had a particular fondness for were taken off the shelves after a while . . . including creamy éclairs.

I got out of the car when I reached the shop and headed straight for the lolly aisle. It wasn't unusual for me to make a trip to the supermarket solely for junk. But it also wasn't unheard of for me to go to the shop to buy something I really needed, like toothpaste, only to completely forget and go home with a stack of lollies instead.

I began eating the éclairs as soon as I was in the car. My figure was yet to catch up with my gluttony, but I was still very unhappy with it. I was 170.5 cm tall and weighed 64 kg. Although my weight was in proportion to my height, what I lacked and desired more than anything was a washboard stomach like the ones I'd seen on the women who adorned the magazines I read.

I continued to sabotage my efforts. I had tried dieting on nothing but 'healthy food', but that never lasted for very long, and I would find that I was eating too much of the good stuff anyway. I had tried eating nothing at all, but then I read about how anorexics sometimes grow facial hair. Infertility was also a risk. I had considered throwing up after every meal, but bulimia really didn't appeal to me. Apparently, it ruined your teeth. And, of course, Denise Austin's *Super Stomachs* video routine didn't work. I didn't know what to do.

The type of body shape I aspired to was always the kind I saw on women in my *Girlfriend* magazines, and apart from Naomi Campbell, they were typically white women – the Cindy Crawfords of the world. Not all these women were stick thin – I loved the hourglass look – but I was doomed for failure. These women were built differently to me. Looking back now, after hearing Cindy Crawford's 'I wish I looked like Cindy Crawford' quote, *of course* those bodies were unachievable. Airbrushing and Photoshop had never even entered my mind.

I was confident in the fact that I had a lot of willpower – I *was* capable of committing to those daily *Super Stomachs* workouts. But when it came to food, that willpower – and everything else – flew straight out the window.

I started pasting evidence of my gluttony in my diary. On one particular day, I pasted a receipt – there was nothing on it except junk. Next to the receipt were a series of empty wrappers: Picnic, Snickers, Crunchie, Nestle Crunch, Crave and a Milkybar. The timeframe in which I consumed all of that junk is unclear, but I had written something about having more left for tomorrow.

Over the page: another receipt. On it were Fantales and Kool Mints. And next to it was a menu of what I'd had for lunch that day: fried rice and Mongolian lamb, and a vanilla thickshake. Commentary followed about how much I enjoyed it, but that I was feeling sick and had a headache and my sides were aching.

It's real sad, you know, my teenage self had scrawled on the page. *It's like a drug addiction. It ain't right.*

Turn a couple of pages and the empty Kool Mint and Fantales wrappers were pasted on the page, along with a Mars bar wrapper.

Flick forward a few more pages and there's a white Magnum wrapper, a Coca-Cola label and a choc-and-toffee drink. I mention that I'd eaten a hamburger that day, and two slices of pizza at 10 pm.

Then comes New Year's Eve and a stocking stuffed with empty wrappers, including a KitKat, Snickers, Cherry Ripe, Mentos and more.

According to my diary, I couldn't eat it all, and strangely I mention that Sophia helped me. This was strange because beautiful Sophia didn't eat much. She had always been skinny, and I would often look at her svelte shape and think to myself, *That's how you could have looked if you didn't have this problem.* I threw away some half-eaten chocolate because that was it: I was done with junk. Once New Year hit, I was going to be healthy. This was the last hurrah. *Humph.*

I think my resolve lasted till 2 January.

CHAPTER 15

Choices

I had a good thing, but my heart was elsewhere.

January, 1998. Levi pulled me closer and kissed me gently. He wasn't my type, but I liked him anyway. I traced my hand across his abdomen and let it linger a little lower. My new boyfriend was far from a bad boy and had no problem admitting he was never in the popular group at school. To him, popularity was tantamount to selling out, because if you valued chasing the acceptance of others above anything else, then you weren't his type of person. Why would anyone want to do that? Levi wasn't the type to conform.

I met him in Wollongong on New Year's Eve 1997, and we were immediately attracted to one another. I had just finished high school and was deciding what to do next, which university I might go to and what course I might do, given I didn't get the marks to study journalism. It turned out Levi was from Greta, about an hour down the road towards Newcastle, and had a sister living in Muswellbrook.

I ran a hand through his long, curly surfie hair that he often wore in an unruly mop on top of his head. Although he looked like a surfie, he was actually more of a muso. He sang and played guitar in a band that used to battle against Silverchair – a losing battle, but a battle all the same.

He was upset when he saw a copy of Silverchair's debut album, *Frogstomp*, sitting in my CD collection at home. At first, he reeled back in surprise – he was well aware I was into hip hop, so what was I doing with a Silverchair album? Then he sadly accepted the fact I was into Silverchair, his nemesis, with a shake of his head. Within seconds, he had moved on and leaned forward to give me a kiss. That was Levi: kind, sweet, even-tempered.

He always made me feel so special and told me I was beautiful every day. When he first asked me out, he made me promise I would never cheat on him.

'My ex cheated on me,' he said. 'I couldn't take it if you did as well.'

I kissed his neck and let my lips inch their way down his body. He had agreed to leave his underwear on while we played around in his bed. I wasn't ready to sleep with him and he put me under no pressure to do so, but asked me why.

'Maybe I'm a virgin,' I said.

'I can tell you're not a virgin.'

I pulled away from him slightly and cocked my head to one side. 'How can you tell?'

He smiled and gave me a kiss. 'I just know.'

'No, really, how can you tell?'

'You're a little bit too experienced to be a virgin,' he said.

We left a trail of clothes on the floor and made our way to the shower. While we were in there, we heard the door open. 'Who's that?' I asked.

'Oh, it's probably just Dad.'

'Are you going to introduce me to him later?'

Levi shook his head, slowly but deliberately.

I was a little offended. 'You don't want me to meet your father?'

'Not just yet.'

I thought he might have been embarrassed and wanted to make sure I was a keeper before he introduced me. He explained much later that he was actually pissed off with his dad, who had a key to the apartment Levi was renting from him. His dad used to come and go as he pleased, as if he still lived there. Levi assured me he was proud to call me his girlfriend and would have been happy to show me off to anyone.

Levi used to come to Muswellbrook for three days at a time and stay at his sister's house so he could see me. There was one weekend when he wanted KFC for lunch. I was on one of my ridiculous diets and couldn't think of anything worse. He drove to KFC and bought a bucket of chicken for himself, and then we went to a sandwich shop so that I could get something healthier.

'Can I please have a ham and salad sandwich?' I asked the woman behind the counter.

She looked me straight in the eye. 'We don't have that here.'

Levi and I looked at each other. *Bummer*, I thought. *What else can I get?* I chose not to challenge her too much, even though I could see she had ham to one side and there was lettuce, tomato, beetroot, cucumber, carrot – all the ingredients to make up a salad sandwich – on the other. There were even loaves of bread behind her.

'What about tuna and salad?' I asked.

'We don't have that either,' she said.

I put my hand in Levi's and we turned to leave the one sandwich shop in Australia that had no sandwiches. 'Okay,' I said. 'Let's go somewhere else.'

As we went to walk out, I could hear the person who had been in line after me ordering. 'Can I have a ham salad sandwich, please?'

'Sure,' the woman behind the counter said. 'Coming right up.'

Even twenty years later, Levi could recall this incident with the same level of disbelief he experienced in that moment. 'I wish I had said something,' he told me, but he had been shocked into silence.

Not every weekend Levi and I spent together in Muswellbrook included a racist who refused to make me a sandwich. But it was on the weekends when Levi *wasn't* in Muswellbrook that I would get into trouble.

I walked over to the DJ and requested 'Push It' by Salt-N-Pepa. I requested the same song every time I went out because DJs always had it in their catalogue, and they rarely played one hip hop song in isolation. Next, I stood at the bar, ready to order a drink.

'Hey, Marnz.'

I could have recognised that voice anywhere. I turned around.

'Hi, Tyce.'

'What are you up to?' he asked.

'Nothin' much. I was just at a party.' I pointed towards Marie and Jane. 'We thought we'd head out for a bit.'

'I'll buy you a beer,' Tyce said. He reached into his pocket and pulled out a pile of loose change. Placing the money on the counter, Tyce sorted through the coins, adding them up as he went along.

I hate beer. *How do I tell him nicely that I'd prefer to buy my own spirits?* I thought. I knew he wasn't working. Muswellbrook employers weren't as keen to put their trust in him, it seemed. Before I could come up with a plan, he had ordered two beers and handed one over to me.

Smiling, I accepted the glass anyway.

My obsession with hip hop had infiltrated most things in my life, including the types of alcohol and cocktails I preferred. There were a lot of brands mentioned in rap: Cristal champagne, Alizé liqueur, Rémy Martin and Hennessy cognac, Patrón tequila, Tanqueray gin. At the time, asking for Alizé and Cristal, a Tupac favourite, was met with blank looks in Muswellbrook, so quite often I'd order Snoop Dogg's signature gin and juice.

Tyce and I headed to the dance floor to the sounds of Tone Loc's 'Funky Cold Medina' – a song about a drink popular in Medina, Washington, that mixed liquor and cold medicine and was a supposed aphrodisiac.

We danced opposite one another until an even slower song came on. He pulled me towards him. With his arms wrapped around me, we moved in time to the music. I lifted my head away from his shoulder and looked up at him, savouring the moment. He leaned forward and kissed me.

As the night was drawing to a close, we left the Prince together and got onto the courtesy bus provided by the pub. I was holding Tyce's hand as we sat on the back seat when I decided it was time to come clean.

'I've got a boyfriend,' I told him.

Tyce tried to wrench his hand away from me, but I wouldn't let go. I held onto him tighter. The look in his eyes betrayed his emotions. I didn't expect him to be so upset, so hurt.

'Marnz, I thought you were alone. I wouldn't be with you like this if I knew you had somebody.'

'Levi and I haven't been together for very long . . .'

'I don't care how long you've been together. A day is a day too long.' He moved his body away from mine. I leaned in closer.

'Tyce,' I said softly, 'I've been crazy about you for . . . forever. How could I resist?'

He turned to me suddenly. 'Come home with me.'

I looked down. I wanted to, I really did, but would he respect me afterwards? And what about Levi? I looked up and made a split-second decision. My heart belonged to Tyce.

'Okay,' I said.

We got off the bus at his parents' place. He lived with them in a white weatherboard house in South Muswellbrook. I would often drive past his place and glance out the window, hoping to catch a glimpse of him on the verandah. There always seemed to be someone sitting outside.

The blue sedan his parents owned was parked out front. Tyce promised to drop me off at home in the morning and took me inside the dark house. His bedroom was closest to the door. Once we were tucked safely beneath the covers, he held me in his arms.

'I want you to break up with your boyfriend,' he said. 'I want you to be mine, nobody else's.'

Thoughts clouded my head. What if he didn't want anything to do with me in the morning? I wanted to stop him. Not because I didn't want to make love to him, but because I couldn't shake the nagging feeling it wasn't going to lead to a relationship, that he would lose respect for me. But how could I stop him now? It was too late. I had let things go too far.

♪♫

Tyce's parents were right there in the house while we were in his bedroom. I was aware that his mother was an alcoholic. It was common knowledge around town, and Mum would often be on shift when Mrs Carrington was brought in to the hospital after she'd had too much. Mum used to talk about how well Mr Carrington looked after his wife.

Tyce was the baby of the family. His sister, Laura, has always treated me with warmth and kindness. His brother, Xander, was extremely good-looking. Neither lived at home.

For some reason Mrs Carrington was sleeping in the lounge room with her husband. I heard her giving Tyce a hard time when he got up in the night to go to the bathroom.

In the morning, it took some effort to lift Tyce's heavy leg off mine, but he didn't stir. I had to be at my casual job at Best & Less by nine o'clock, so I got up to leave. I would have to hitchhike back to the party I'd been at the night before to get my car.

Once I had made it outside and closed the door behind me, I heard a click – the door was being reopened from the *inside*.

I turned with a big smile on my face, thinking it was Tyce.

It was his mother.

'Who are you?' she asked, clearly unimpressed. She didn't remember me, though we had met before.

'Mawunyo,' I said softly, my head to the ground.

'Who?' she asked a little louder.

'Mawunyo,' I repeated, terrified.

'Go,' she said, her arms outstretched as she shooed me away. 'Go!'

I felt like such a cheap little hoochie. I turned and walked all the way to the party headquarters in the rain. Not a single car stopped to pick me up on the way, despite my attempts to hitchhike.

As soon as I made it back to the house, I grabbed my belongings and got ready to drive home. An older guy there told me he'd seen someone who looked like me hitchhiking a little earlier.

'She had hair like yours – except she had a whole heap of beads in her hair,' he said.

'No, that was me,' I replied. 'The beads must have been beads of rain.'

When I got home, I had just enough time to shower and throw my uniform on. It was one of those typical retail outfits – a black skirt and white shirt. I pinned my name badge on and strode through the doors of Best & Less, minutes before my shift was due to start.

As I stood there folding underwear and serving customers every so often, Tyce was on my mind.

When I finished my shift, I went back to his place, still dressed in my uniform. I apologised to his parents for coming into their home in the middle of the night. His mother was much cheerier than she had been earlier that morning. She smiled and accepted my apology. The look on his father's face suggested he found the whole thing slightly amusing.

Their lounge room was very tidy. They had a couple of couches and a television. There was no carpet in the main living area; instead, the floor was made up of shiny lacquered wood. A photo of Tyce, Laura and Xander as babies sat above a cabinet.

'Is Tyce . . .?' I pointed to the bedroom.

Mrs Carrington nodded. I went into his room and he was awake but still in bed. I sat at his side and ran a hand through his hair. He looked up at me and smiled, pulling me closer to him. We kissed, and my heart melted all over again.

Tyce wasn't home when I called a day or so later. His mother excitedly gave me his cousin's number, so I called him there, but he wasn't interested in talking to me.

'I'm in the middle of playing Nintendo,' he said. 'Can you call me back?'

I didn't call him back. I was too hurt. When Tyce's cousin laughingly told me at a party a week or so later that Tyce was drunk the night we went home together – insinuating that his being so legless was the only reason he'd taken me home – I was gutted.

I broke up with Levi, without admitting I'd cheated. It would have hurt him too much. And I knew all too well what it felt like to be hurt.

♪♫

I eventually forgave Tyce and went round to his place on a few occasions. Sometimes we would sit on his verandah and just talk. Mrs Carrington was clearly fond of me despite that earlier encounter, and she was always so welcoming – greeting me warmly at the door, offering me a cuppa, making me feel like I belonged.

While I was on one of my health kicks, I ran over to pick Tyce up so we could go jogging together.

'Look after my boy,' Mrs Carrington said to me, smiling warmly as we left the house. Tyce challenged me to keep a speedy pace as we ran across Muswellbrook. I had to stop every now and then to catch my breath. He had put on weight and didn't look himself, but he was a lot fitter than his appearance suggested. In my eyes, he was still attractive. My feelings for him hadn't changed.

The next time we went jogging, we took a similar route and were about to split up and go our separate ways when I stopped and looked at him. I desperately wanted to tell him how I felt, but I was scared, and what if what I was feeling wasn't really love anyway?

The moment passed, and he was gone.

We drifted in and out of each other's lives. It wasn't long before Tyce started dating a girl named Penny. She was blonde and skinny. He couldn't have found someone more different from me if he'd tried.

I cried for weeks when I found out Penny was pregnant with Tyce's child. I had always thought that one day *I* would be the mother of his children. It tore me apart to accept that that would never happen.

I was out at the Prince not long afterwards when I ran into him. Half-heartedly, I congratulated him on his news.

'Thank you,' he said.

I just needed to know one thing. I wanted to know if he was happy. 'Do you love her?' I asked.

'Yes.'

My eyes welled up. Tyce was in love with Penny. Tyce, the guy I thought about 24/7, was having a baby with someone else. Tyce, the only guy I'd had feelings so deep for that no one else stood a chance – not even Levi, who was so kind and sweet and really into me. He never stood a chance because the only thing I knew was my love for Tyce, and how much I wanted to be his. And now it was clear Tyce didn't care about me at all. I guess it didn't matter then if I told him how I felt.

'You're the only guy I've ever been in love with.' There, I said it.

'Marnz, I loved you too. You know at Miranda's party, I wanted you to be mine.'

I got up and ordered a gin and juice at the bar and followed that up with a pre-mixed can of bourbon and cola. Once I'd sculled that, I moved on to West Coast Cooler.

Tyce summoned my attention as a group of us sat huddled in the outdoor area of the pub, smoking weed.

'My cuz says we can use his place tonight,' he said softly, his deep brown eyes looking at me expectantly.

'No way!' I said.

'Gee, thanks!' He laughed.

I placed a hand on his arm. 'Tyce, I want to, for me. But I couldn't do that to you . . . Penny . . . and your baby on the way . . .' I got up. By then I was feeling dizzy. I made my way to the bathroom and locked the cubicle behind me. With my pants half down, I fell to the floor and started balling. After a while, I could hear people talking.

'We can't get her out of there . . .'

Then, Tyce's voice.

'Marnz,' he said softly. 'Marnz, are you okay? Come on out of there.'

'Fuck off,' I said. I immediately regretted my outburst, because after that he disappeared. He was gone. It was well and truly over.

I ended up having to be carried home that night.

The next day, when I got home from my casual shift at McDonald's, I called Tyce to apologise for my behaviour at the pub the previous night. Mrs Carrington answered the phone. What she said next, before she put me on to Tyce, shocked me. 'You know, I always hoped that you and Tyce would end up together.'

After a long pause, I said, 'I guess you never know how things are going to turn out . . .' By that I meant, *I guess we had no idea things would end this way, but they have. Oh well, that's life, and I guess I need to move on.*

Mrs Carrington began to repeat my words excitedly. *Oh shit,* I thought. *She thinks I mean there's still a chance for us.*

I tried to backtrack, sputtering out a couple of nonsensical words – but it was too late. I'd said what I'd said. I didn't mean it the way it sounded. I didn't mean to suggest that the final chapter between Tyce and me might not have been written yet. I really didn't. But in the end, the words of young, heartbroken me would turn out to be prophetic.

CHAPTER 16

Music & Me

*Extracurricular activities are often mistakenly thought of
as the cherry on top. They're actually the bulk of the dessert.*

I was a student at Charles Sturt University in Bathurst, but
I hadn't joined the Mitchell Mafia. I wasn't studying journalism.
Not yet anyway. I'd gained an extra five points on my TER based
on the fact that I was from the country, bringing my score to just
over fifty. That gave me enough points to enrol in a short-lived
Bachelor of Arts in Communication (Media and Cultural Studies)
course at the university.

When I met Candace, it was clear we were going to be the best
of friends.

'My name is Candace,' she said. 'I spell it the same way as it's
spelled in the Bible.'

She was also from Ghana but was born and raised in Australia. She was studying theatre and media and wanted to be an
actor.

'I want to play specific types of roles. I don't want to be cast as a villain – I want to be the good girl. And I hate it when the Black characters only have Black love interests on the big screen, and white people only date other white people. Whatever happened to interracial dating?'

Candace had a wry, understated sense of humour, which I loved. She once went on about 'the life of a poor uni student'.

'The other day I was buying a muesli bar at the supermarket,' she began, 'and the muesli bar was a dollar forty-five. I only had a dollar twenty on me – but I had twenty-five cents in my account. So, I split the purchase by paying the dollar twenty and putting the rest on EFTPOS. I did it as if it was the most normal thing in the world. The cashier didn't know what to do.'

One of the many things we bonded over was our mutual love of hip hop.

'I'm so sick of the music at the bar,' I said to Candace, rolling my eyes. 'It's the same old thing every bar night.'

'Yeah, well, this is Bathurst,' Candace said. 'We are out in the sticks.'

'We should organise our own hip hop night,' I suggested.

Candace started to get excited. 'That's a great idea. My brother is in a band. We could hire a DJ and get them to perform.'

We'd hatched the plan but underestimated how difficult it would be to convince a sceptical student union that a 'Hip Hop and R'n'B night' was worth investing in in Bathurst – a country town famous for its car races at Mount Panorama, copious numbers of pubs and what we referred to then as 'rah-rah music' – Grinspoon, The Screaming Jets, Aerosmith. It was as if they'd missed the memo that hip hop was king.

The student union backed us after we convinced them of the merits of a hip hop night as an alternative 'social and cultural event' to the band nights, lunchtime trivia, club functions and theme nights already on offer. We got down to planning and arranged for one of our uni friends, an Indonesian Muslim guy who was also heavy into hip hop, to design the posters. We settled on bright orange – a colour you couldn't miss – and included a graffiti-inspired toon. We put the posters up all around campus and down the main street of Bathurst. I went around to lecture halls and told people why they should show up.

On the day of the actual event, Candace and I went shopping and bought matching outfits: black, grey and white tracksuits. The tops were short-sleeved and zipped up at the front. We walked into the event like queens. Colourful disco lights lit up the room. 'Ghetto Supastar' by Pras, ODB and Mýa blew the speakers up as we mingled with the crowd and watched as it got bigger and bigger and bigger, until the room was filled with body upon sweaty body, bopping around to the hits the DJ was spinning. By the time the band made it to the stage, the crowd was hyped. They sang a few R'n'B covers and a couple of originals, throwing down the dance moves.

Candace and I were blown away by just how big the event was.

I ordered a gin and juice at the bar and we continued our royal tour around the venue. It went so well that the university let me put another one on the following year in Candace's absence – she'd had enough of Bathurst and had transferred to a university closer to her hometown. Sedudzi designed and illustrated the posters for the second one – bright green this time, with a cartoon he drew. He even came to Bathurst for the event.

To give a sense of how significant these events were, I was in Sydney years later when someone introduced me to a woman who had gone to uni in Bathurst.

'We used to have Hip Hop and R'n'B nights there,' she told me. 'It was only ever once a year, so I used to hang out for them.'

'I started that shit,' I told her. 'Me and my friend Candace came up with those nights.'

I had my own hip hop show on the community radio station on campus, but also took every opportunity I could to get some training in journalism. I had applied to transfer to Journalism a year into my studies at Bathurst but had been knocked back, so I continued to do work experience in TV and radio, and, even though it was broadcast journalism I wanted to specialise in, I also made sure I had articles in print. I put a folder of references together and made sure my grades were on point, and I applied again a year later. With my foolproof application, they just couldn't say no that time around. Finally, I was a journalism student at Charles Sturt University. And I added a minor in Public Relations.

When the Sydney Olympic Broadcasting Organisation (SOBO) came knocking at CSU, looking for media students to join their ranks for the 2000 Olympics, I put my hand firmly and squarely up.

I was selected as one of just a hundred students recruited to work at the Games. My job as a Trainee Broadcast Liaison Officer involved providing technical assistance and support to broadcasters from around the world who were providing Olympic coverage to their respective nations.

When I found out I would be working alongside Bruce McAvaney, Mum's favourite commentator, I put him on the phone to her.

'I hear you think I'm pretty terrific,' he said.

'*Who is this?*' she asked.

Apparently, according to Mum, I hadn't explained to her who was on the other end of the line. The exchange went terribly. Mum was so embarrassed afterwards, and to this day hasn't forgiven me. She still thinks Bruce is the bee's knees, though, and he really is a top bloke. They could have been great friends.

I was working more than ten hours a day for the sixteen-day duration of the Games.

I was based at the main stadium but also spent a few days at the basketball venue, where I met members of the US Dream Team – Tim Hardaway, Kevin Garnett and Ray Allen. The team that year also included Allan Houston, who played for the New York Knicks. I was so dazzled by his good looks I couldn't bring myself to say hello. I just stood in front of him and stared.

I was watching from the stands at the Olympic Stadium when Cathy Freeman won the women's 400-metre final, and even got to congratulate her afterwards. Despite the divisions in Australia, Cathy's victory brought us all together, and in that one moment nothing else mattered. And I finally had the opportunity to meet my childhood hero Carl Lewis. Meeting him was so incredible – a pinch-yourself moment if there ever was one – that if I didn't have a photo of the two of us together to prove it, I may have wondered whether it really happened. He was so warm and kind, and while there was no proposal, I had to ask myself: *Could life get any better?*

I was on a blissful ascent, pursuing my journalistic dreams, and I had successfully applied to study abroad for a semester in the United States. What could possibly go wrong?

CHAPTER 17

No Church in the Wild

For me, calling myself a Christian meant I was a believer,
not Christ-like. And that was the problem.

It took five years after I lost my virginity till I was mentally and physically ready for sex. I had taken a guy I had just met back to my dormitory at uni. I was now comfortably at the stage where I was like the men who bagged bitches they didn't give a shit about. The only guilt I did feel was associated with my religion. My faith was inherited, and it was an inexperienced faith. My soul was longing for more, and the seeds were there for what would develop into true faith, but at that point it took a back seat to having a good time.

We hadn't used protection, so I went to the sexual health clinic in Bathurst in search of the morning-after pill. They sent me to the hospital, where a doctor handed me the drug, but not before giving me a lecture on why I shouldn't be having unprotected sex.

It wasn't long after that that I had my first Pap smear. It came back abnormal. I was sent to a gynaecologist for a colposcopy. The news wasn't good.

'I've got what?' I said to the doctor. I couldn't quite believe what I was hearing.

'You've got pre-cancer,' the doctor repeated. 'Pre-cancer of the cervix.'

I was speechless.

'You'll have to have a LLETZ to remove the abnormal cells – it's a relatively minor operation with a good success rate . . .'

I tuned out. Pre-cancer. What if that turned into cancer? Cancer at the age of twenty-one. I was meant to be a Christian, yet I was caught up in a lifestyle of indiscriminate fornication. This was my punishment for breaking the laws of the Bible. I'd been told all my life that Jesus died for our sins, but what about *this* sin, *my* sin – living like He never existed?

I told the doctor I was due to leave Australia for the United States soon. I had convinced the Head of School to let me study abroad for six months. She was reluctant to allow it, because I hadn't been a journalism student for long.

'I would advise you to have the operation before you go,' he said.

I couldn't believe this was happening. One of the thoughts that immediately entered my head was, *Will I lose all my hair?* I'd been growing it since Year Seven, and it only sat just below my shoulders. Imagine having to try to grow it again from scratch. The tight, tight curls breaking through the follicles on my scalp, piling on top of each other to form a tiny afro, defiantly natural, right before I poisoned the roots with hair relaxer in a bid to straighten the kinks. My hair was important to me. I was devastated.

I blinked, taking in the bleak walls of the operating theatre at the hospital in Bathurst. I couldn't help but feel a profound sense of loss. It was as if the doctor had cut away more than some abnormal cells. I felt like my spirit had also been hacked away. It's the one time in my life where I remember keenly not wanting to die, thinking my life was worth something. I was so young, I had so much to look forward to – I wasn't ready to leave the planet, and yet cancer, for so many, equalled death. And I had pre-cancer. *Pre-cancer.* I was alone in that operating theatre in Bathurst, away from family. My best friend, Candace, was long gone.

'Now, I want you to avoid any vigorous exercise for the next week,' the doctor said. 'And no sexual intercourse or tampons for a month.'

I nodded. Sex was the last thing on my mind. I had spent the past week working myself up into a frenzy about what could lie ahead for me. It would be an understatement to say the depth of my knowledge on cervical cancer had been limited up until then. I had since done some research, but that had only served to heighten my anxiety even further. I simply couldn't deal with getting cancer.

I walked out of recovery and made my way back to my dorm. I would find out later that the surgery was a success and I was going to be okay. But remnants of the stress I'd felt in that moment remained. I had had a close call. I wasn't invincible. Life wasn't a given.

PART THREE

CHAPTER 18

They say if you can make it here, you can make it anywhere.
But what if you don't?

I had pushed my troubles to the back of my mind: my pre-cancer diagnosis sat uneasily but firmly behind me; the near-misses with Tyce were in the rear-view mirror; and I'd defeated the odds by becoming a journalism student. I was ready for a new adventure.

As soon as I stepped foot onto American soil for the first time, I *felt* different. It began with the man who grabbed my luggage as soon as I'd passed through customs, who showed me a degree of acceptance I'd never felt back in Australia. It was also the fact that this man was Black – as were so many others I'd glimpsed as I made my transfer at the airport. I immediately felt like I *belonged*, that I'd arrived at my spiritual home.

'Are you here to go to school?' the porter asked me.

'Oh, no,' I said with a smile, not realising at the time that

Americans referred to uni as 'school'. 'I'm here to study at university.' He wished me well, and I was on my way.

When I walked the streets in America, nobody batted an eyelid. Blending in was refreshing for a change. It wouldn't be until I opened my mouth to say a few words that people would realise I was from somewhere else – and then I would ham up my connection to Australia. The conversations usually went like this:

'Oh, where are you from? England?'

'No, Australia.'

'There're *Black* people in Australia?'

I'd respond with a giggle, and lay on the charm, suggesting they should pay the place a visit.

I couldn't wait to discover Black America, to find my way into the centre of it. Stripped from the Motherland, Black Americans had built their own rich and diverse culture, influenced by the continent that bears their roots, but conceiving a radical new way in a new place. There's the style – from Air Jordans to high fashion; many African-American celebrities double as fashion icons, popularising looks and sparking off trends. The creative names – I've come across Ladonna, Lacresha, Laquan, Lashawn. The innovative hairstyles – Black Americans have taken styling afro hair to a whole new level: laying edges, the perfect fade, coils for days. The food – I now have African-American friends in the soul food industry in Sydney who talk about how their ancestors were given scraps – leftovers and undesirable cuts of meat – and how they transformed them into iconic dishes like ham hocks and collard greens; barbecued ribs and cornbread. Nothing was wasted. Soul food is a cuisine borne of necessity and innovation, with many of the dishes adapted from ingredients common in West Africa, such as black-eyed peas and okra. The music – gospel, blues, jazz, R'n'B, hip hop – all originally Black artistic expressions. Chuck Berry is considered the father of rock'n'roll.

While the terms hip hop and rap are often used interchangeably, hip hop *isn't* a synonym for rap. It's an entire culture, with four main elements: DJ'ing, rap, breakdancing and graffiti. A fifth element – 'consciousness' – is also worth mentioning. Conscious rap is often political and Afrocentric, and depicts the struggles of ordinary people, but with an aversion to crime and violence. Jamaican-born and Bronx-bred DJ Kool Herc is widely considered the father of modern rap, his spoken interjections on record preceded by West African storytellers known as griots, talking blues songs, jailhouse toasts (poems outlining outlandish misdeeds), and the dozens – ritualised word games where insults were exchanged. When the Sugarhill Gang released 'Rapper's Delight' in 1979 – the year I was born – more and more people became cognisant of rap, and eventually it would take over the world.

Hip hop music found a lifelong fan in me when it reached Muswellbrook. While the lyrics of some tracks forced me to question my value as a woman, others brought me great joy, or livened up a party. There were songs that made me pause and reflect; some were enlightening, others poignant; *all* were captivating.

In 2001, the year I arrived in New York, I thought that *cool*, when it came to Blackness, was something squarely in the domain of African Americans. Twenty years on, I realise being African is dope as hell – Afrobeats, which has its cultural origins in 1920s Ghana, is a massively popular music genre that, like hip hop, has been exported around the world. African recording artists like Davido, Wizkid and Burna Boy have climbed international charts and continue to pump out certified hits. There are few people who wouldn't want to move to the fictional Kingdom of Wakanda, and politicians in America, including Speaker of the House Nancy Pelosi, have been photographed wearing Kente cloth at official gatherings.

That's now. But back then, while it was cool to be Black, it wasn't so cool to be *African*.

Another reason I was excited about my trip to America was connecting with family I'd never met before. I was ecstatic when my father told me he had relatives in the Bronx – the birthplace of hip hop. I begged him to contact my aunt so I could get to know my extended family and experience the city at the same time. (Dad is an only child, so my aunt was in fact Dad's cousin.) Mum got in on the act, and eventually Dad relented.

Mum and Dad paid for my ticket over, and I saved thousands and borrowed thousands more on a student loan to finance the rest of my trip. My mum was almost as excited as I was, and even Dad was taking more of an interest in me than usual.

One of the reasons I'd chosen to continue my journalism studies at the State University of New York at Oswego was the fact the uni had *New York* in its title. In reality, it was closer to Canada than New York City, which I technically knew but didn't quite understand the gravity of before I arrived. I might as well have been at the University of North Carolina Wilmington – also affiliated with my uni, and also on my list of potential places to go.

I'd also relied a little too heavily on the opinion of one of the girls from uni, Allison Langdon, who had studied there before me. What I neglected to take into account is Allison is white. Her experiences at Oswego, situated on the frozen shores of Lake Ontario, were going to be vastly different to mine. To her credit, she had told me how segregated the campus was, and how every cultural group had their own student union. There was the Black Student Union, the African Student Organization, the Caribbean Student Association, the Asian Student Association, the Chinese Students & Scholars Association, and the Latino Student Union, to name a few. And, of course, there was the Student Association – for the white students.

It was the thick of winter when I arrived on campus. Even so, I wasn't expecting it to be incomprehensibly cold. Having hardly ever experienced snow before, I considered going to New York during winter more of a positive than a negative. It had snowed in Bathurst once while I was there, and my elation was heightened by the fact it was such a novelty – though the snow had quickly melted away before I had the chance to really enjoy it. Sustained snowfall over months was different, though, and I soon grew tired of it.

Among the first people I met were other Australians (as is often the case when you go abroad), who were also studying at SUNY Oswego. One of them introduced me to an Australian on staff, a slim brunette, who said she had a question for me.

'Do you think Australia is a racist country?' she asked. ''Cos race is such an issue here in America. I thought I'd ask you.'

I locked eyes with her. The look on her face indicated that she thought it was a silly question – *of course* Australia couldn't be as racist as America.

'When you've got a country built on stealing land, raping, murdering and pillaging the people who lived there first, taking their children away and stripping them of basic human rights to the point where their descendants are still having to deal with intergenerational trauma and marginalisation – I don't know, what do you think? I certainly experience racism in Australia, but I know my Indigenous brothers and sisters have had it much worse.'

The woman's face went a deep shade of red, and before I knew it, she'd shrunk back into the crowd. I never saw her again.

My roommate, Julieta Sanchez, was a Latina from the Bronx. She was short and pretty, with some interesting quirks. Every time we'd watch TV, whenever there was a voice-over saying who would be starring in a particular movie or show, she would drop in her own name. '*Tomb Raider*, an adrenaline-fuelled roller-coaster ride, *starring* . . . Julieta Sanchez'. Julieta was friends with other Latinas, including one who loved to drop the word *nigga*. The hairs on my arms stood up every time I heard her say it. I had to say something.

'Is that really your word to use?'

'I'm from New York, and that's how we do it in New York,' she explained. 'I've got cousins who have skin as black as yours. We've always called each other niggas.'

I'd later cop Angie Martinez's debut album, *Up Close and Personal*, where she dropped the word like it had an expiry date – there's even an interlude track called 'Silly Niggaz'.

Through Julieta, I met Dante Perez. He was friendly, Hispanic and also from the Bronx. He wore glasses and the growth on his upper lip was wispy thin, not quite a moustache. He had a caramel complexion, and always had a maroon Yankees cap fixed to his scalp. Slightly geeky and loyal to a fault, he'd look after you once you were in his circle. If he didn't have time for you, you'd know that too. Dante loved everything Australian – despite never having visited the place. There was the time when he said to me, 'I hope you're having a *g'day mate*.'

'Dante, you're using that expression all wrong.' I laughed. 'You don't say "Hope you're having a g'day mate" – it's used as a greeting.'

'Oh dang, Mar, I just tried to remix that expression, put a fresh American spin on it, but I guess I face-planted.'

Another friend I made at uni was Talisa, an African-American girl from Brooklyn. She wore her nails long and colourful and carried herself with sass. My other close girlfriend was Dani, born and raised in Jamaica, Queens, but originally from Nigeria.

I would also meet Kordell, who was from Inglewood, California. His nickname for me was 'Australia'. He always wore his hair in cornrows, and he walked with a certain swag.

It was through these friends that I discovered Blackplanet (basically a Black people's Facebook before there was Facebook). We planned union events and boogied at informal dances, and Dani and I would hang out with her network of Christian friends for some faith-based fellowship.

I would watch TV in my dorm room, and couldn't get over how many Black faces filled the screen. I even loved watching the commercials, because Black people were represented there too. I can also recall my shock at seeing World Vision-type advertisements for kids living in poverty in the United States – Black kids hungry and homeless in one of the richest nations on earth.

My favourite channel was BET – Black Entertainment Television – an entire *network* dedicated to Blackness, featuring news focused on Black issues and events, Black drama series, and music videos from Black artists across gospel, pop, hip hop and R'n'B. Black lifestyle, Black celebrity, Black fashion. I had never seen anything like it. My favourite BET show was *106 & Park* – a music show named after its Manhattan address. But *106 & Park* wasn't just *any* music show. At its core, it felt like a celebration of Black culture. Recording artists would come on as guests, and the live audience always played a big part in the show. At the time, A. J. Calloway and Marie 'Free' Wright were the hosts. I loved Free, who was also a rapper – she was beautiful, and like her name suggested, had an openness and warmth about her, as if she could be your best friend.

While there were magazines fulfilling similar roles when it came to celebrating Black culture – *Ebony*, *Vibe*, *Essence*, *The Source* – television as a medium brings people directly onto the screen in your lounge room. It has a powerful ability to re-inforce the relevance of its message, carry its energy, and bring you into its community.

Julieta and I were watching BET one day when P. Frank Williams showed up on the screen. He was being interviewed.

'I know that guy,' I said to Julieta. I had called Frank all those years ago when I was studying for my HSC. Back then, Frank was a contributor to *The Source*. He was now the executive editor. He had done a lot in between, including working for the *LA Times*, covering news, pop culture and music. Frank was also one smart cookie – he'd received his Master's in Journalism from one of the best programs in the country: Columbia University. I decided

I was going to pay him a visit during spring break, when I'd thawed out from the Oswego winter.

At SUNY, I tried out for the student-run television station as an anchor for their 'Live at Five' news bulletins and was selected ahead of a number of local students. The bulletins were dry because very few of the reporters actually filed stories – everyone wanted to be a presenter. Dani captured the sentiment of many of the journalism students when she told me where she saw herself: 'I don't want to be out there in the field. I want to be reading the news, that's it. I don't want to be *gathering* news. I want to be *on* the news.'

I, on the other hand, was – and am – the opposite. While I want to present my own work and have always enjoyed broadcast, reading the news isn't where it's at for me. I've always wanted to be 'live on scene'. I wanted to cover stories of international significance – imagine reporting from the steps of the Lincoln Memorial when Martin Luther King Jr delivered his 'I Have a Dream' speech, or being in front of the Victor Verster Prison the moment Nelson Mandela walked out, fist in the air. I wanted to pen beautiful scripts and tell stories in new and visually striking ways. I wanted to write about social justice. I wanted my journalism to make a difference, and ideally, I wanted to tell these stories in long form.

The one thing I did enjoy about reading the news was walking into a dorm room on campus with Dani and having a guy I didn't know wave at me and say hello, only to catch himself and say, 'Oh, man, I thought I knew you – but I've really only seen you on TV.' It made me feel like people could be drawn to me, that I was a friendly presence, a part of their day.

I also scored a gig on student radio, hosting a hip hop show. I suspected my Aussie accent could be jarring, so I developed this bizarre hybrid where I said things like *laast* instead of *lahst* and *paast* instead of *pahst*, but that only made me sound even more strange. I really should have just embraced the Aussie, because I got a phone call one night from a listener.

'Where are you from?'

'Australia.'

"Cos you don't sound *that* Australian. I have friends who are Australian, and you don't sound like them. Your accent is a unique blend of weird.'

I adopted my nickname 'Marnie', which is what my friends at uni called me, for my on-air appearances, and then I used it more widely in America when I introduced myself. Mawunyo was just too hard, I told myself. But, subconsciously, it may have been an attempt to conceal what I could of my African identity.

My excitement was peaking as I waited for my cousin, Emmanuel, to pick me up from LaGuardia Airport during my mid-semester break from university – I had finally made it to the city.

'Hi,' I said once we were face to face, smiling warmly. 'I'm Marnie.'

'Hello,' he replied without a smile in return. He was tall, slim and well dressed. 'Your father hasn't been in touch with us for twenty years, and now suddenly you need a place to stay and he decides to give us a call.'

I was stunned. I had really been looking forward to meeting my extended family. I wanted to be in the Bronx and connect with the relatives I'd missed out on sharing my childhood with. Growing up in Muswellbrook, most of my friends had a network of grandparents, aunties, uncles and cousins in town they could hang out with on a whim. I only had my immediate family. I tried to explain to Emmanuel why meeting him and his family meant a lot to me. At the same time, I wondered whether he was only expressing his own thoughts, whether the general consensus among the rest of his family was different. There was no doubt they would have discussed my visit.

Emmanuel guided me to his polished Acura and steered it towards the Bronx. He drove a luxury car, even though he still lived at home with his parents. 'Biggie used to rap about Acuras,' he said with pride. He was playing Jadakiss on the sound system. The song 'Put Ya Hands Up' came on.

'Oh my God, this song is hot,' I said. 'Can you turn it up?'

Emmanuel looked over at me, impressed that I was impressed, and cranked the volume. 'Put Ya Hands Up' would become part of my ever-expanding New York soundtrack, a song that stayed on repeat every time Emmanuel drove me around in his Acura.

As we drove through the highways, bridges and side streets of New York, I gazed out at the bright lights, one borough fading into another. By the time we reached the apartment, Emmanuel had warmed to me and was a little friendlier. We talked about music and the always-on nightlife, and what it took to make it in New York, and how he was studying medicine.

'Cómo estás?' Emmanuel greeted a man as we walked out of the car park. 'That's how you say *How are you?* in Spanish,' he told me once we were out of earshot. 'That's how you greet Hispanic people around here.'

My first impressions of the Bronx were similar to my first impressions of America: it felt like a homecoming. If 'hustle and bustle' were the first words out of your mouth when you thought of New York City, then Manhattan brought the bustle and the Bronx backed it up with the hustle. There were the street carts selling hotdogs, the frankfurts floating in lukewarm water all day – not that I would be buying any. It was the sweet smell of roasted nuts covered in candied cinnamon and sugar that drew me in. I'd always buy the nuts, folded in waxed paper bags, which sat alongside bagels and doughnuts pressed against steamed glass. New York might have felt like the centre of the universe, but it was hard to find a decent coffee. It was often brewed too bitter for me, as if to accentuate the fact that the people drinking it were also strong, tough. New York had no patience for the weak.

The Bronx was teeming with sidewalk vendors selling scarves, sunglasses and Yankee hats in every colour, every style, every variety imaginable. Others spruiked knock-off handbags and bootleg DVDs. Every shopfront felt like it hid a back room, and then a room beyond that. I'd catch a glimpse – children playing in the recesses, elderly shop owners going through stacks of receipts and invoices, people playing chess. There was always something just below the surface, drama being played out, dreams conjured up, arguments unresolved.

I could *feel* the city. I could feel it in every inch of my soul. We walked towards the building that would become my home for a period of time and boarded the elevator, squeezing next to a woman with a young, scowling girl and a man who couldn't help but comment on the girl's blue eyes, which were offset by her dark complexion.

'She's gon' be breaking hearts with those eyes,' he said. 'Her eyes are all that and a bag of chips.'

'Yeah, she got them eyes, but she don't know how to *act*,' the mother said, yanking the girl's hand towards her.

The tower was one of several in a tight-knit complex known as the River Park Towers, the tallest buildings in the Bronx. They were built in 1975 so residents in the area could have affordable housing options, and most of those who lived there were working-class. The building my aunt and uncle were in – 40 Richman Plaza – was forty-four-storeys high and had a modern feel to it.

Emmanuel opened the door to the modest two-bedroom flat. With no corridor to greet us, we walked straight into a lounge/dining room. My eyes took in the two cream-coloured couches. On closer inspection, I figured they used to be white but had taken a minor battering after years of use. The floor was carpeted, and the walls sparsely decorated. It was a very cosy-looking room with a large television against the wall and a half-empty CD rack standing alongside it. A dining-room table took up a third of the space, and a large window brought in light and allowed a view to the street.

Emmanuel introduced me to his father, my uncle-in-law. He was a very short, slim, clean-shaven man who was full of youthful energy and overflowed with confidence and an air of self-importance. I could also detect a little roughness. He drove taxis for a living and came across as street smart, but he considered himself smart-smart too. My uncle received me warily. I had two other cousins, Kendrick and Ransom. Kendrick flashed me a smile. He was the youngest of the boys and was in his final years at the local high school. He would later tell me how his accent was the thing that initially set him apart at school, so he passed it off as Jamaican to avoid getting teased too much by the other Black kids, who thought Africa wasn't so cool. My uncle would point out how ridiculous this was.

'When I'm walking the streets of the Bronx, I see so many people who look exactly like people I've run into in Accra,' he said. 'A lot of these African Americans look like Ghanaians. And they probably are. They just don't know it.'

Kendrick sported a muscly physique. In the way that rappers talk about new money versus old money, Kendrick's muscles looked like new muscles, as if he'd had to work for a long time for that body; it hadn't come easy. His brother, Emmanuel, looked like he couldn't be bothered, eschewing the gym in favour of his naturally slim physique. Kendrick would sometimes have his hair in cornrows. That day, he sported an afro. Ransom was away at uni the day I arrived.

It would be a couple of days before I met my aunty. She worked in a different borough and stayed there most days of the week, so it was mainly just me and the men of the family.

When I did meet my aunt, she greeted me warmly. She was a tall, dark-skinned woman and towered over her husband. Despite this physical disparity, she was very submissive in his presence. I was astonished to hear her address him as *Mr* Rockson. The level of respect this woman afforded her husband was mind-blowing.

After a few days, my uncle became quite fond of me. He introduced me as his daughter whenever we went anywhere together. I was also much taller than he was, and I recall one man asking if we were husband and wife.

My uncle was so convinced of his intellectual superiority that he never missed an opportunity to tell me.

'I'm very, very clever,' he would say, and then proceed to give a step-by-step explanation of how he had managed to smuggle each member of his family – all illegal immigrants – into the country. He'd hustled his way to America, the land of opportunity.

'I don't understand why *your father* would migrate to another Third World country,' he said.

'Australia isn't a Third World country.'

'Yes, it is.'

'No, really. It's not.'

My uncle demanded respect and was revered by each member of his family. On one occasion, one of the boys was using the bathroom while I was getting ready to go out, so I went into my aunty and uncle's room to use the mirror. He was absolutely furious when he found out. He didn't explain to me why he'd been walking around the house sulking; he left that up to my aunty.

'That is his *private* space,' she told me gently. 'You shouldn't go in there.'

Manhattan had a different feel to the Bronx. The foot traffic felt chaotic, but there was a real *flow* to it, a rhythm that absorbed you into the crowd. I'd sometimes upset the flow, and catch an elbow, or have someone step on my heel. One time, my shoe flew right off and I had to scramble to find it. There was cursing. I'd interrupted the flow. There was always a sharp word reserved for people who violated the city's unspoken rules.

Manhattan was filled with sights and juxtapositions both curious and shocking – a homeless person dressed in a garbage bag begging for change outside a Prada store, Middle Eastern grocers selling halal meat and prayer rugs next to a cineplex. It was a city of random encounters, where tourists, locals and people desperate to make it in whatever field they specialised in converged.

The Source magazine's offices were on 215 Park Avenue South. I stepped off the subway and walked towards the building and looked up – this was it. This was where the magic happened. I took the elevator to the eleventh floor, where the security guard greeted me. He introduced himself as Haywood, and you could tell he was a kind soul. He reminded me of my dad in stature, and if security guards are meant to make you feel safe and secure, rather than harassed and intimidated, then Haywood won hands down.

When I was reunited with P. Frank Williams, but in person this time, it was clear I was in the presence of greatness. Frank was one of those people who lit up the room. He was tall and attractive, yet he made you feel completely at ease, to the point where you'd open up and tell him things you didn't expect to reveal. You'd walk away thinking, *Hang on a minute, he didn't tell me anything about himself, but he now knows my life story.* He wasn't just a journalist – he was one of the best minds the industry had to offer.

At twenty-nine, he was young to be the executive editor of a prestigious publication like *The Source*. Since his tenure at the magazine, he's gone on to become an Emmy- and NAACP Image Award-winning producer, putting out shows such as *Unsung*, a music biography series, the documentary *Who Killed Tupac?*, and the true crime show *American Gangster*.

I admired everything he'd done for the culture – he lived and breathed it. He *was* the culture. A cursory spin through his social media pages is a catalogue of his encounters with industry heavyweights: Snoop, Jay-Z and Ice-T, among others.

I tried to build my case for why he should take me on as an intern at *The Source*. I had read the magazine for years – not only was it considered the hip hop Bible at the time, it was also the highest selling music magazine on newsstands in the US, outselling the heavily subscriber-based *Rolling Stone* at newsagencies.

I explained how the degree I was pursuing in journalism was considered prestigious in Australia. When I told him my minor was in public relations, it was as if Frank put two and two together and came up with an idea he figured could work. He stood up and led me into the office of *The Source's* PR queen, Kymberlee Norsworthy.

Kym had Beyoncé's complexion and wore her long brown hair in locs, which she would often twist around her finger. Her voice was West Coast crisp; there was warmth behind it, but also drive and intention: you usually knew where you stood. Like Frank, she's very intelligent, with a Master's in Journalism from Temple University in Philadelphia. She had worked with E-40 at Jive Records, having grown up in the same neighbourhood as him in Northern California. She'd also worked for Def Jam records, and as the Senior National Publicist at Interscope Records, which owned exclusive distribution rights to the iconic hardcore rap label Death Row. When I met her, she was the Principal and Lead Publicist of her own company, Worth Ink, with her main client being *The Source*, including *The Source* Hip Hop Music Awards.

Nowadays, Kym does publicity for faith-based artists and doesn't miss the hip hop scene at all. She's had an impressive career, and it was inspiring to see a Black woman at the top of her game.

At first, Kym looked at me as if she didn't quite know what to do with me. Then I told her about the Hip Hop and R'n'B nights I had organised at uni. Frank had emphasised that I was good peoples, really into music and a woman of colour, and his recommendation was key to Kym's decision to take me on, but the story of how Candace and I had built these events in a country town from scratch sweetened the deal. She saw me as driven – always thinking about how I could contribute more. And now I'd be coming back to *The Source* during summer as their newest intern.

I loved the Bronx. One of the guys at *The Source* told me with a degree of reverence that I was staying in the 'Thug Area' of the borough, but I never felt unsafe there, and, in any case, Emmanuel assured me that the 'Thug Area' was actually a little further up the road. While on spring break, I discovered a gospel church in the West Burnside area where I was staying with my relatives. The church was a world away from what I was used to. Where the Presbyterian church was stiff, structured and formal, this church was loud, vibrant and laid back – and all Black. The choir lit up the room with their powerful voices. Where the Presbyterian church relied on the warbling vocals of its elderly parishioners, this church had a young choir, and you can bet they rehearsed during the week. Their voices weren't just in unison; they formed rich layers that complemented each other, and their arms lifted heavenward to praise the Lord.

The choir wore maroon stoles. Most of the women were attired in minimal accessories and sensible shoes, the men wearing gold satin sashes. They danced, clapped and belted out the lyrics to 'How Great Thou Art', building up gradually from the choir conductor's lead vocals.

Oh Lord, my God, / When I in awesome wonder / Consider all the worlds Thy hands have made, / I see the stars, I hear the rolling thunder, / Thy power throughout the universe displayed.

When the choir reached the chorus, the entire room erupted. People were dancing in the pews and in the aisles, arms lifted, singing for everything they were worth, repeating:

Then sings my soul, my Saviour God, to Thee, / How great Thou art, how great Thou art.

The pastor, who had made his way to the front of the room, encouraged the already hyped congregation to raise their voices.

'Somebody give Him praise,' he said. The congregation, dressed in their Sunday best – modest gowns, long skirts, tailored suits with matching pocket squares – responded enthusiastically. 'I can't hear you!' he said. 'Give the Lord praise. Remind the Devil that you're free. Praise the Lord.'

People were waving their hankies in the air, stomping and 'flapping their wings', just the way Mum does when she dances.

Fists were raised. A child ran down the aisle alongside the pews, the organ providing a soundtrack to the beautiful chaos.

'Amen,' said the pastor. 'That's how you let the Lord know you're thankful. That's how you praise His holy name . . . Please be seated.'

People took a minute to find their seats, the melodic roar that had filled the room turning to a reverent whisper.

'Is anyone visiting this church for the first time?' the pastor asked. I put up my hand. 'Where are you visiting us from, sista?'

'Sydney, Australia.'

'Wow-ee,' he said. 'We've never had anyone visit us from as far away as Australia before. Welcome, sista.'

He instructed the congregation to turn to their Bibles as a young person walked to the front of the room to read the Scripture. He then launched into a call-and-response sermon, where *Amen*s and *Hallelujah*s filled the room.

'Are we not feeling blessed today?'

Parishioners clapped and hollered, 'Yessir!'

'The Lord is mightier than our sorrows – can I get an Amen?'

'Amen!' the congregation called out, responding to each scenario he posed, each declaration he made. 'Alright! Preach!'

'Now tap your neighbour and say, "I'm highly favoured",' the pastor said.

I tapped the woman sitting to my right. 'I'm highly favoured,' we said in unison.

Not only was there room for participation here, it was expected. I couldn't help but get swept up in the chorus of enthusiasm. There was no falling asleep in this church. The pastor's voice rose an octave with almost every sentence as he got more and more animated. When he got extra-excited, he'd actually sing some of his words.

Once the service had wrapped, a young kid walked up to me.

'Excuse me, ma'am,' he said. 'When you go back to Australia, can you please buy me a Coogi sweater?' Biggie Smalls used to rap about wearing the Australian brand.

I smiled. 'Yeah, sure.'

I needed a hairstylist, and there happened to be one in the apartment block, but after witnessing a girl having her beautiful long hair singed off at the ends with a hair straightener and then a couple of inches chopped off, the burned ends falling to the floor, I decided to look elsewhere. I found another stylist nearby, where I could get my hair relaxed and blow-dried straight. I had never seen my hair that straight before; they knew how to get it just right. Two decades on, my hair is natural and I don't mess with relaxer anymore – and wish I never had.

It was in that salon that I was taught to dry wrap my hair, which involved smoothing it around my scalp before bed and covering it with a bonnet before I nodded off, so it looked good not only the following day but long afterwards. It was strictly a style to sleep in, but Talisa, my sassy Brooklyn friend from uni, had no problem walking the streets with her hair wrapped – bobby pins keeping her straightened hair in check. While Dani thought that women who did that were, in a word, 'ghetto', Talisa rocked her wrapped tresses and looked good doing it.

My hairstylist was a woman who appeared to be in her forties and who, upon learning I was from Australia, said, 'That's where a lot of our music comes from in church.' She was referring to the megachurch Hillsong, that was started in Baulkham Hills in Sydney and has exported their original worship songs all across the world.

The salon was busy, with many customers coming and going after hooking themselves up with a blow-out and silk press, or a twist-out, or a wash'n'go. In Australia, Black salons in the city sell hair extensions, but there were separate stores for that in America. There were also salons dedicated just to braiding, often owned and staffed by African migrants.

I was getting my hair blow-dried when a couple with a young girl walked in. They said hello and heard my accent.

'Where are you from? England?' the man asked.

'No, Australia.'

'Oh,' he said without the usual fanfare. 'That's where the English sent all their criminals and degenerates.' It was the first time the mention of home had been met with a degree of scorn. And he didn't stop there. He went on about convicts and slammed Australia for its 'poor treatment of Indigenous people'.

I listened, and couldn't really disagree with him. I love Australia, the country that raised me. Australia is home. But I felt the weight of conviction that day, sitting in a hairdresser's chair in Brooklyn.

CHAPTER 19

Element

A choice without options isn't a choice. It's a trap.

I was back in the Bronx for summer, having wrapped up my semester abroad at uni, and had started my internship at *The Source*. Not even the oppressive heat could make me wilt. I felt like I was on top of the world.

While my aunty and uncle shared one of the rooms in the two-bedroom apartment, Emmanuel and Kendrick slept in a bunk bed in the other. Ransom and I shared the lounge room. He was just home from uni for the summer, so he slept on the floor while I spread a sheet on the leather couch. I was not an early riser, nor did I get up as soon as my alarm clock went off. I was a serial-snooze-button kind of gal, and it drove Ransom up the wall.

I hadn't shared a room since I was paired with my sister when we were kids, and I didn't realise how selfish I was being. I was also oblivious to the fact that Ransom's annoyance had been gradually intensifying with every press of the snooze button. I was oblivious because he never said a word. I didn't know I had made an enemy, and he was plotting his revenge.

One day, my cousins crowded around me, and they posed the cruellest of questions: 'If your parents were drowning, and you could only save one of them, which one would it be?'

'I'd save them both,' I said.

'You can't save them both. You can only choose one. Who would you choose first?' Emmanuel zeroed in. 'You'd save your mother, wouldn't you? You'd leave your father to drown.'

'No, I wouldn't,' I insisted. 'I wouldn't leave Dad to drown.'

'You're lying,' he said. Being related to my father, Emmanuel wanted to catch me out. He wanted to prove some strange, sadistic point about my loyalties – or lack thereof.

I told my mother on the phone what they'd said to me, and she was furious. How *dare* they ask me to pick between my parents.

While my relationship with Ransom had slumped to a low point, Kendrick, too, seemed to have it in for me. Initially, we got on well, but he turned on me the day we couldn't get into the apartment. Neither of us had a key and there was no one else home. He broke the lock, and when his father asked what had happened, I told him. That made me an enemy. To Kendrick, I was a snitch.

After a night of dozing in and out of sleep, I sat up on the couch. Ransom had been getting back at me by setting his alarm so it would go off at half-hour intervals throughout the night.

It didn't seem to bother him that he also missed out on a decent night's sleep.

I suddenly looked at the clock, registering the time. I was going to be late if I didn't get up immediately and make my way to work. I reluctantly peeled back the covers and headed for the shower. I had a full day ahead of me at *The Source*.

When I stepped out of the shower, I wrapped a towel around myself and stood in front of the mirror. I had been bleaching my skin, just my face and neck. Not because I wanted to be white, but because I wanted my face to look like other parts of my body that rarely saw the sun and were much lighter. My skin had a beautiful glow to it, as far as I was concerned. I didn't like the smell of the cream I was using and was worried that someone might recognise the scent, but that wasn't enough to stop me from bleaching. Mum had introduced me to Shirley Beauty Cream, which I put on at night, and Skin Success, which I used during the day.

I would never bleach my skin now – I'm thoroughly against it. Luckily, I didn't use the creams long enough to do any permanent damage, and my face is back to its gorgeous, chocolatey best. Back then, though, I thought the more light-skinned I could be the better.

Historically, it was a survival mechanism. The darker your skin, the harder life would be. In 2001, I, too, felt that light-skinned was always considered better, especially when it came to women. Black female stars were mostly light-skinned – Beyoncé, Halle Berry, Alicia Keys ... In movies, caramel and redbone leading ladies would often be paired with leading men with slightly darker complexions. It was rare to see a woman paired with a man whose skin tone was lighter than hers. Black was still beautiful, just so long as you were on the *lighter* side of Black. This imagery and messaging – colourism, really – seared its way into my consciousness. I wanted to look like a leading lady. I wanted to be beautiful. And I thought then that that meant lightening up my skin just a little.

My theory that light-skinned was always better would be dramatically challenged on a subsequent trip to Miami. Despite being a Black woman myself, I hadn't had many opportunities to hang out with other Black women. Having grown up in a country town where there weren't any girls my age of African descent, and then going to uni in the country, it actually made sense. It also made sense that I would have far more to do with Black men – I was attracted to them, they were attracted to me. We got down.

This lack of interaction with Black women caused me to be a little wary of them, given all the negative images in the media. Black women were meant to be angry. Black women were meant to be verbose. Black women were meant to be confrontational. These are all stereotypes, of course. The women I met and hung out with in Miami were kind, real and gorgeous inside and out.

I'd run into Lanelle, Tariana and Velinda while hanging out at the hotel bar, and we hit it off immediately. They were from New Jersey and were letting their hair down on a summer girls' trip. Lanelle wanted to check out the Black Film Festival, so off we went to see *My Girlfriend's Back*, a romantic comedy starring Malik Yoba and Tangi Miller. We hit the notoriously wild Miami clubs afterwards, but it was the next day when we went to the beach that my mind was blown. While I had slip, slop, slapped my way to oblivion and tried to find shade under a beach umbrella to avoid the sun's rays as best I could, Lanelle, Tariana and Velinda were straight-up trying to get a tan. They were already Black but were trying to get even blacker.

'Why would you want a tan? You've all got gorgeous complexions,' I marvelled as I jostled to position myself in the shade.

These women were stunning. They were proud of being Black and were comfortable in their own skin. It was something I admired and carried with me. Black women are friendly. Black women are gentle. Black women are beautiful, in every shade.

♪♫

I rustled around in the suitcase I was living out of and picked an outfit. Some days, I would get dressed up; others, I would wear jeans. I decided on a suit that day. I picked up my Philips CD player – the new model with an FM tuner, so I could listen to the hip hop and R'n'B station HOT 97 FM, with Angie Martinez hosting breakfast in the mornings.

I got to the station, shoved some coins into the machine, retrieved my ticket and headed down the stairs into the labyrinth of tunnels that is the subway system. There was only one thing about New York that I really couldn't stand: rats. I cringed when I saw a fat one run across the railway tracks. I had never seen a rat until I went to New York. Mice, yes, but never a *rat*, and certainly not like the ones that infiltrated the subway system. New York was a city constantly purging itself – pyramids of trash would appear every night outside restaurants and bodegas, and magically disappear by morning, but not without providing some quality nourishment for opportunistic rodents.

There were no spare seats when the train arrived, so I grabbed onto a pole. Having lost reception to HOT 97, I put on a CD instead, nodding my head to New York native Fredro Starr. I'd grown up listening to Sedudzi's Onyx albums, so when Fredro broke away from the group and went solo, I copped his debut album *Firestarr*. Fredro Starr is hard as hell and *real*, and at the time I was yearning to express my own authenticity. Onyx sounded angry, they sounded hungry. 'Last Dayz', as an example, is a brooding, gritty song about the impossible situation Black communities are placed in and how sometimes throwing your hands up in the air, embracing the chaos and creating some of your own is the answer. New York might have been on its best behaviour for me, but Fredro Starr made me feel like I was coasting on the surface of a dangerous city, which for many it was.

Even the daily commute on the subways could be an adventure. Sometimes in the evenings, when the train wasn't so crowded, I would look up after hearing music that was drowning out my own headphones. Right in front of me would be a group of African American and Hispanic street dancers moving up and down the aisle. They would use the poles on the train to vault themselves into somersaults, or hold acrobatic poses while pumping their hip hop soundtrack. One of them would momentarily break free from the others to ask commuters to put loose change in their large styrofoam cup.

I hopped off the train once I had made it to Manhattan. I could feel the steam coming through the vents beneath my feet as I strode along the pavement in time with the other passengers, passing a few buskers on the way. In Sydney, while there's definitely bona fide talent out there, most buskers could get away with a mediocre act. New York buskers were next level. Often I'd walk by thinking, *I could be listening to the next big thing.* They ranged in scale only when it came to their equipment and means, not talent – everyone from children drumming on overturned buckets to full-blown jazz ensembles. There were vocalists with small amplifiers, acapella singers, tap dancers, breakdancers, jugglers, Dolly Parton impersonators. Everyone appeared to be hustling in New York. Everyone was on the make.

I walked briskly up Park Avenue South until I got to number 215 and took the elevator to the eleventh floor. Midway up, I was joined by a guy, also making his way to *The Source*, who complimented me on my complexion, of all things. *But it's not really my complexion,* I thought.

'Hi, Haywood,' I said to my all-time favourite security guard. He grinned and welcomed me to work.

The majority of the employees at *The Source* were people of colour. For some reason, there were quite a few white people on the sales and marketing team, but apart from maybe one junior white editor and Dave Mays – the founder, who started the publication as a newsletter when he was a sophomore at Harvard – everyone else on staff was either Black or Latino, including the other interns. I was living in a Black world, and loving it. Each day at *The Source*, I had to pinch myself. *This is real. This is really happening. I am living the dream.*

Rapper Foxy Brown was on the cover of the June issue of *The Source*. The magazine cover was blown up and erected in front of the office. Each month, when a new edition came out, the poster would change. The tagline on the Foxy Brown issue was *How she survived love, drugs and drama.* Surviving drugs and drama? Sure. The idea that Foxy had to *survive* love was a fascinating one. *I hope one day I'll experience love without having to 'survive' it,* I thought.

I walked into the office and was greeted by Frank with a 'Wassup, Marnie.'

Frank dressed casually at work and wore a durag most days – I wasn't sure if he had hair for the longest time, until he showed up sans durag one day, his hair looking fresh and naturally styled. It was obvious from the moment we met that he thought of me as a kid. Every time he invited me to one of the many events *The Source* either threw or was a part of, he would stop for a minute and wonder out loud, 'Hang on a minute – you're old enough, right?'

'A group of us are heading out tonight. Mystikal will be there. You interested?' he asked.

Am I ever! Dani is going to lose her shit when I tell her – she loves Mystikal. There was something on every night of the week. I accepted most invitations, even though it got on my uncle's nerves. I would be at work all day and then out most of the night.

'Hold on, you're old enough, right?' Frank said on cue.

'I'm twenty-one,' I told him for the umpteenth time. He nodded in approval.

I was Kym's only intern, and thanks to her commitment to making sure I got the most out of the experience, I got to do a lot of things the other interns didn't. While they spent most of their time stuffing envelopes and going on coffee runs, I got to be more hands-on with the magazine and was invited to industry parties.

Later on that day I approached Frank in his office. I desperately wanted to invite Dani to the Mystikal event that night, but I didn't know how to broach the subject. I'm sure I could have just asked and the answer most likely would have been yes, and even if it was no at least I would have tried, but for some reason I felt like I was asking a lot.

So I decided on a tactic. 'Am I going to be the only girl there tonight?' I asked.

'I don't know, I think Kym will be there . . . What's up? You don't want to go? You don't have to if you don't want to.'

No! I thought. *I can't wait. I just want my friend to come too.* 'I just don't want to be the only girl there, that's all.' I decided not to push it.

Frank took a photograph of me and Mystikal, with our arms slung over each other's shoulder, but I couldn't help thinking Dani should have been on his other arm. I felt super guilty. Also at the event was Atlanta R'n'B group Jagged Edge, who were behind the hit single 'Let's Get Married', and newcomer R'n'B singer Jaheim, who was signed by DJ Kay Gee from Naughty by Nature to the record label he'd created.

I was having a chat with a *Source* contributor when we, of course, got onto the topic of hip hop music.

'Who's your favourite artist?' I asked him.

'The late, great Tupac Shakur,' he said. 'Always Tupac.'

Really? Tupac . . . One of the greatest hip hop artists of all time, yes, but I had expected him to name an artist who was more underground. I was genuinely surprised that someone who was working for *The Source* would go for one of the most famous names out there, until it occurred to me that *The Source* was what helped artists like Tupac become famous. At a time when *Rolling Stone* wasn't dedicating pages to hip hop artists, *The Source* dedicated the whole magazine to the culture.

'Who's your favourite artist?' he asked me.

'Well, for ages it's been Lil' Kim. And I like Snoop Dogg and E-40 as well, but I need to find someone new. I'm listening to Fredro Starr at the moment – I quite like his new album. And I've always liked Onyx—'

'Your favourite artist is *Lil' Kim*?' he broke in, seeking clarification. The look on his face changed, as if he was in some sort of danger. I turned my head and when I looked back, he was gone. I'd never seen anyone disappear faster than that guy. What was his problem? Was it Lil' Kim's sexually explicit lyrics? Did he think I was bold and adventurous by association? He was never in any trouble.

Each day at *The Source* was more exciting than the last. I was contacting record labels for bio information – I had direct access to major labels: Bad Boy, Tommy Boy, Interscope, So So Def, Def Jam, Roc-A-Fella, Columbia, Jive. I was liaising with journalists from MTV and BET. I was researching previous *Source* Hip Hop Awards so Kym would have that info handy to provide background in press releases. Frank invited me to that year's ceremony, which was about to be held in Miami for the first time, to distance it from the drama that had descended upon the awards in LA. (A couple of fights had broken out backstage and in the audience; the police eventually had to shut the entire production down.)

I had quite a bit of autonomy, for an intern. Kym gave me a copy of the keys to her office, because every now and then she worked off location from her home office in Jersey City. Kym could be quite warm, and on one occasion she handed me a pile of promotional CDs after a record company sent her two of each. But I walked into Kym's office one day to find her in a less generous mood.

'Why haven't you got the papers?' she asked. *Huh?* I thought, giving her a questioning look. 'It's your job to get the papers each day and go through them to see what, if anything, has been written about *The Source.*' That was news to me. I decided not to challenge her and bought the papers the next day, doing as she asked and cutting out any relevant articles.

While Kym could be a tough boss, she did offer me some amazing opportunities. Once, she put me at the forefront of helping her organise a press conference where LL Cool J, Lil' Bow Wow, Jermaine Dupri and Trick Daddy would appear. The goal was to get as much media there as possible and to have them write favourable articles about the upcoming *Source* Awards. The nominees would be announced at the press conference. I faxed off press releases to those on the guest list and called the media bodies to gauge the level of attendance.

The press conference was being held in the penthouse suite of the Hudson Hotel in Manhattan, and we arrived at the hotel early in a yellow cab.

'I see you've got your little suit on,' Frank said to me as I walked into the suite. Just about everything in the room was white – the walls, the furniture, the accessories. It felt like a '90s video set.

I was dressed up in the same cream-coloured outfit I had worn to the Mystikal event, but instead of buttoning it up, I wore the jacket open and had a tight-fitting brown-and-gold shirt on underneath.

I had started on a course of Xenadrine diet pills that I'd picked up from a health food store in Manhattan. They had an ingredient in them – ephedrine – that I didn't know at the time had been linked to severe side effects, including heart attacks, strokes, seizures and psychosis – even death. I also didn't know at the time that ephedrine was known as 'poor man's speed' because of its effect on the central nervous system. The pills were also filled with caffeine, and I was constantly riding a buzz. The warning on the packaging instructed users not to add any additional caffeine to their diets, but I was still drinking coffee and Diet Coke, plus I was eating chocolate. I had way too much energy, but I was dropping the kilos and that's all I cared about.

I saw Jermaine Dupri and Lil' Bow Wow at the press conference. Lil' Bow Wow was just a kid at the time, but they were both very small in stature. All the rappers who were invited to the press conference showed up, but I didn't see hip hop legend LL Cool J. It turned out we had walked straight past him – he'd been sitting upstairs near the entrance and we hadn't even recognised him. Kym said it was the first time a rapper had arrived before she did.

Despite this, Kym was satisfied with the press conference and pleased with the turnout, but it proved to be the moment things started to unravel between us. I wasn't satisfied and, as only a precocious twenty-one-year-old high on diet pills would do,

I blamed her for not giving me added responsibility. The ridiculousness of this makes me laugh now, but at the time I was deadly serious – I could have helped turn the press conference into an extravaganza.

I had just written a press release – one I was really proud of. In it, I had outlined how in the next issue of *The Source* there would be a report on the latest topic to cause a stir: Christian rap was becoming mainstream.

It took a while for me to appreciate the genre. While I loved rap and I was into hymns and some gospel music, the combination struck me as odd. But while rap and religion could be poles apart, sometimes they overlapped – sometimes they were two sides of the same coin. Kanye West exemplifies this, and has been repping God on wax since 'Jesus Walks', featured on his debut album, *The College Dropout*. Even he acknowledges in the song that mentioning God in his lyrics could cost him commercial airplay. (It certainly didn't – 'Jesus Walks' charted in the Top 20, was certified Gold and won a Grammy for Best Rap Song.) The grittiness of the type of rap I was listening to was part of its whole appeal, and it took a dose of maturity and life experience for me to gain an appreciation for Christian rappers.

Kym marvelled at how good my press release was, and I could hardly contain my smile, until she commented, 'Periods go in front of quotation marks.' Then she proceeded to dress me down. 'That's so basic. It's Punctuation 101.'

I looked down at what I'd written, confused. How could I have got that wrong . . . after all these years? Could *she* be wrong? I could have *sworn* I'd been taught differently. Puzzled, I changed it. Later I would discover it's an American thing. Punctuation, like so many other quirks, wasn't the same in British and Australian grammar. But that didn't take the sting away from my embarrassment.

I also bumped heads with Kym when I asked if she could add my name to the magazine's masthead.

'Interns aren't on the masthead,' she said. It seemed an odd thing to do, but *The Source* had always included interns on its masthead. In the end I would have to give up that fight, and on reflection, stuff like that wasn't important. What *was* important was the experience I was getting, and Kym was very generous in letting me do so much. When one of the other interns saw my press release and witnessed the free rein I was being given – while she was sorting mail and doing coffee runs – she looked me straight in the eye with a twinkle of awe.

'Whoah. You're going to be big time,' she said. 'I can just see it. You're destined for greatness.'

When I was asked, yet again, where I was from – this time by a music reviewer at *The Source* – I felt the question I really needed to answer was: *Why do you have that accent?*

'Australia,' I replied.

'By way of Africa!' Tracii McGregor, the VP of Content and Communications, announced. Here was someone who embraced Africa in all its glory, and was proud of her Jamaican roots.

'Yeah,' I smiled nervously. This attempt to erase my African identity seems absurd to me now, but at the time, it just didn't seem that cool to admit that I was from the continent, as obvious as it was – because where were the African role models? Where were the Africans doing big things on the world stage? To even ask these questions I was showing my own naivety.

I needed only to have looked as far as my own country, Ghana: the beacon of democracy in Africa and the first country, in 1957, to achieve independence from colonial rule in sub-Saharan Africa. With a population of about 31 million, compared to Australia's 25 million, Ghana's land mass is about 3000 per cent smaller than Australia's. For such a relatively small country, Ghana packs a lot of punch. It has considerable natural wealth, including gold and cacao. In 2021, Ghana's president announced that the country would become less dependent on exports and would stop exporting cocoa to Europe to focus on producing chocolate locally.

I need only have studied Ghana's first president, Kwame Nkrumah – a legend, a revolutionary – voted in December 1999 by BBC listeners in Africa as the 'Man of the Millennium', and for good reason. Nkrumah campaigned for the political unity of Black Africa, and viewed Ghana's sovereignty as important for the 'total liberation' of the entire continent. More than thirty other African countries followed Ghana's example within a decade, declaring their own independence. Nkrumah was responsible for building new roads, schools and health facilities across the country, and his policy of Africanisation – reclaiming

Africa from its colonial past – created better career opportunities for Ghanaians.

I need only have looked at the rich music history, with Highlife music originating in Ghana. It paired the melodic and rhythmic structures of traditional local music with Western instruments and provided a soundtrack to independence. Later, Reggie Rockstone rapped in the local language Twi and pioneered Ghana's own version of hip hop: Hiplife.

Ghana's praises deserved to be sung. But it was a time when Africans in the West were taught to be ashamed of who they were, where they came from and what they represented. Images of Africa and Africans were either non-existent or damn near embarrassing. The assumption was that everyone on the continent was either in a state of crippling poverty or engaged in brutal civil warfare. World Vision ads highlighted starving children, wilting in their mothers' arms, while news bulletins in the '90s featured horrific tales of the Rwandan genocide and child soldiers in Sudan. It was important news, and I've made Rwandan friends, one of whom sat me down one day and opened a photo album filled with members of his family lost to genocide. 'He's dead. She's dead. All of them are dead. Those children are dead as well. That person there – dead.' It was heart-wrenching. The world needed to hear these stories. But I've even had to stop friends and family from making jokes that feed into stereotypes.

The truth is, Africa is a diverse continent, but it's often regarded as being monolithic. There's a lot to be said about the images put forward by some media outlets. I work in the media – I've seen how it works up close. They often repeat the same negative images over and over again, with no reprieve for weeks on end, and those images make their way into the consciousnesses of people who don't know any better. And if racists can teach the oppressed to hate themselves – the job is done for them.

CHAPTER 20

Quiet Storm

Good luck is the epitome of fortune.

I looked up at the massive television screen in front of me at the nightclub: Destiny's Child busting out the dance moves. Beyoncé, Michelle and Kelly dressed in pink. *Bootylicious.*

I'd had three drinks but was feeling incredibly tipsy. I spotted a familiar face – an executive assistant at *The Source*. Let's just say he didn't look like an assistant – he looked like the type of guy who *had* assistants. He was a tall, broad-shouldered Black guy, intimidating to look at, mainly because he didn't say much. He would stare you down with a gaze that made you feel like you didn't belong there, and whatever came out of your mouth had better be good, because patience was in short supply.

He was huddled in the corner with a group of people smoking weed, so, filled with Dutch courage, I walked over and sat down next to him. He offered me a puff of his blunt, and I took a few hits. It was the most potent marijuana I'd had in my life. That, combined with the alcohol, put me in quite a state. The new 112 song 'Dance with Me' came on: *'If you're sexy and you know it clap your hands...'*

I drunkenly clapped my hands. *'If you're sexy and you know it clap your hands...'* I clapped again, a smile baked on my face.

One of the other interns was leaving the party, and suggested I leave too. We walked to the closest subway station together. I watched as he waved goodbye from the platform opposite mine. Feeling wasted, I hopped onto one train and then got off to catch a connecting one to the Bronx. I slumped to my knees, barely missing a puddle of dirty water. I turned on my back, shuffled up against the wall and caught the stench of warm, greasy food – hotdogs and chips – mixed with wafts of perfume and aftershave from women and men passing by nonchalantly. Overpowering all of this was a stench not unlike an open sewer.

My ears rang with the deafening screech of the subway trains on the rails, and the barely coherent announcements echoing off the concrete walls. I looked across at the rubbish, piled up in slick, distended garbage bags. *What am I doing here? How do I get home?*

Tyce entered my mind. A full-bodied wail escaped my lips. I was in New York City, hopelessly drunk and high, curled up on a subway platform, and I couldn't be with the man I loved. The tears started to fall.

I then thought about how, at twenty-one, I had narrowly avoided cancer. The pre-cancerous cells had been scraped away and I was in the clear, but the anxiety had lingered. I wasn't through with this life yet, my hopes, these dreams.

I sobbed as I contemplated a life without love, without the man I wanted to be mine. I didn't want to be alone.

Before long, I looked up to see a couple of male police officers. 'Female . . . Black . . . intoxicated . . .'

Any protest I put up was futile as they shoved me into the back of a police van.

I blacked out.

♪♫

I woke up around five o'clock in the morning and panicked. *Where am I?* The night before came rushing back. The drinks. The weed. The subway. The police. *Hang on, why am I waking up in a hospital bed?*

The police, who I'm sure initially planned to take me back to the cop shop, must have panicked when I blacked out, so they dropped me off at a hospital.

My uncle was going to be furious – I might have stayed out late in the past, but I always made it home. On top of that, I had to be at work in a few hours. I pulled myself together and dressed to leave the hospital.

'Wow, you look like a different person,' a nurse said to me. I must have been quite the sight when the police brought me in.

I baulked when I saw the bill. *What on earth did they do to me? Pump my stomach?*

The staff at the hospital had obviously found my Australian driver's licence confusing. On the admission form they had written down my first and middle name, *Mawunyo Grace*, and had followed that up with my street address, but instead of jotting down Muswellbrook as my place of residence, they had written 'Bronx'. I walked out without paying. There was no chance they would find me. I told myself I would make up for it one day when I could afford to make a difference to that hospital.

My uncle had refused to cut me a key because I wasn't 'going to be around for very long', so I had to knock on the door when I got to the apartment in West Burnside. One of my cousins answered it. I walked in, showered and got dressed for work.

Kym looked shocked to see me that day, all in one piece.

'You look great,' she said, perplexed.

It wasn't long before I tested her nerves again. I made an innocent comment – one that I hadn't intended in any way to be disrespectful. I can't remember what I said, but I do remember being surprised by her reaction.

'You're so sarcastic,' she said. 'Look, I don't think this is going to work between us.'

I couldn't believe what I was hearing. I had worked my butt off at *The Source*. I gathered my things to leave and headed to the subway.

I took a train back to the Bronx. I was furious as I entered the apartment, only to find my uncle standing there.

'Where were you last night?' he demanded.

'I was in hospital,' I said.

'Why?'

I tried to think up an excuse. 'I wasn't feeling very well. I collapsed.'

He tapped on his temple with his index finger. 'I'm very, very clever.'

Oh yes, how could I forget?

'Were you drinking?' he asked.

'No,' I lied, desperate to maintain the facade of the gospel-church-going niece.

'I don't understand how a reasonable young lady who doesn't drink would suddenly collapse and end up in a hospital overnight.' He stared me down. 'You were losing your virginity.'

What? Now I was angry. My virginity was long gone, and what business was it of his anyway?

'I was at the hospital,' I said. 'Look, I'll prove it to you.'

I called the hospital I had been admitted to. 'Did you have someone by the name of Mawunyo Grace there last night?' I said to the nurse. She confirmed I was there. I handed the phone to my uncle. As soon as he started to ask her *why* I was there, I grabbed the phone and slammed it back onto its cradle.

'That's *it!*' he said. 'I want you to pack up your things and leave. I want you out!'

Shit.

I packed up the suitcase I'd been living out of. Where was I going to go? Maybe I could call Frank and ask if I could stay at his place in Brooklyn. I hopped into the elevator and rode it down to the ground floor. I went to the subway station and tried to call Frank from one of the payphones. No answer. I blinked back tears as I considered my predicament. Bunking at Frank's place was a silly idea anyway, I thought. Distressed and tearful, I sat down on a bench and put my head in my hands. I was stranded in New York, home was a twenty-four-hour plane ride away, and I was increasingly running out of options.

CHAPTER 21

Phone Home

Kindness will always be remembered.

Somehow, I'd lost contact with Talisa. My aunty later told me one of my friends kept calling the apartment, asking where I was. I assume that was Talisa, but unfortunately, with all the drama, she was one of my SUNY friends I never saw again after summer.

There had been no offer from Dani for me to stay at her place. Her parents had been devastated when she decided to convert from Islam to Christianity, and their relationship was rocky, so she couldn't invite a friend to stay.

Dante Perez, however, didn't care about what his mother thought. They didn't get along, and he'd been giving her the silent treatment over some incident that happened when he was a kid. He also lived in the Bronx and didn't hesitate to take me in when I told him what had happened. I was in an absolute state when he took the subway to pick me up from my station so we could ride together back to his apartment. He had two single beds in his room, and he'd made one up for me. It felt weird being couped up in a room with him, and it also felt weird being the only person in the house talking to both him and his mother, who had the nicest red pedicured toes I'd ever seen.

I sobbed and sobbed over the situation I found myself in. I had embarrassed my parents – Dad in particular. I had been so excited to meet his relatives; I had longed to feel that connection to cousins, aunties and uncles, and they had dismissed me as a bothersome tramp, unfit to live under their roof. I blamed myself, though, oblivious to the role they had played in making me feel so unwelcome. And my once-in-a-lifetime opportunity at *The Source* had disintegrated before my eyes. Dante comforted me in that endearingly awkward way of his, showing a great deal of empathy, which only made me cry more.

'Oh, Marnie Mar,' he said. 'I got you, Mar.'

Dante tried to convince me everything was going to be okay, but I felt I had brought shame to my family and disgraced myself. *How could things have gone so wrong?* I thought, caught up in a cycle of remorse and disbelief. *And how can I possibly make them right again?*

When I called my parents and told them everything, Mum was furious that my 'father's relatives' had thrown me out of their apartment. She refused to believe that I deserved it and blamed Dad, making me feel even worse. She organised for me to fly to California to stay with *her* relatives for a while before coming back to Australia. I had had enough of relatives, though, and was not looking forward to it.

I arranged to meet with Emmanuel, who pulled up to see me

in his gleaming Acura. I made up a silly sob story that I knew he would sympathise with, harkening back to the day I had *actually* lost my virginity. I told him I had fallen pregnant and lost the baby, using the situation with the blood clots to fabricate a ridiculous scenario.

'And that's why what your dad said upset me so much,' I said.

'Do your parents know about this?'

Well, of course not. I just made it up now.

'Yes.'

'Don't tell anybody else about this – ever,' Emmanuel said. And with that he drove his Acura back home to tell his father to allow me back into their home. I only stayed for a week. I was very wary of them all by now.

My aunty made the most curious of statements when I returned. 'Your uncle likes you. He likes you a whole lot. He even wanted you for his son,' she said, referring to Emmanuel.

'We're *cousins.*' I was horrified. She looked at me as if to say *so what?*

I solemnly took up my position again on the couch, my uncle's demeanour suggesting that while he'd approved my return, it wasn't with open arms.

I realised I still had the keys to Kym's office and set out to return them. Her manner was softer when I walked in through the door.

'I want you to come back and work for me,' she said, 'not because I feel sorry for you. I really like you, Marnie. You've got a lot of potential.'

I went back to work at *The Source* again, ever so briefly, but something inside my mind had shifted. I felt so out of it; nothing made sense. Even now, I find it hard to remember the details of this period. I only had a couple of weeks left of my internship to round out summer, but my parents had changed my flights, so I wasn't going to be in New York for much longer. I would be heading to LA, and then home. My American dream was about to be over.

Hours before I was due to leave New York, I dropped by *The Source* with flowers for both Frank and Kym.

Frank was really happy to see me when I walked into his office. He had sent me an email, asking me where I had gone, but, as far as I knew, he wasn't aware of what had transpired between me, my uncle and Kym.

We hugged each other. I didn't want to let him go. I sat opposite him and told him my uncle had thrown me out . . . in the *Bronx*. The way I spat out the words was embarrassing. What was I saying? I loved the Bronx, but I made it sound like the worst place in the world. The look of disappointment in Frank's eyes was too much to bear.

I started to ramble, saying things I didn't mean. The mental fog closed in – I had no idea where these words were coming from or what I was getting at. The first waves of panic arrived. 'I've got to know myself a little better over the past few months,' I said, 'and I don't like what I've learned. I thought I was independent, but I'm not.'

My hysteria rose an octave. 'I screwed with you, I screwed with Kym . . .' I don't even know what I *meant* by that. *How* had I screwed with him? *How* had I screwed with Kym? I was taking responsibility for things I hadn't done. I had worked hard at *The Source*. I had embraced this incredible opportunity. I had been so happy to be there. *What am I saying? What am I saying? None of this is making any sense.*

I thought I saw tears in Frank's eyes. Tears of compassion? Tears of rage? If they were tears, they soon dissipated. Frank had lost interest in my monologue. He looked down at his pager to check a message. When he looked up again, his demeanour was calm. He didn't raise his voice, but his tone was strictly business.

'Do you realise how many people would kill to be in your position right now?'

Was he suggesting I wasn't worth it? This was too much for me to take. I couldn't handle him thinking this opportunity was wasted on me. So, I continued to talk even more shit.

'You know where I'm from,' I said. 'I knew more about hip hop than anybody else in that area, and now suddenly I'm working for a magazine where there are people who know far more than I do . . .' I rambled on. What I was saying wasn't even true in my own family, let alone 'where I came from'. I was making no sense whatsoever. I wasn't on the *verge* of a breakdown – I had entirely broken down. What Frank had witnessed was the beginning of my unravelling, but we were both in the dark about what was really going on.

Frank stood up and gently steered me towards the door. 'I've got work to do,' he said. He smiled at me. 'See you in the industry.'

I was completely cut. I looked at him, alarmed. It was as if I'd been punched in the gut by the kindest person I knew. I was a ball of pain and confusion. I'd lost everything.

None of it made sense. Everything had come to a head in that moment; all my self-doubts had bubbled to the surface. He didn't know I had failed my HSC, but *I* knew. I was an imposter. I wasn't good enough to be at *The Source*. I wasn't even of good character. I was a mess of a human being.

Before I left New York, I stopped off at the clothing store where my cousin Ransom was working. I smiled at him as I picked out a t-shirt for my brother John with the words *Da Bronx* scrawled across it. Ransom was acting strangely. One of his workmates approached and asked if I had found what I wanted. 'Yeah, I'm all good,' I said. It was then that Ransom said something that made me realise the tension at home, everything I'd blamed on my own behaviour, wasn't my fault at all.

'This is my cousin from Australia,' he said. 'We treated her mean.'

Wow, I thought. *Just . . . wow.* 'Well, what goes around comes around,' I said cheerily. 'You should come visit us in Australia.' I'm not sure I've seen anyone look more scared. There was no way on earth he would ever visit his cousins in Australia.

♪♫

When I arrived in California, I was no more than a zombie, emotionally exhausted and physically drained. All I could think about was the mess I had left behind in New York.

My West Coast relatives were so happy to see me. I hadn't been expecting that sort of reception after the one I got in New York. I heard my uncle tell my mother on the phone that I was really quiet, which is a clear indication that I wasn't myself. My uncle was the sweetest man you could ever meet, along with his amazing African-American wife and their three children.

I had a few uncles in California who'd married African-American women, one of whom was the spitting image of Whitney Houston. They took me to Long Beach and out to a theme park. I tried my best to smile, but I couldn't be happy. Deep down, I was just so sad.

My uncle took me outside and warned me to be careful, pointing to a bullet hole in the car next door. We were in a safe neighbourhood, but they had lived in Compton – one of the girls was born there and would proudly make this clear whenever given the opportunity. It sounded cool – that's where NWA are from – the 1988 album *Straight Outta Compton* featuring cutting-edge hits like 'Fuck tha Police' and 'Gangsta Gangsta'.

Were it not for the generosity my family in California showed me, I would have left America not wanting to meet another relative for as long as I lived. I humbly accepted their kindness.

My aunty-in-law was a force of nature. She knew how to whip up a storm in the kitchen. Her soul food was on point. Her peach cobbler was the bomb. She also introduced me to sweet potato pie, and her fried chicken was better than the Colonel's. She ran her house in a very strict manner. Her daughters weren't allowed to relax their hair – and what gorgeous hair they had. I couldn't believe how long, thick and curly it was. If only I had never relaxed my own hair, *Marnie with the good hair* would have been *Marnie with the great hair*. She also kept a strict cleaning roster – her kids were expected to pitch in.

'My kids can *actually* call themselves African American and mean it,' she said, 'because my husband is African and I'm American.'

When Kordell, my friend from SUNY, came to take me out for the day, my aunty insisted it was a date.

'No, we're just friends,' I said. 'He's got a girlfriend.'

'*Mmmmhhhhmm*,' was her reply.

Kordell took me to the Magic Johnson Theatre in Crenshaw, where we watched *Baby Boy*, a John Singleton film about a young man coming of age in the hood, starring Tyrese Gibson and Snoop Dogg. The title role was meant to go to Tupac, before he was tragically murdered in Las Vegas. We drove via Kordell's grandmother's place in Compton, and then we went out clubbing in Hollywood, at a place called Florentine Gardens. When we hopped into the car, about to head home, he tried to kiss me.

'But you've got a girlfriend!' I protested.

'Oh, we're seeing other people.' That was a bold-faced lie if ever I'd heard one. I was really disappointed at first, but then it was as if I threw my hands up in the air and thought, *Oh well.*

'A little less teeth, baby,' he said, as I went down on him.

'Sorry,' I mumbled.

'That's aiiight, Australia.' He smiled. 'Just make it better.'

What the fuck am I doing?

My self-loathing had compounded by the time he dropped me back at my uncle and aunt's place. But at least I was met with warmth on the other side of the door. I thought that by the time I left America I was almost back to being my old self again. But I wasn't. New York, it turned out, was just the beginning of my breakdown.

CHAPTER 22

Were You There

There are lessons, even in the midst of crazy.

I looked at the newspaper article about pop star Aaliyah dying in a plane crash. I'd heard the news a few days earlier, and now here was a newspaper article confirming the details of the accident. I shook my head at the tragedy and sadness of it all. I'd already been feeling out of sorts that day. I wasn't myself, but I couldn't pinpoint what was wrong. I scanned the room and my eyes settled on a navy blazer slung over an empty chair.

'Is that yours?' I asked, looking over at Channel Nine sports supremo Ken Sutcliffe.

He gave me a friendly smile. 'Yeah, it's mine.'

'You shouldn't leave your blazer lying around like that,' I said. 'It's a nice jacket. I could flog it.' Even as I was saying that, I found myself again wondering, *What the fuck are you doing?* It didn't make any sense. Why would I hark back to my months-long teenage shoplifting spree? Not that Ken knew anything about it, but why would I want to highlight something – even to myself – that I wasn't proud of? It was so long in the past. Besides, I obviously had absolutely no intention of flogging his jacket.

'You wouldn't get very far walking around with that thing on,' he said. 'You'd be pretty easy to spot.' He pointed to the Channel Nine logo emblazoned across the front of the blazer.

'Oh yeah, I guess you're right,' I said.

I had found it reasonably easy to land a gig at the 2001 Goodwill Games because of my involvement in the Olympics the year before. I was a runner. It was my job to 'run' around and make sure everything 'ran' smoothly. I was based at the swimming venue and, given Australia's obsession with swimming events, I was surrounded by many high-profile media personalities. However, deeply affected by my experiences in New York, I found myself doing and saying the strangest things. I was a ball of confusion. It was as if someone had flicked a switch and lifted the usual filter that stands between me and acts of stupidity. In place of that filter was reckless abandon and a strong inclination towards self-sabotage.

I walked outside and ran into a familiar face. 'Hi, Ray,' I said excitedly.

'It's Mike, actually,' he said. His expression was so stern, it could have cut me in half if it were a knife.

'Oh, I thought you were Ray Dinneen. I grew up in the country, so I used to watch you on NBN television—'

'I'm Mike Munro.' His tone was curt.

Okay. Mike it is, I thought to myself. *Gee, but I guess he looks nothing like Ray Dinneen.*

Where is all this coming from?

My supervisor, Bernie, approached me. 'Here's a list of what we need from the supermarket.'

'Bernie, I'm ruining my reputation,' I said.

'What are you talking about?'

I shrugged, distressed. 'I don't know, but I'm ruining my reputation.'

'You don't have a reputation,' she said. Her tone was kind, but I looked at her as if she'd lost her mind. Little did I know I was the one losing mine. I took the list and the car keys.

'Do you want to come?' I asked one of the other runners.

'Yeah, sure,' she said, and followed me to the car.

I parked it in the shopping centre car park and we headed into the mall, splitting up the list once we entered the supermarket. I pushed the trolley up and down the aisles. I couldn't find a single item on my list. I stopped occasionally to stare at the rows and rows of groceries, products of every variety and description, yet I couldn't find what I was after. I became increasingly frustrated.

My runner companion snuck up behind me. 'How'd you go?' I jumped. 'Your trolley's empty,' she observed. Her tone was kind. 'Here, give me your list.' I handed it to her and watched gratefully as she started to fill the trolley with a few items.

We headed back to the car park. 'Oh shit,' I said. 'Did you pay attention to what level we parked on?'

'Nah, I wouldn't have a clue,' she replied. We walked round and round and round, looking for the white car. My head was spinning. I was becoming increasingly agitated.

'Here it is,' my companion yelled out after what felt like hours. With relief, I followed her voice and unlocked the car.

As we were pulling into the parking spot back at the swimming venue, I accidentally accelerated, running into the wall in front of me. *Shit!* I turned the engine off and hopped out of the car. 'Oh my goodness,' I said, looking over the damage. 'Please don't tell Bernie.' It was a split-second decision, and yet another one I'd come to regret. When Bernie found out what I'd done, she was far more disappointed that I didn't tell her I'd crashed the car than she was about the damage.

'Why didn't you tell me?' she asked.

I didn't know what to say. I looked down at the ground. 'See, I told you. I'm ruining my reputation.'

'You don't have a reputation,' she said.

Ken Sutcliffe looked me up and down. 'You will never work for Channel Nine again.' *My career is over before it has even started,* I thought. Technically, I was employed by Turner Sports, not Channel Nine, but what he said floored me and torpedoed my confidence. I was a blooming flower no longer.

Afterwards, I went and sat with the crew. One of the older crew members who had up until then been really nice to me looked at me with disdain.

'Your job is really easy,' he said.

'Yeah, I know.'

'Well, then how come you can't do it?' I shrank further into my shell.

When I got back to the hotel, I walked up and down the stairs, looking for my room. I walked around and around and around the building, going up and down the stairs, into the lobby, everywhere. I was so confused; the fog was closing in. I knew the level I was staying on, but where was my *roooooooom*? Eventually, I found it and collapsed on my bed.

I called my mother.

'How's it all going?' she asked.

'Mum. There's something wrong. I don't feel right.'

'What's going on?'

'I don't know. I crashed the car – and didn't tell my boss. I got lost in the shopping centre. I got lost in the car park. I got lost trying to find my hotel room. There's something wrong.' By then there were tears streaming down my face.

'Come home,' she said. 'Get on a plane and come back home. Did you take your little Bible with you? Have you been praying?'

I ignored her questions. 'Muuuuuuuum!' I screamed down the line. 'I can't come home – the Games have only just started.'

'Change your flight and come home,' she repeated. 'And read your Bible.'

I did as I was told – the 'change your flight' bit at least. I was due to fly out of Brisbane the next morning.

That night I went down to the hotel bar.

'Hi.' I looked at the bar staff, tears still in my eyes. 'Can I please have a Hennessy on the rocks?'

He looked at me. 'That's a pretty tough drink – you don't want to mix it with anything?'

'Nah,' I said. 'I'm a pretty tough chick.' I giggled to myself.

'Okay, a Hennessy on the rocks it is.'

I took a sip. I was already feeling light-headed and woozy, but this took me to another level. I headed back upstairs and put on the TV. I flicked through the cable television channels and landed on a concert – the Up in Smoke Tour, headlined by Snoop Dogg, Dr. Dre and Eminem.

'If you love dick, tell me about it,' Snoop Dogg said to the audience.

'I love dick,' I yelled, throwing my hands in the air.

'Say it again,' Snoop said.

'*I love dick!*' I screamed.

Knock, knock, knock – an angry rap on the door.

'Oh,' I whimpered to myself. I walked towards the door and opened it slowly.

'Will you keep it down?' Outside was an angry youngish-looking white dude with prematurely grey hair. My eyes went wide as he scolded me for making too much noise.

I went to bed after that.

The next morning, I made my way to the airport. I thought about how for the last few days I had had no control whatsoever over what I was doing and saying. The crew member was right – my job was easy. All I had to do was make coffee, buy supplies and groceries, and run errands. It *was* a simple job, but I still couldn't do it. Not in the state of mind I was in. If what I was doing was bizarre, what I was saying was even more so. I thought back to what I'd said to Ken Sutcliffe when I saw his blazer hanging over the chair. It just didn't make sense. Things would have been much worse if Bernie hadn't been so understanding. She didn't know what was going on; I didn't know what was going on; and yet she handled the situation as if she was a trained psychologist. I, on the other hand, was a complete mess.

I had to switch off the music I was listening to on the plane. Every time I heard a song, I felt as if it related directly to me somehow. Every lyric, each bar, made me think the song was written about me. 'Every Breath You Take' by the Police. *Am I being watched?* Madonna's 'Papa Don't Preach'. *Am I in trouble?* But my dad didn't preach enough!

I was too scared to read the paper. Each time I absorbed a headline, I linked it to something that was going on in my life. If I stumbled across a television talk show, I was convinced the topic of conversation was directed towards me. It was as if the whole world revolved around my absurd existence. Something was terribly wrong.

Sedudzi picked me up from Central Station in Sydney and put me on a train to Muswellbrook. I looked around and couldn't find my phone. It was an original Nokia. It was on me – then it was gone. I made it to Newcastle before being intercepted from the train by my parents. They took me back home, but not for long.

I'll never forget the look on my dad's face right before I was taken away to a mental hospital. I was ranting and raving about his shortcomings as a father and threw a newspaper advertisement I had found onto the floor in front of him. It featured lines from the Dorothy Law Nolte poem 'Children Learn What They Live':

If children live with criticism, they learn to condemn. / If children live with hostility, they learn to fight. / If children live with ridicule, they learn to feel shy. / If children live with shame, they learn to feel guilty.

Underneath this were the words, *They may not remember what you said. They may not remember what you did. But they will always remember how you made them feel.*

'That's how you made me feel,' I railed. 'Like I'm nothing. Like I don't matter.'

He looked at me wide-eyed, his lips pressed together. I had never seen that expression before. I walked out of the room before he could reply, but I don't think he was about to anyway.

The next thing I can remember is being in hospital triage. I was days away from my twenty-second birthday. I had weeks to go before I was due to finish my degree. But everything ground to a halt.

CHAPTER 23

They Ask Me

If faith can shift mountains, isn't believing the easy part?

The overriding emotion I felt was fear. I had no idea what was going on and didn't understand how any of this could be happening.

As I was being led away from the reception area at the hospital, a man in a cowboy hat sped past me, closely followed by a male nurse running after him.

There were two main sections in the psychiatry ward. I only knew of one when I first arrived. It was the place they put you if they considered you to be a risk to yourself or someone else.

They took everything away from me. I wasn't allowed my aerosol deodorant. *What on earth am I about to do with a can of deodorant?* I thought at the time. Now, I realise they took it away for the same reason those products aren't allowed on planes – they're highly flammable and could be made to ignite or explode, or operate as a flamethrower. They confiscated my shoe-laces. I wasn't allowed batteries. And I definitely wasn't allowed my Gillette razor. Anything that they deemed could be used as a weapon was confiscated and locked away.

I was scared of the environment and I was scared of the other patients. It was difficult to tell them from the nurses because the nurses didn't wear uniforms, so I regarded everyone with suspicion. There were far more male nurses there than you would find at a regular hospital.

My first night in that place was horrible. I could hear somebody screaming. Each time I drifted into a restless sleep, I would hear another shriek and be jolted awake.

Every so often I would hear footsteps making their way down the hall. One of the nurses would shine a flashlight through the little square window in the door. Then the footsteps continued down the hall. I felt like I was in jail. I no longer had my freedom.

Mum was by my side as soon as visiting hours resumed. I couldn't shake the feeling that something had happened to my father. The last time I saw him he didn't look himself. *I* had put that expression on his face. *I* had upset him.

'Mum, where's Dad?' I asked.

She looked at me sadly.

No, really? Where is he? Oh my God. Oh my God. Is he dead?

'Is Dad dead?' I asked.

Oh my God. Is Dad dead? Oh my God. Wait. Did I kill him? Is that why I'm in here?

'Did I kill Dad?' I was panic-stricken. Confused. Horrified.

Mum's eyes welled up. 'Are you so wicked?' she asked.

Hysterical, I ran from the room, screaming. My chest felt

hollow, except for the small pocket of air caught up in my ribs. I couldn't breathe. My heart pounded. *Oh my God. Is my father really dead?* I screamed louder. Two nurses grabbed me and threw me into a small room with thick glass walls. I jumped up and down on the foam mat and continued to scream. One of the nurses jabbed me with a needle while the other held me still. They left the room, slamming the door behind them. I had never been in such agony. *Dad. Dad. Dad.* I could see a group of nurses from my isolation room. I waved to get the attention of one of them, who looked at me with contempt.

'Is my father dead?' I asked her, mouthing the words through the glass wall. She nodded. I fell to the ground and started screaming again, tearing at my hair. I couldn't believe it. *How did this happen? What the fuck? Dad. My dad. He was dead?* I cried. I continued to tear my hair out. I pounded at the ground. *How can I go on living? My life is over. I can't live knowing I've killed my father.* I had never felt such anguish in all my life.

♪♫

Dad came to visit me later that day after he had finished work. He was very much alive, and I have never been more relieved to see anyone in all my life. I bounced up on the bed and looked directly into his eyes. *It's really him. He's here!* I smiled at him.

After a few days I was moved to the other side of the ward. I was allowed to sit outside. My mother could even take me out on daytrips. Mum was at her religious best. She would lead us in prayer, asking God to heal and deliver me. She'd hand me the Bible and tell me to read aloud from particular verses.

'Go to Psalm twenty-three, verse four.'

'Even though I walk through the valley of the shadow of death, I will fear no evil, for you are with me.'

'Okay, now read Psalm twenty-seven.'

'The Lord is my light and my salvation – whom shall I fear? The Lord is the stronghold of my life – of whom shall I be afraid? When the wicked advance against me to devour me, it is my enemies and my foes who will stumble and fall. Though an army besiege me, my heart will not fear.'

'Isaiah forty-three, verse two.'

'When you walk through the fire, you will not be burned; the flames will not set you ablaze.'

'Now, Psalm ninety-one, verse seven.'

'A thousand may fall at your side, ten thousand at your right hand, but it will not come near you. You will only observe with your eyes and see the punishment of the wicked.'

I wasn't finding these verses particularly comforting. Fire. Flames. An army besieging me. The wicked advancing to devour me. It didn't matter that I wasn't the one who was stumbling and falling, there were still people stumbling and falling, there was still punishment. I felt on edge and vulnerable. And I was hardly a poster child for Christianity. Didn't I fall into the category of the wicked? Was there salvation for someone like me?

The hours crept by so slowly in that place. I was extremely bored. I figured if I was in jail I could at least read a book. But my mind was so jumbled, I couldn't concentrate on anything.

The food was disgusting. I'd look down at the microwave dinner in front of me – over-cooked vegetables, processed mash, leathery meat. It was as if the powers that be simply didn't care – we were just a bunch of crazy people and lucky to be fed at all. The catering staff would slide the plate in my direction and then quickly turn away. They didn't make eye contact or say hello. It was as if they were scared of me. *Of me!*

When I looked in the mirror, I didn't see myself any longer. My hair was a mess, my appearance unkempt. But it was my face, my eyes, that I found the most difficult to recognise. I had a vacant look. I was no longer there.

My sister commented on my hair when she came to visit.

'That's not like you,' she said to me, not unkindly. 'You usually like to look nice.' I hung my head in shame.

All I could feel was guilt. I felt like this was payback for all the things I'd done wrong – the stuff I had stolen, the men I had let defile me, my blatant disregard for the God I claimed to believe in. This was all because I had lived a double life. This, I felt, was the time of consequences. My judgement had arrived.

It was my birthday. And I was in a mental hospital. All the work I had done, the battles I had fought to get this far with my university degree, and it was all going to come to nothing, weeks before I was due to finish. How on earth did my life come to this point? It was hard enough being Black – but Black and crazy?

My mother brought a birthday present to the hospital. I tore off the wrapping. It was a Bible. I already had a Bible, one I obviously didn't bother to read. I would try to read this one.

Each day, Mum would read chapters with me and we'd pray together. My minister from the Presbyterian church came to visit.

He said that although my dad didn't outwardly show emotion, he was deeply affected by what was happening. This made me feel really sad.

The doctors at the psychiatric hospital said I had suffered a drug-induced psychosis. Except I hadn't taken any drugs. It was incredibly confusing and distressing. Mum was pretty much the only person who believed me when I said I hadn't taken anything, and it was many years later that I made the link between the diet pills I'd been taking, Xenadrine, and my breakdown. At the time, the pills, which I had purchased in the United States, were illegal in Australia. (They've since made their way into the Australian market.) Maybe I was predisposed to mental illness, but those diet pills have caused me a world of pain. This episode would mark the beginning of a long struggle with mental illness, and next time, I wouldn't need any substances to reach breaking point.

Roughly a week later, I was allowed to go home on a day visit. I called Bernie and told her where I had spent the last few days. By then the Goodwill Games were over.

'I'm so sorry I wasn't myself at the Goodwill Games,' I said. 'I want to make it up to you.'

'There's no way you can make it up to me,' she said. I whimpered. 'By that I mean, there are no events on a grand scale like the Goodwill Games where you could make it up to me.' She paused and drew in a sharp breath. 'Oh. Oh dear.'

'What is it?'

'Oh,' she said. 'Switch on your television.'

As I did, I watched as a plane flew into one of the Twin Towers. *Is this my fault somehow?* I thought to myself. *I was just in New York. What could I have done to cause this?* My paranoia was working overtime. I was once again at the centre of the world, the prime mover of every event, and even a terrorist attack that I clearly had nothing to do with was my fault somehow. Later that afternoon, I went back to the hospital.

Less than two weeks after I was committed, I was discharged. Without the constant prayers and faith that God would deliver me, I may have been stuck in that place for a lot longer. I'd read nothing there but my new Bible, and eventually I'd focus on the more comforting parts of the passages Mum told me to read. *The Lord is my shepherd; I shall not want. I will fear no evil, for you are with me. I will say of the Lord, 'He is my refuge and my fortress, my God, in whom I trust.'* The psychiatrists at the hospital asked me a few questions before confirming I was alright to go, making sure I was myself again, but the experience changed me forever.

'You're so lucky to be going home,' one of the other patients said to me. I hadn't made friends in the hospital, but this guy had noticed me come, and now he was watching me leave.

For others the stay could be months, years, if not a life sentence.

I was also lucky enough to make it out in time to graduate.

I changed my life from that moment on. I decided I would never drink again. Nor would I take illicit drugs. And celibacy would also become a way of life. I was determined to be a different person.

I also realised that, yes, I had never heard Dad utter the words *I love you*, but then I had never said them to him either. So I decided I was going to tell him. We had arrived back home and were sitting together in the family room, in much the same way we were on the day I'd been taken away – the day I unravelled.

I looked over at him.

241

'I love you, Dad,' I said. Nothing. 'I love you, Dad,' I said again. Still no response. 'I love you, Dad,' I said for the third time.

'Mawunyo, I love you too,' came his reply. Finally, the declaration of love I desperately wanted. And it only took twenty-two years and me repeating myself three times. I smiled.

♪♫

I was filled with so much emotion on my graduation day – I had made it. Despite everything I'd been through, I was to receive my degree in journalism. When I read the card Sedudzi had placed in my hands, the tears that had threatened began to fall freely.

Dear Mawunyo,

On this your graduation day I congratulate you on your excellent achievement. Your successful completion of four years of university study both here and abroad is a testament to your amazing strength, will and perseverance. Made all the more special because to get accepted into uni was a struggle in itself. I have witnessed your rise and know it has not been easy. You have gone through so much pain and life experience that would have crippled weaker people, and come out the other side a better person. This is what I am most proud of you for, and I will always respect and admire Mawunyo Grace Aku Gbogbo. Although at times we don't get along the best, the best is yet to come for us. I pray that your future is as bright as you have made your past. The Olympics, Goodwill Games, Oswego, Hip Hop R&B nite, the ABC, and you somehow found time to get a degree. Happy graduation sis!

Much love from your biggest little brother,
Sedudzi
God Bless.

CHAPTER 24

Amazing Grace

A second chance is far more aligned to gold than silver.

'You need a job,' Mum said.

We were visiting Sedudzi at St Andrew's College at Sydney Uni, where he was studying commerce. Not long ago, Mum had finished her own degree and was now finally a registered nurse. Watching her, a mother of four, complete a degree while working full-time was inspiring, and it also made me feel like I had no excuses whatsoever when it came to pursuing a dream. But by then I was already someone who was always on the grind.

'Yeah, I know,' I said to Mum with a casual smile. Now that I was officially a journalism graduate, it was probably time for me to start looking for work.

'Let's go get you a job,' Mum said.

Again, I smiled and shrugged my shoulders. 'Okay.'

'Let's go to every television station in Sydney until you have a job,' Mum went on.

'Yeah, sure.'

'Where do you want to go first?'

'Well, I've always wanted to work for Channel Seven,' I said. 'Or Channel Nine.'

Sedudzi's girlfriend, who was also visiting, piped up. 'Channel Seven is over at Epping, it's a bit of a trek. Channel Nine is at Willoughby on the North Shore. But the ABC is just up the road in Ultimo.'

'Okay, let's start there. Let's go to the ABC first and then go from there,' Mum said.

So, Mum and I got ready to leave, picked up our suitcases and took a bus from Newtown to Ultimo.

After arriving at the ABC's headquarters, we made a beeline for reception.

'Hi,' I said to the two security officers – a man and a woman – behind the front counter. 'Is Heather here?' Heather worked in Human Resources and was the only person I knew to ask for. It turned out she wasn't there that day, which turned out to be a very good thing.

'What is it you're here for?' the grey-haired security guard asked me, peering through his glasses.

'I just wanted to see if there were any positions available,' I said. I didn't expect the blast that followed.

'What is it about people walking in off the street looking for work?' the man said. 'You're supposed to look in the paper and apply for a job that's been advertised. That's the normal way to go about things.'

He then disappeared for a brief period for some reason. And that, too, was a very good thing. The woman smiled at me and got on the phone. Within minutes, the NSW news editor, Paul McIntyre, was on his way downstairs to meet with me.

As we were strolling through the foyer, waiting, a Black woman with long, braided hair said hello.

'You brought your mother with you for an interview!' she said. 'I wish my mother would come to an interview with me.'

Paul McIntyre was a tall, handsome, softly spoken Kiwi. I'm sure he gave me a slightly odd look when he noticed I was with my mother, as he should have, but he didn't say anything about that . . . or our suitcases. Instead, he steered us both towards the ABC cafe, where we sat down at a table.

'What's your name?' Paul asked.

'Grace,' I blurted out, opting for my middle name. My CV had *Mawunyo Grace Gbogbo* prominently printed across the front of it, and given everything I'd just been through, I reasoned it wouldn't hurt if I disappeared for a while. I also figured that Grace was a much easier name to contend with.

Paul had a look at my resumé, and we chatted about my experience. 'I'm willing to do anything,' I said. 'I'll make coffee, sort mail – whatever you need.'

'I'm actually looking for two employees at the moment to work as news operations assistants,' he said. 'We call them NOAs.' He explained that TV was at Gore Hill, and we had walked into the ABC's radio headquarters. 'You won't need to do coffee runs, but you will have to transcribe copy when journalists file from the field, and assist the chief of staff with anything else that needs doing. The idea would be to eventually train you up to be a journalist yourself. It's kind of like being a copyboy – but for radio. Is this something you'd be interested in doing?'

'Yes, of course,' I said.

Mum sat at a distance, her eyes directed away from us but her ears attuned to what was being said.

Paul told me he actually liked it when people came in through the door and applied for jobs. To him, it showed they were serious. He was also very impressed with my resumé and the fact I'd worked at the Sydney Olympics. He had a bunch of applications on his desk, he said, but he wanted to hire me.

'When can you start?' he asked.

True to his word, Paul let me know when there were opportunities to do some reporting.

One of those first opportunities included working as the national overnight reporter, which involved ringing the cops right across the country and filing stories on any police incidents that had happened overnight.

When I pitched a story to write in my own time, about boxer Anthony Mundine's upcoming world title fight against American Antwun Echols, it was commissioned by the radio current affairs program, *AM*. I interviewed way too many people for the story, including Anthony and Antwun. I was working hard, long hours in my NOA role, which meant I was pushed for time, and I filed way too close to deadline. It wasn't completely up to scratch, so the executive producer of *AM* told me he sold the story to ABC NewsRadio. I was devastated. I never did hear it air. On the plus side, the EP found the interview I did with Antwun Echols on the server and commented on just how good it was. It turned out the fight lived up to the pre-bout hype. I was in the arena when Mundine, a proud Bundjalung Wiradjuri man, won by unanimous decision and took the world title belt.

But the world would become a strange place, again, and I needed some time out. Paul visited me at home. He was so kind and understanding at a time when I was particularly down, and offered much-needed words of encouragement: 'I've heard people say stuff about other people – that they're not going to make it. I've never heard anyone say that about you. You're going to make a great journalist someday.'

After two years working in the Sydney newsroom, I was posted to Tamworth as a junior journalist. My job there was to report on news stories in the New England North-West region and read the local news bulletins on radio. It was an exciting opportunity, and I embraced it wholeheartedly. I arrived just before the annual Tamworth Country Music Festival. Growing up in the country, I always thought country music was a bit daggy. I was also unaware of how much Dad loves country. But once I was in the Country Music Capital of Australia – 'Australia's Nashville' – I couldn't help but get swept away by it, and grew to like the songs and artists that dominated the country music charts.

I met a young Jessica Mauboy, who at the time hadn't reached the heights of fame she would later find after finishing runner-up on *Australian Idol*. She was only fourteen years old – young, quiet and with none of the on-stage glamour she now exhibits, but when she sang, she blew the audience away. She won the 'Road to Tamworth' competition that year.

I also filed stories about country music singer-songwriter Sara Storer, who nabbed a record-breaking seven Golden Guitar awards in one night, including Female Vocalist of the Year and Album of the Year.

During my time there, I'd end up covering three festivals. At one I met Jimmy Little backstage at the Golden Guitar Awards. I read him a few lines of 'Just a Picture', a song I was working on. I had evolved from writing poetry to writing song lyrics. It seemed a natural progression, and it made sense given my passion for both music and writing. I decided early on, though, that I was going to leave the music part of things to the experts. I'd collaborate on songs. I'd be the Bernie Taupin to someone else's Elton John – or so I hoped.

Jimmy Little listened to my lyrics and offered some feedback.

'It sounds like it's about someone longing for a person they really miss,' he said in a considered and thoughtful manner. This was a profound thing to say because I had had Tyce in mind when I was writing it, but in an effort to be creative, I had made the subject in the song dead – because Tyce was essentially a dying ember to me at the time. After Jimmy Little's comment, I changed tack. I figured the song would be about missing somebody, but it could still be played at funerals.

In addition to reporting, my job also involved reading news bulletins on the radio. Mum came to Tamworth to visit on a number of occasions and loved hearing me on the wireless. I sounded good for the majority of the time I was there – I was fine for at least eighteen months – but then I was paired with a voice trainer in Sydney who was meant to make me sound even better. But he was the type of person who, I was told later, broke people down in order to build them back up – except I already had such little confidence, I couldn't be built back up so quickly and convincingly.

He said stupid shit, like the time he mused about whether the reason I was so crap might be because I have a cleft palate. (I don't.) I was also given a disparaging mentor who was extremely critical of my skills. I was under so much pressure, and it all got too much for me in the end. I would get really nervous on air, and my voice would quiver. It reached the point where a regular listener sent this email to the newsdesk:

Please give my regards to Mawunyo Gbogbo. I was concerned yesterday, as she didn't sound her usual self and today I think I understand. She is obviously struggling but determined not to let it get the better of her. It will pass, whatever it is.

The email, the heart and kindness in it, made me cry. I was told years later that the voice coach I was working with was eventually asked to leave the ABC because he had upset too many journalists. Needless to say, another breakdown would visit me in Tamworth, and I was out of action for a short period of time. Gathering myself, I returned to Sydney soon afterwards to resume my news operations assistant role.

Mum and Dad finally decided to go their separate ways once we'd all made the move from Muswellbrook. I hadn't known they had actually been separated while still living under one roof for some time. Although they seemed to have stayed together for as long as they did for us kids, I don't think they did us any favours. In fact, for me, it was to my detriment. Having two parents who fought so much was worse than having parents who didn't live together. But that was the decision they made.

I returned to Sydney to resume my old job. Being a NOA had been a great foot in the door, but I was craving bigger and better things at that stage. Writing to me was everything, and I was on the lookout for ways I could continue to exercise that muscle and develop my talents in my own time. I ended up enrolling in a Master's in Creative Writing degree across the road at the University of Technology Sydney. I didn't see the point in doing a Master's in Journalism. I already had a degree in that discipline, one I'd fought so hard to get.

I continued to find ways to do what I loved while holding down my day job. I contributed to a current affairs program on 2SER FM – the community radio station on campus at UTS – and I started writing reviews for a website with a specialist focus on hip hop and R'n'B content. It was the stuff I was doing *outside* of work that kept me stimulated and was more closely aligned with my training, ironically.

I'd also, during this period, decided to pay a visit to the Motherland.

CHAPTER 25

A Mighty Fortress

While you were gone, the heart of the Motherland beat on.

Despite my reluctance to leave my homeland as a young child, it took twenty-two years for me to return to Ghana.

Sedudzi, Sophia and John went back with Dad. I went back a year or so later with Mum. Finally, after all these years, we would reunite with Aunty Rita, but while we had always thought that would be on Australian soil, it wasn't to be.

When I initially looked back on that trip to Ghana, my first impression was that all we did was go to church service after church service, because that's where Mum wanted to be and that's all she wanted to do. But having visited Ghana again since, I realise, given we didn't have a car and Mum hadn't been back to the country for a couple of decades, we did a hell of a lot. Church was a part of that, but we were also tourists in the country of my birth, and there were insights to be had.

'You have to be very careful what you name your children,' the pastor said at one of the services we attended. 'Children can take on the nature and characteristics of the people you name them after.'

I asked Mum if she'd named me after anyone.

'Yes, I named you after a girl who was very successful. She was also very, very naughty.'

'Why would you name me after someone who was naughty?'

'I wanted you to have character,' she said.

Suddenly everything was starting to make sense.

'Before we begin this tour, we will look into the history of this former slave fortress.'

With our feet back on Ghanaian soil, Mum and I were about to be confronted with the realities of the past. I tried to prepare myself mentally for the tales of horror and atrocity that were sure to come, but I soon learned nothing could prepare you for the tragedy of the slave trade.

'Elmina Castle was built in 1482 by Portuguese traders. All the rooms on the ground floor were originally used as a warehouse to store goods bartered for with gold and ivory. But it was in the early sixteenth century that the focus shifted from the gold trade to the human trade.'

The tour guide marched us into the first of the dungeons. I tried to imagine what it would have been like to be herded through this same dungeon, but in shackles and chains. I had to crouch in order to make it through the arched entryway. Once inside, I gazed at the pitted walls in the small, dark dungeon.

'This is where roughly two hundred female captives were kept at any one time. Families were separated. And the Africans were deliberately split from those who shared the same language, making it impossible for them to communicate.

'Where we are standing is the place the captives were forced to sleep, eat and defecate. That explains why many of them died right here. Disease was rampant and the sick were not attended to.'

I looked around. There was very little ventilation in the dungeon. The stench must have been unbearable. Even at that moment, centuries later, it was unpleasant.

'The captives were given food once, sometimes twice, a day, just enough to keep them alive. If they were fed more, they would be stronger and more of a threat to the guards.

'In addition to being tortured and intimidated, the women were under constant threat of rape at the hands of the soldiers. Some would be personally selected and marched upstairs at the request of the governor.

'Those captives who were considered "rebellious" were murdered.'

I shook my head in horror and dismay. My attention shifted to the others on the tour, a mixture of Black and white faces. Many were overcome with emotion, some shedding tears.

'While these atrocities were taking place in the dungeons beneath the castle, upstairs was a missionary sanctuary where the slave traders held church services. While the slave traders were upstairs praying, the captives were downstairs praying to that same God.'

We trudged through the male section of the dungeon, where we heard more about the plight of those captured. It wasn't too hard to imagine the captives shackled together in that very room. The tour guide then led us to the 'Door of No Return'.

'This is the door the Africans passed through before boarding the slave ships that would transport them to Europe, the Americas and the Caribbean.

'Up to twenty-five million people were forcibly removed from Africa and sold into slavery.'

I walked through the Door of No Return and gazed out over the waters of the Gulf of Guinea below. Frozen in the moment, overcome with sadness, I thought of the fate that had awaited these captives. And then I thought of their descendants, the people from whom I had gained so much of my Black pride. Ghana is a nation with its arms open to the African diaspora, inviting people back to the country's shores, most notably during the Year of Return in 2019, which attracted the likes of Rick Ross, Cardi B, Ludacris and 6LACK, among others. I turned around and walked back through the Door of No Return, like so many before me never got a chance to do.

As my mother and I walked through, a woman approached. We exchanged names and said where we were from. She was American.

'You sold us,' she said to me and Mum. There wasn't accusation in her voice, just disbelief. 'You sold us,' she repeated.

The guide had been telling us there were Africans who had sold some of their own into slavery – at times for little more than alcohol.

Speechless, we stood for a moment, facing one another, in silence.

CHAPTER 26

January 26

Let's get political. Political.

I spent the next two years when I returned to Australia working my day job as a NOA, while writing and reporting on stories outside of work at both the community radio station attached to my uni and the hip hop website. Paul had moved on as the NSW news editor some time ago and a number of different people began cycling through the role. I was jockeying to do more within the walls of the ABC, so I wrote to my new manager, who was a fair, no-nonsense boss. I pestered him repeatedly for opportunities. Eventually, he said, 'Look, do you hassle the boss of the *7.30 Report* the way you hassle me? Or what about the boss of *Lateline*? Have you been hassling him too?'

It was a light-bulb moment. 'Actually, no. No, I haven't.' That was about to change. I ended up landing a recurring role with *Lateline* as their Acting Foreign Affairs Editor. And I worked as a producer and journalist for *7.30* that summer, filing a story about The Gap, an ocean cliff in Sydney's east with the reputation of being Australia's most notorious suicide spot. My story provided historical and statistical information on The Gap, and highlighted the local council's proposed suicide prevention plan, which had failed to attract the additional 3 million dollars needed from the state or federal governments. It included a heartfelt interview with a mother who'd lost her daughter to suicide there, and a man who lived nearby who'd been recognised for his role in coaxing hundreds of people away from the cliff's edge, inviting them back to his house for a coffee, or even a beer, ultimately saving their lives.

In March 2008, the ABC launched CNC – the Continuous News Centre. They advertised a number of producer/presenter positions. These were entry-level jobs, but it was a great chance to learn the craft, so I applied for one of the many roles they had going.

My manager, who wasn't doing the hiring but could see what was happening under the man who was, looked me straight in the eye, telling me in no uncertain terms that there was no way I would even be considered for one of these roles. I asked him why.

'Look at the people who are being hired,' he said. 'They all have something in common. Something that you don't have.'

'What's that?' I asked.

'They're blonde!'

'Oh,' I said, immediately dismissing his observation. 'I'm sure I'd still be in with a chance.'

'What? You and all the blondes?' he replied.

My manager was clearly frustrated – frustrated that I couldn't see what was happening right in front of me, and frustrated that it was happening at all.

When the guy who was doing the hiring asked one of my blonde friends why she wasn't applying for one of these roles, she pointed to me.

'What about Mawunyo?' she said. 'She really, *really* wants to do it. I'm not ready.' The man turned his head, looked at me and then looked back at my friend. It was clear that I just wasn't blonde enough. Funny thing is, I had been completely unaware of what was going on. Had my manager not pointed it out, plain as day, I may have missed it. I hadn't really thought too much about the battles I might have to face, on top of my own insecurities and mental health issues, in pursuing my career. But of course racism would be one of them.

Almost fifteen years later, I reflected on this moment when I applied for a job as a journalist/producer at another media organisation – a role that, had I had that training years earlier, I would have stood a good chance at getting. I got a call from the boss there after I'd submitted an application. We had spoken weeks earlier, so he thought he'd pay me the courtesy of calling me directly.

He told me he couldn't hire me. 'I would get *murdered*,' he said, pointing out that I just didn't have enough on-air TV experience. I cried when I got off the phone.

But God moves in mysterious ways, because that very day I was asked if I'd be available for an interview for an internal role at the ABC – a dream job for me – and I was offered that one instead.

But I had to go through the trenches to get there.

While the man in charge of 'hiring blondes' had moved on and been replaced with people who were more inclusive, for years, I'd still be working in an industry where people of colour were brought in and then expected to blend in – be different, just don't flaunt that difference. I was such a rarity in my workplace that I was quite often 'othered'. A few years ago I had to defend myself against a high-profile presenter who, to her credit, later offered a heartfelt apology after challenging me because I wouldn't let her touch my hair.

'But you let me touch your braids!'

'No, I didn't. You just did it. I would never let you.'

I forwarded an article to her from Everyday Feminism – a website speaking her language, given she's a feminist – that outlined how Eurocentric beauty standards mean that white women feature in the media so much more often than Black women, and that the Black women who *do* feature in the media often have chemically straightened hair. So the invisibility of my hair type sends a message that it's unappealing and inferior.

The article also pointed out that to many Black women, our hair is not just hair – it's a source of empowerment. But the irony of the whole situation was that I was wearing a wig that day. Having her hand sliding across my scalp could have wound up ripping my wig off. That was just one of many reasons why I didn't want her to touch it, and I was disappointed by her initial reaction.

And people underestimate how often Black people have to put up with this sort of thing – I mean, it's even happened to me at the butcher shop.

When I feel objectified by so many people who find my hair fascinating and exotic, and who are offended when I assert my boundaries, it reinforces just how invisible Black people are in the media landscape.

Case in point: each time I catch the end of *Sunrise* as it morphs into *The Morning Show* on Seven, I'll watch as the camera pans back, highlighting a team of at least seven powerful media identities – all white – peering back at me from the screen. It seems unfair to me that in a country like Australia, where Indigenous people are Black, I rarely see Black people represented when I switch on the television. But then again, we're still arguing about changing the date of Australia's national day, so it's hardly surprising. (These days I'm more likely to wake up with *Today*.)

A friend who used to work for a commercial news website got a phone call from a colleague when she posted a photograph of a Black woman alongside a quirky headline about a freak accident the woman had been involved in.

'We don't put Black people on the homepage,' the colleague said, almost apologetically. 'It's terrible, I know.' I guess that's unless the Black person is a criminal or a celebrity or a *celebrity criminal*. My friend was horrified.

Now, you'd think that when I'm in the room, my colleagues might catch themselves before saying racist things, but I've had to deal with a number of other high-profile presenters who think it's their God-given right to use the n-word.

In 2018, I was doing a stint as a reporter in audio current affairs at the ABC, filing stories for *AM*, *The World Today* and *PM*. One of the presenters, who was filling in as the host of *PM*, repeatedly echoed Alan Jones as she sat at her desk, after 2GB was found to have breached the Commercial Radio Code of Practice when he used the term 'a nigger in the woodpile' on air.

'Nigger in the woodpile, nigger in the woodpile, nigger in the woodpile,' the presenter said over and over again. 'What does it mean? I just don't understand what it means.'

'Can you stop saying that?' I called out across the room.

'But I just don't understand what it *means*,' she said.

Two journalists, one of them also high-profile, came over and thanked me for telling her to shut up.

This wasn't an isolated incident. Just a couple years ago I was sitting in the office, minding my own business, when I could hear another presenter of some standing having a giggle with his producers about white coffee and black coffee, snickering about how in America the PC mob were saying those labels are considered offensive.

'Well, it's not as if we call it "nigger coffee",' the presenter said as his producers laughed. 'Can I offer you some nigger coffee, anybody?' he went on.

I walked over and told him to quit it.

'Quit what?' he responded.

I was incensed – furious at him but also his producers, who were enabling him. He emailed me later to apologise unreservedly, saying I was right to call him out. *I can kick into that kind of mode in an ironic fashion, but you are right, it is not funny or necessary . . .*

I wish I could say that's it. Sadly, the incidents I've witnessed or been subjected to are too numerous to mention.

As someone who didn't defend herself as a child when that racist primary-school bully Elliot Robertson thought fit to call me a nigger in class, I'm hardline. If you're not Black here in Australia, the n-word isn't yours to use – it's as simple as that. If, as a white person, you insist on arguing this point, it may be time for you to examine your attitude and call it what it is: racism.

And it isn't just media members who are guilty of racist attitudes and behaviours – the public at large needs to take a long, hard look at itself. I was brought to tears on more than one occasion when working on a late-night radio program for two years from mid-2015. Part of the job involved direct contact with the audience – people calling into the program from right across the country. I have never been subjected to such a sustained onslaught of racist views in my life – and that's saying something. These callers had no idea I was Black (I used my nickname Marnie), so they thought they could say whatever they wanted, and, boy, did some of them not hold back. I had to keep reminding myself after every shift that not everyone listens to the radio in the middle of the night, and not everyone who listens picks up the phone and calls the station. I had to convince myself that these comments weren't representative of the whole of Australian society. Had I not had these conversations with myself, I would have found it difficult to keep going.

We have a long way to go in this country. A long way.

CHAPTER 27

Hood Scriptures

Often danger is marked with a big red sign.
Even when it's not, there's still a sign.

Wanna hear my Mawunyo fantasy? I'd met DJ Bravo when I was out clubbing one night. He'd been trying really hard ever since to get into my pants. He was a hip hop DJ who had released successful mixtapes. I wasn't interested . . . until he told me his 'Mawunyo fantasy'. He set the scene – me in a white dress down to my ankles. Both of us in an elevator. *Do you want to hear more?* he texted. *Yes*, I typed back. And on it went.

His girlfriend had dumped him, apparently after finding emails he'd written to me claiming they'd already broken up. Eventually, he got what he wanted. We were both single at the time, so I went for it. It was amazing, so I went back for more. I had been celibate for about six years and had broken my drought after meeting a guy who was visiting Sydney with the US Army. Bravo followed.

At the time, I was still writing reviews for the hip hop website in my spare time, and for free, since I felt underutilised at work. Writing reviews can be tricky. As far as I was concerned, a good reviewer could slam with sophistication; that is, discerningly take apart a piece of art with class and wit, without needing to get into the trenches. My reviews were brilliant when I liked something – a concert, an album, a single. But if I didn't like something, I'd often think, *Well, at least they're trying.* I would return the CDs because I didn't like having a go at artists who meant well. When I did attempt to write reviews about something I didn't like, I found myself back-pedalling within the same review. It would start out slamming an artist for a pathetic album and end with me contemplating how much the artist had evolved from track one to track eleven, and how it really *wasn't* a bad album after all – if you just listened to it over and over again and gave it a chance.

I've since stepped up my game. I believe being credible as a reviewer is of utmost importance, and giving an honest opinion about whether something resonates with you or not – and being able to explain *why* – is key to that credibility. Giving your true opinions is a way of showing respect for your audience: a silent bond exists between the writer and reader that, while what you're saying is subjective, it's the truth as you see and define it.

Back then, though, I really struggled. But at least the 'things I did like' list included the Snoop, Ice Cube and Bone Thugs-N-Harmony concert I reviewed. I also got to interview the rapper Coolio. When the founder of the website asked me to write a review on DJ Bravo's new album, though, I panicked. *What if I don't like it? Worse still, there's an obvious conflict of interest – I'm sleeping with the guy.* I chose to take on the challenge, though, with the website's founder accompanying me to Bravo's apartment to film our interview for additional content.

'Act like you've never been here before,' Bravo said beforehand. 'When you walk in, look around and say "nice apartment", and don't just go to the bathroom – ask me where it is.'

The camera was set up as Bravo and I took our seats and got down to business.

I hit him with my first question. 'How would you say your mixtapes have evolved since the first one you collaborated on in the early days?' And we were off. 'There are quite a few safe hits on your latest album – what are your hit predictions?' I was warming up. 'How did you go about selecting which tracks would appear on the record? Was the culling process swift and decisive or more difficult? Anything you left off that you would have liked to include?'

'Ask him a personal question,' the founder said from behind the camera.

I racked my brain for an appropriate one, paranoid that I would reveal my position – or ask one that would result in me learning the answer to a question I wasn't prepared to hear. We were on camera, after all. 'You've had a lot of success over the years and have worked with some of the music industry's biggest stars . . . what stands out in your mind as your career highlight?' Oops. That wasn't personal enough. I'd thrown the word 'career' in there.

'Ask him something personal,' the founder repeated. I scanned my list of questions. Nothing. *Do you have someone special in your life?* I thought to myself. *What do you like to get up to in your spare time?* My brain went into overdrive. *Are you fucking anybody?*

In the end I successfully avoided asking anything too personal or revealing, and it was a wrap. The interview was over. I wrote a glowing review of the album – which I actually *did* like – but I thought I'd better add a slightly disparaging line to throw readers off the scent: 'The inclusion of Che'Nelle's "I Fell in Love With the DJ" seems a little self-indulgent.'

Bravo loved the write-up. But the 'I Fell in Love With the DJ' line caught his eye, prompting him to defend himself by saying he put it in there because it was a reggae track and he needed to change the pace up a bit. *How come you didn't write anything in there about how great you think my cock is?* he texted.

A couple of months later, I was in the mood for a booty call and got in touch. He had a new girlfriend. *Oh okay*, I texted, and was about to move on with my life when he texted back, asking if I wanted to get together anyway. Two words: *Hell no*. He persisted. I told him how my father had cheated on my mother, and the kind of havoc that had caused, and how it had affected my childhood. There was no way I was going to be 'the other woman'. *No way.*

It took him a few weeks to wear me down, but wear me down he did. His persistence, combined with my weakness and memories of just how good it was to get down with him meant I gave in.

He unleashed his inner crazy during those surreptitious dalliances. He loved to role-play and – knowing I was religious and harboured a huge amount of guilt over what I was doing – he'd tell me to address him as the Creator when we were mucking around, which, of course, I refused to do. Thinking I was Catholic, he also asked me to hold rosary beads and say Hail Mary's while we were in full flight. Again, no.

'Are you an atheist?' I asked him, given his predilection for mocking religion with his Christian-themed role-play suggestions.

'I'm British,' he laughed. 'High Church Anglican – we're closer to God than anyone!'

What started out as a bit of illicit fun turned into an on-again, off-again affair that lasted a couple of years. That is, until he came around one day for a session and afterwards told me that that was the last time.

'My girl and I are getting serious,' he said. 'I'm going to be good.'

Having never heard of a mistress being dumped, I was devastated. I felt like I'd been sucker punched. It was a strange mix of emotions, given I had never had romantic feelings for him – I'd long ago switched off those feelings – but for some reason I took the news particularly hard anyway. I thought about driving out to The Gap and putting an end to my miserable, duplicitous existence – I mean, could I *really* call myself a Christian? And I knew an awful lot now about The Gap. It's all fun and games until the side chick gets discarded.

I teamed up with a singer I'd met on Twitter and a music producer I'd worked with on a couple of other tracks to write a song inspired by the affair: 'Plays Me Like a DJ'. In the second verse, I thought about the consequences of not listening to your first instincts, of failing your conscience: *The things he tells me sound rehearsed / He doesn't miss a beat / Like a scratched CD in a jukebox / I just want to switch him off / I've changed the locks that chain my heart / The key he holds won't work / It never ends on a good note / When you forget the lies you spoke.*

'Did you listen to *Conversations* yesterday?' Dad asked me.

'No, I missed it, who was on?'

'The Channel Seven boss, Peter Meakin. Richard Fidler was away so Peter Meakin was being interviewed by one of the Chaser boys, who asked him why Channel Seven was so white and male. He said he didn't think it was very male anymore, but agreed it was pretty white – he said that's because he's reliant on the people who come through the journalism schools, and they're mostly white Anglo-Saxon Protestants. He said he typically doesn't get applications from people of colour.'

'Well, I'm going to change that,' I said.

I listened to the podcast and then emailed Peter Meakin straightaway, guessing what his email address might be, and got a prompt response. He said they didn't have any positions going but requested some scripts to check out my writing and offered to meet with me after.

Sedudzi helped me prepare for my meeting, reviewing emails before I sent them to Peter and helping me brainstorm story ideas.

I met with Peter in October 2009. He asked for story ideas, which I delivered in droves. He disparaged most of them, constantly telling me I was 'so ABC'. I didn't know what he meant by that for a long time. He meant my story ideas were too serious, not tabloid enough.

In the end, my visit to Seven didn't result in a job. It just wasn't my time.

I was on a visit to Melbourne when I experienced another break-down. I was in hospital when it hit me – *really* hit me – what it meant that Jesus had died for my sins. I had, again, hit rock bottom. I'd been trying to go it alone, walk my own path, but I needed Him – I always had. And it turns out He had never left my side. *The Lord is my light and my salvation.* Christ had died *for me.* I cried and cried and cried. I got down on my knees and sang 'Amazing Grace' – *really* sang it – like I was understanding each word for the very first time:

Amazing grace! How sweet the sound / That saved a wretch like me. / I once was lost, but now am found, / Was blind, but now I see . . .

I certainly felt like a wretch. I didn't deserve His love. I didn't deserve mercy. But God loved me anyway. I was forgiven. And it was time I forgave myself.

This was a pivotal moment for me and my faith – it would become far more durable, more resistant to the vagaries of life's circumstances. I wiped away my tears, and broke into 'Because He Lives':

Because He lives I can face tomorrow, / Because He lives all fear is gone; / Because I know He holds the future, / And life is worth the living / Just because He lives.

In Hebrews ten, verse twenty-two, it says: 'Let us come near to God with a sincere heart and a sure faith, because we have been made free from a guilty conscience, and our bodies have been washed with pure water.'

I'd been an all-or-nothing person my entire life. Fail a diet? Might as well binge. Fall into temptation? Might as well give up, because perfection is just too hard to achieve. But God wasn't asking for perfection. That was something the world expected of Christians, not God.

I had an interview a few days later for a job at what would become ABC News 24. When I got out of hospital and made my way back to NSW, I decided I couldn't do the interview. I called Gaven Morris, who was then the Head of Continuous News, and told him so. 'I've been really sick,' I said. 'I just got out of hospital. It's a bad time for me. I can't do the interview.'

'Just give it a chance,' he said.

So, I went in. I did the written current affairs test. One of the questions was *How many characters can you tweet?* I had no idea.

In the end, I didn't get the job. Things would have been very different for me if I had landed that position. But it just wasn't meant to be. My time had still not arrived.

PART FOUR

CHAPTER 28

Reunited

*When you think you've reached the final chapter of a great book,
but then discover there's a sequel – that's the joy of
unrequited love requited.*

Tyce was a latecomer to Facebook and a complete novice when it came to all things social media. For a while there, I thought he must be bisexual because he had on his profile 'Interested in men and women'. Turns out he thought it meant just for networking purposes.

We'd had limited contact since becoming Facebook friends. He expressed excitement when I first added him. My own excitement was tempered by the fact that he was in a relationship at the time.

When he posted a picture of himself on his page posing with a gun and it showed up in my newsfeed, after he'd already put up a series of unsettling status updates, I messaged him and asked if he was alright. I also suggested he tone it down.

Two months later, I logged onto Facebook, and had a look to see who was also logged on. I saw the little green dot next to Tyce's

275

name but I chose not to initiate a conversation. The last time we'd spoken he'd told me he'd broken up with his partner. I'd tried to comfort him, but at the same time I wondered why he couldn't love me like that.

A few minutes later: *ping.*

It was Tyce.

He thanked me for listening to him when he needed a friend. We exchanged a few pleasantries, told each other we cared. Then this message came through, taking me completely by surprise:

Tyce: *I remember looking at you for the first time, thinking, 'She is the most beautiful girl I've ever seen.' And I still do, your heart is beautiful too. That's why I will always have love for you. I'm smiling but I wanna cry. I've still got a crush on you.*

Me: *Really? You thought that? Lol. That's really sweet of you to say. It's sad how we never really got a chance to explore our feelings for each other. It took me a really, really, really long time to get over you, and I don't even know whether I am truly over you. I'll always have love for you too.*

Tyce: *There have been so many times I wanted to tell you since high school how I feel about you. I never stopped loving you. You make me feel like it's okay to be me. Your so smart and humble. I think you are so special cause your you. I love you. There, I said it, and it came from my heart. I love you.*

Whoa. Oh my God, I thought, reeling. *Tyce loves me? Oh. My. God. Not in the past tense. He isn't just saying he had 'love for* me' but that he was in love with me. *Tyce was and is in love . . . with me.*

It took a while for that to sink in. The man I'd obsessed about since we were teenagers. The guy who stole my heart. And he was in love with me? I didn't know how to react. I went to a place between disbelief and unspeakable joy, and with that came the tears.

I got up from my laptop and went to my room. What could I possibly say? So many years had passed. He was a father, he'd been to jail, he didn't know the difference between 'your' and 'you're'.

I put on some hymns and sang through my tears. I looked heavenward. What was I supposed to do with this information? So much time had passed since we had first kissed, since I had fallen for him. I had never wanted anything more than to be his.

A few hours passed as I contemplated my next move. Eventually, I decided to go with my heart, because ultimately, my head was telling me the same thing. I went back downstairs and sat in front of my laptop.

Tyce, from the bottom of my heart I love you too. And I've wanted to hear you say those words for more than fifteen years, and it breaks my heart to hear you say that now. I was just crying like a lil' baby. You have to understand I'm a completely different person to the girl I was when I fell hard for you as a sixteen-year-old. I've changed a lot. I've been through some unimaginable things, and I don't doubt you could fall in love with the girl I was then, but could you love me now – jaded, scarred and not so innocent?

I don't know if you remember this, but I'll never forget the day we went jogging together and were about to go our separate ways. We stopped and looked at one another, and I wanted to tell you then how I felt, and I've always regretted that I let that moment pass. I wanted to tell you then that every time I see you my heart melts, that when I look into your eyes I get lost in your world and I just want to be around you, hear your laugh and see you smile. Nothing makes me happier than knowing you're happy, and when you're not doing so well, it makes me sad. I don't think you realise how gifted, talented and clever you are and how much you have to offer. You'll always have a special place in my heart, no matter what.

Tyce replied minutes later:

I'm so blessed. How could I forget us jogging? We was deadly. Those lovely Black legs. And I didn't realise until we went our ways that something wasn't right. I felt such a fool! I didn't tell you how much I wanted you. That I loved you and I wanted you to feel the same for me. All my life I have wished that I said something.

As for loving you now, well, the Bible tells me, 'Those without sin cast the first stone.' Time has passed and things have happened.

Throughout my life, on many occasions, I have thought of you and I ached to bump into you (tears).

You don't know how much I adore you, and I am looking at you in awe at what you have achieved.

I want to be more like you in areas of my life. I love you, Marnz. Thank you for shining your light when I was in a dark place. WOW, you did feel the same for me. I'm so happy to hear that from you.

We chatted for hours, keeping each other awake all night. After spending a period of time in Queensland, Tyce was back in Muswellbrook – his mum had been diagnosed with terminal lung cancer. I expressed my sadness, and I told him about the time she'd confessed she'd always thought the two of us would end up together. Tyce reacted to this with surprise and glee. We planned our first date, arranging to meet up the following Friday. I couldn't wait to see him again.

Tyce loved me.

CHAPTER 29

It Was a Good Day

Love is a drug, so pure, so potent.

Our first date took place more than fifteen years after our first kiss. It was a strange feeling, made all the stranger because after a flurry of text messages and poems we'd written to each other, Tyce had already decided that he was moving to Sydney to be with me.

I wasn't sure what to wear but settled on a new dress I'd only worn once before. We were meeting on Good Friday and planned to start our date off with church. We had arranged to meet each other halfway, on the Central Coast.

I was telling Tyce I couldn't find any service times that would work at the church we wanted to go to, but there was one in Charmhaven that had an extension service at the Laycock Theatre in Wyoming.

Me: *That's if u're absolutely sure u wanna go to church. Kind of a weird thing to do on a first date, I know. Lol.*

Tyce: *'In my most desperate darkest hour I called out to the Lord and he answered me.'*

Me: :-) *I guess that's a YES for church!*

Tyce: *Yeah, I wanna thank Him for sending one of His brightest lights into my life. His will be done.*

I watched as Tyce strolled through the gates at the Tuggerah train station, wearing a green collared shirt. I had a sudden pang of worry that once he saw me again, once we'd spent the day together, he wouldn't love me anymore.

He smiled as he walked over and enveloped me in a huge embrace.

'*Ohhh*,' he groaned. I could hear the smile in his voice.

I held onto him tightly. When we eventually let go of each other, I took a good look at him. He was missing a few teeth, towards the front on the top and bottom, but he looked cute. I was still strongly attracted to him.

'Do you have any idea how hard it is to talk to a girl who looks like you?' he said once we started to make our way towards my car. He must have approved of the effort I'd made to look half decent. To think he'd felt this way back in high school . . .

I set the GPS and we drove to the Hope Unlimited Church. We got there as the worship music was wrapping up, but the sermon had yet to start. Once we'd navigated our way around raised hands and swaying feet to reach a couple of empty seats in the middle of an aisle towards the back, Tyce and I sat down, our hands clasped together tightly.

'When Jesus was crucified on the cross, there were two men on either side of him,' the pastor began. 'Both of them deserved to be there. Today, I want us to think about these two criminals.'

This is going to be interesting, I thought, resisting the urge to squeeze Tyce's hand. The pastor launched into the sermon, speaking about how one of the crucified men was forgiven for his sins right there and then – even in his darkest hour the thief recognised that Jesus is Lord, and asked to be remembered when He went into His kingdom. 'Today you will be with me in Paradise,' Jesus had assured him.

When the sermon was over and we returned to the car, I put on my iPod touch, playing a mix of my favourite tracks at the time. The Weeknd was on as we pulled away.

'What did you think of the sermon?' I asked Tyce.

'I thought it was good,' he said, much to my relief. 'When you're a criminal, you feel like the lowest form of scum there is.' Tyce put his head down.

'The only difference between you and a whole heap of other people is that you got caught,' I said. 'People do really dodgy shit all the time and get away with it.'

'I guess that's the thing with Jesus – all sin is the same in His eyes,' Tyce agreed. One of my favourite songs came on, Nate Dogg's 'Music & Me'. 'Nice! Old skool.'

We went for a walk by the ocean and reminisced about the '90s. I was saying how much I loved Sir Mix-a-Lot's 'Baby Got Back', because it celebrated women with big butts. 'Not that my butt is that big,' I added.

'Oh, you've got ass,' Tyce said.

I was flattered, but compared to the women in the video clip, I really didn't.

We made our way to the local RSL club because the fish-and-chip shop by the water was yet to open. Tyce paid for the all-you-can eat buffet for the two of us.

'So do you have any more kids, other than the two you have with Penny?' I asked.

'Yeah,' he said. My heart sank, but it wasn't a deal-breaker. 'I tried to kidnap my son, Tyce Jnr, but the taxi didn't arrive in time.'

I laughed in spite of myself.

We talked a little about his lengthy criminal history. It had been a few years since he was last locked up. 'I enjoyed my time in there this time around,' he said.

'Why?'

''Cos in jail if a guy doesn't like you, you know about it. There are always people trying to kill you, and being on your guard all the time makes the time go faster.'

Despite all the trouble he'd been in, Tyce had also spent three years working in the mines, which I'd known nothing about. He had even managed to get a degree.

'You know, I blame you for some of my six-month prison sentences,' he said. 'I'd go to the pub and start thinking about you married off, far away somewhere, and someone would say hello to me. I would turn around and be like, "What the fuck do you want?"' and lay into him. You were my first big crush.

'Before then, girls didn't mean a whole lot to me. Do you remember when we used to dance in the quadrangle?' I only had vague memories of this. 'There was one time in Year Eight when you touched my hand and I thought, *She likes me.* I dumped my girlfriend 'cos I wanted to ask you out. But I didn't. There were so many times I walked up to you and then turned back around again. My boy Travis was like, "I'm just going to tell her," and I said, "No! I'll tell her myself." But I never did.' Tyce paused. 'Don't tell anybody this, but I used to play Brandy's 'Sittin' Up in My Room' and think about you.'

I was surprised – to think that Tyce used to pine away for me to that tune was incredibly heartwarming. If the lyrics were anything to go by, he was a mess for me, and he was waiting for the day that I would be his.

It was then that 50 Cent and Olivia's 'Best Friend' – a song about two friends, both wanting more – came on. 'This can be our song,' he said.

We moved to the pokie area, where Tyce asked me whether he should bet on black or red. I'm not a fan of pokies, and although Good Friday was a great Friday because I got to spend it with him, his smoking, drinking and gambling put a dampener on what was otherwise a glorious date. My phone rang, and since it was Dad I decided to answer it.

After I ended the call, Tyce walked up and said, 'Hi, my name is Tyce. I see you haven't got a ring on your finger, are you single? I'm single too. Will you be my girlfriend?'

Of course there was only one answer to that question. I smiled and said yes. Tyce looked relieved. 'I thought you were going to say no just then.' Even after all those years, after the conversation we'd just had, he thought I was going to reject him.

When we left the club, Tyce and I walked for a while and then sat on a bench outside the mall.

'Were you trying to sleep with me back when we first kissed?' It was obvious he was. I just wanted to make sure. I'd believed him at the time that he was 'just going in for a feel'.

'Yeah. I know what I'm doing now,' he laughed, and then admitted that he'd been a virgin then. I was shocked. 'I thought that if we had sex, then we would be joined together forever, that we would get married. I was pretty silly back then, I thought that's just how it worked.'

'I thought sex was all you wanted,' I said. 'Malcolm told me you said you tried to have sex with me.'

'I never said anything to him – or any of the boys! I knew if I did it would get back to you, so I deliberately *didn't* say anything.'

All this time I had thought the worst of Tyce. I started crying, thinking about all the time we'd missed out on.

He also revealed how much he loved my body. 'The white girls at school used to walk around with their skirts hitched up around their necks. But Mawunyo was never like that. You wore your skirt just above the knee.' He looked me over with approval. 'If I failed any Maths exams, that was your fault. One plus two equals . . . tits. Seven plus one equals . . . tits.'

My laughter mingled with my tears.

He feigned being in a classroom. 'Miss, can you please tell Mawunyo to leave the room?'

'Why? What did she do wrong?' I asked, playing along.

'It's her breasts, Miss. I can't concentrate.'

The body that I myself didn't appreciate as a teenager was the one he loved. I'd had a breast reduction a few years earlier. I had altered a part of my body that caused me pain – a bad back, an inability to wear decent clothes, the discomfort I felt even running around the block. It had been a feature that Tyce had not only noticed but desired.

'I remember one time you made some food in cooking class, where you sprinkled some sugar on top. It tasted so good. And in woodwork class, I just wanted to take you out the back to the storeroom and have my way with you.

'The poor girls I went out with.' He shook his head. 'They didn't do anything wrong – they just weren't you. Marnz was up here.' He lifted his hand. 'No one came close. I had you on a pedestal.'

I continued to laugh through my tears.

'I'll give you my resumé,' Tyce said, thinking he still needed to win me over. 'I'm smart. I can change a light bulb without a chair. I can mow the lawn. I wash dishes – I don't think it's the responsibility of the person who cooks. I can do backflips from a wheelie bin. I can do a kickflip on a skateboard. I'll look after you when you're sick and make you a cuppa. I can cook too.'

'What can you cook?'

'Sausages,' he said, and I laughed.

He told me I was the only girl he had ever taken back to his parents' place.

'Mum was always saying, "You should have stayed with Mawunyo," and I was like, "Mawunyo doesn't want me."'

'Well, you didn't want to talk to me after I went home with you that night,' I said, referring to his preference to play Nintendo at the time.

'Why did you come back to the house?' he asked. 'I got in so much trouble. Mum and Dad were pissed off that I'd brought a girl back to the house. They figured you were just as bad as I was.

'But when you came back later that day, they thought, *She's actually a nice girl*, and then I copped all the blame. My mum hit me in the back of the head with an ashtray. I was so mad at you.'

He was scared he'd get into even more trouble from his parents if he spoke to me. This revelation filled me with relief. It wasn't that he didn't care or had been playing games. Tyce loved me – he really loved me. And, finally, I felt justified in my love for him.

'Your parents are really tight, huh? They're very much in love?'

'Yeah,' Tyce said, 'you couldn't separate them with a steel rod.'

That's the kind of love I wanted. I yearned to spend every waking hour with him, making up for what never was and what still might be.

Tyce also told me about a car accident he'd been in. He was hit by a truck driver going 100 kilometres an hour and had spent four weeks in a coma. He could have died – and what a tragic loss that would have been.

As far as I was concerned, we were soulmates.

CHAPTER 30

The hardest person I find to forgive is myself.
But with standards that high, I limit my high.

We spoke on the phone and texted back and forth until we met again. A lot of our messages were funny expressions of how much we cared for each other:

Tyce: *I love ya like da fat kid loves mudcake.*
Me: *Lol. I love you like a party animal loves to hit the Cross.*
Tyce: *I love ya like a crackhead loves that crack pipe.*
Me: *I love you more than a snake would love legs.*

But here was the thing: while I was finally dating the only guy I'd ever loved, I was still terrified of losing him once he found out some of the stupid stuff I'd done in the past.

He'd already told me he had thought of a romantic, one-of-a-kind way to ask me to marry him. But I wanted him to know all of me; I didn't want to hold anything back.

Me: *U and I need to talk when I get 2 Mbk. I think u're under the false impression that I'm some perfect lil' angel sent from heaven . . . HARDLY.*

Tyce: *Marnz, I have been sent to most maximum security jails in NSW, shot, stabbed, run over, put in the boot of a car. I think you are an angel, babe, always have, always will.*

We joked around a bit, but I emphasised that I was serious.

Tyce: *I'll be honest with you, Marnz, the truth will make us stronger and I respect you as a person. Why lie when the truth will do!*

Me: *That's the way I feel. Always wanted to be in the kind of relationship where you can tell your man anything and vice versa. To me that's really important.*

Tyce: *I have 28 baby mamas, run a child labour camp, pimp 8 bitches and have crack cocaine on my Weetbix. Still love me? Lolololololol.*

Me: *Lol. Yup. :-) Crazy me*

I finally told him everything – about how I'd felt when he didn't call me in high school. About the school counsellor's husband, and how his assessment that men were fundamentally different to women and just didn't love in the same way had scarred me. About how I know now that men can love just as deeply as women, but having been misled, I had switched off my feelings.

About my disordered eating and how subconsciously I might have been trying to destroy the body men found attractive, because it had brought me so much pain. About the pre-cancerous cells, the surgery and the trauma that followed. About how excited I was to meet my cousins in New York, and how they'd let me down. About the cops taking me to hospital after I'd passed out on the subway platform. About how I was thrown out of my family's apartment. About spending my twenty-second birthday in a mental hospital, and my mental health struggles ever since. About vowing to never drink or take illicit drugs again, and how I'd been successful in honouring that vow. About my celibacy. And my promiscuity.

I got this response:

Thank you for your trust, Marnz. I'm grateful you are still with us. The Bible tells me, 'Those without sin cast the first stone.' I've done some things due to being in gangs & jail that I'm not proud of. They are simply things that happened, some of them we had no control of. Those things that happen don't define who we are today. Good deeds don't make anyone a good person, same as a bad deed doesn't make anyone a bad person. When I was in Silverwater Max Jail when I was 19, I lived with bad people 24/7. The eyes of a murderer are the window to a body with no soul, Marnz. I've been in and out since I was fourteen and I know exactly what a bad person looks like, sounds like, behaves like. You are not a bad person, you are a gift to anyone who knows you. What you have told me makes me have more respect for you, Marnz, because like me, our mistakes and trials could have easily sunk us or turned us into a bad person. Instead, we pick ourselves up, we learn, and despite feelings of anger, hatred, sadness and resentment we make a conscious decision to do better. It doesn't matter how slowly we do this so long as we don't stop. You are a light to me, the only light that shined into my darkness. I wanted to shoot people with that gun for what they did to me, Marnz. But you reminded me there are good people in this world and that I am a good person. I'm so grateful to you. I love you dearly and will defend you even against yourself. God Bless You, for He has blessed me with you.

Tyce told me he loved me unconditionally, because it was the only way he knew how to love.

CHAPTER 31

O Perfect Love

Jesus loves me. Dad loves me. Tyce loves me. I love me.

I went to visit Tyce in Muswellbrook shortly afterwards. We had a beautiful weekend together. I stayed at my high-school friend Amber Jones's place while I was in town. I felt that staying in a hotel would have brought way too much temptation to sleep with Tyce, and I just wasn't ready. It didn't matter that we had been together before. I wanted to take my time and do this the right way. I'd already lost him once. My heart couldn't take losing him again. Tyce was so happy to receive a CD I had put together for him of songs that meant something to the both of us. On it was the song I'd written in Tamworth, 'Just a Picture', and it was performed by the music producer who'd come up with the beats. The two verses and chorus went:

When my head hits the pillow / that's when I see your face /
When the lights go out at night / my mind drifts to another place /

In my dreams you smile at me / and run your fingers through my hair / But when I open up my eyes / you're no longer there.

You're just a picture / and some old memories / You're just a picture / smiling back at me.

You're out of focus / but clearly I can see / If you were my picture / you'd be right here with me.

In the times we shared together / your look changed year by year / Now I've only one reminder / of the days when you were near / It's clearly black and white / our love has never been that way / It's rough around the edges / just like you, I'd say.

♪♫

Tyce's mother greeted me warmly when I went around to visit. We held each other in a long embrace.

'I hear you're not well,' I said, telling her I would keep her in my prayers. When I referred to the 'diploma' Tyce had received when he was in Queensland, Mrs Carrington corrected me. 'He has a *degree*. It's a degree,' she said, proudly emphasising his achievement. His degree was in youth work – he wanted to help young Indigenous kids stay out of the juvenile justice system and keep on the straight and narrow.

Tyce went off to do some work in the backyard while I sat outside and chatted with his parents. I explained to Mrs Carrington that I was on long service leave from my job as an associate producer for the television program *Insight* on SBS.

'It's such a privilege being able to hear people's stories,' I said. 'There are times when I'll be typing up a pre-interview and I'll shed a tear or two, because some of what I hear is so full-on. Some people have been through so much.'

It was then that Mrs Carrington started to open up to me. 'I used to live on a reserve,' she began. 'Now, that's not to be confused with a mission. A reserve is much worse than a mission. We were constantly on the run from the welfare men who were there to take children away. Someone would whistle, and as soon as the whistle travelled down to us, we would run. On this particular day, I'd heard the whistle and took off, and then I turned around and realised my brother and sister weren't with me. They'd been taken – stolen – while Mum was out pegging clothes on the line.'

I let the thought sit with me for a moment: *Children. Taken from their parents. Taken from their families. Families decimated. A cycle of trauma for those taken, and those left behind.*

I could see the hurt in Mrs Carrington's eyes, as if it had only happened yesterday. As if, in some way, she still blamed herself for not being able to protect her siblings. She'd gotten away. Her brother and sister didn't. Of course she wasn't to blame – she was just a child then – but I could see how something like that would eat away at you.

The Stolen Generations weren't people in the remote past; these weren't characters in a story. It was still alive in the Carrington's yard. Tyce's mum had seen it with her own eyes, had felt the anguish of losing two siblings to a government policy. I couldn't begin to imagine the torment she'd been through, not to mention what her parents experienced in the aftermath.

'When I used to lecture in universities, there were people who didn't like me based on my skin colour,' she said. I'd had no idea that she used to lecture in universities. 'After listening to me they changed their tune. I don't blame them. They'd had no interaction with Aboriginal people to make them think this way.' Tyce would later tell me that after all the racism his mother had experienced and the pain she had gone through, she had never developed a negative attitude towards white people. To the contrary, even. Mrs Carrington had an enormous heart.

Tyce walked up to us. 'Thanks for waiting and hanging out with my folks,' he said. I told him it was a privilege.

Tyce and I got ready to go to the shops so we could pick up some ingredients for a dish I was going to cook for him and his parents.

'He's like a little kid in the supermarket,' Mrs Carrington warned me. 'You'll have to say to him, "Naaaah – you can't have that. Nah, you can't have that either."'

Tyce was always hilarious when we went out; there was always a joke on his lips. He had me clutching my stomach in fits of laughter in the supermarket. At the same time, I noticed his wallet never did make an appearance when we came to the register.

We went to Tyce's sister's place afterwards, where I was going to make homemade pizzas. Laura Carrington was so happy and excited to see me. She's one of the sweetest people I know.

One of Laura's neighbours who was driving past wound down the window to say hello.

'This is my partner, Mawunyo,' Tyce said.

'I saw her on Facebook,' the woman said. 'And she really is beautiful.'

'Beautiful inside and out,' Laura confirmed.

Laura took a photo of Tyce and me while we were standing in the kitchen in an embrace. 'True love,' she said.

Later, she pulled me aside and said, 'Tyce asked me for twenty dollars to go and see you on the Central Coast, and I said, "Yep, here you go." I was more than happy to help him out since it was you. I've said to him, "Will you please marry this one?"'

Tyce sat outside playing a guitar with only four strings – the fifth had broken and he'd tried unsuccessfully to reconnect it. He wanted to sing a song for me.

'How come your guitar only has four strings?' I asked.

'Because I hit someone over the head with it at the pub. I had a baseball cap on and this guy told me I looked like a gangsta Charley Pride.'

Later, he would tell me something that truly broke my heart.

'You know that car accident I had? When I ended up in a coma?'

'Yes . . .' I said.

'That was a suicide attempt. I ran out in front of that truck deliberately.'

With every revelation, each note of hardship, each story of struggle, I was drawn closer to Tyce. I felt I had to protect him now.

♪♫

That night, Tyce and I went back to Laura's house after she had gone out. Tyce put on the Ray Charles movie starring Jamie Foxx, and we snuggled in front of the TV. Laura's analog TV flickered constantly; it was nearly impossible to watch, so Tyce started talking about his childhood.

'You know, I got teased a lot in primary school.' When he told me who the main culprit was, I was completely shocked. It was a guy we'd both gone to high school with, and someone I considered a complete loser. I couldn't imagine him exercising any type of power over Tyce.

'It was mostly to do with the fact I was a Blackfulla, but also 'cos I didn't have brandname clothing – unless I flogged it from a clothesline. But even then, the teasing didn't stop. My parents didn't have the money to buy us nice clothes. They drank away their money. I experienced and saw things no kid should ever have to go through or see. There was violence in our household. Dad would come home drunk at two in the morning and wake me and Xander up, take us out the back and teach us how to box.

'I behaved the way I did because I was a product of my environment. Growing up, I was surrounded by alcoholics, drug addicts.

'When I was about eight, I remember our uncle chasing us kids with an axe, threatening to kill us. We ran and hid in a room, and the axe came crashing through the door. He left us alone after that. Mum and Dad were too busy at the card table, drunk with all the mob. It was only a matter of time before all hell broke loose and the adults would start fighting. That's how it always ended up. This sort of stuff took place at least three days a week.

'I've never seen my people have a glass of wine with a nice meal and function normally. Fights were the main course. I automatically associated drinking with anger, swearing, things getting smashed.

'When I began to drink I behaved the same way, because that's what I thought was normal.

'I first lost my freedom for assault and robbery when I was fourteen. I spent sixteen months at the Worimi Juvenile Detention

Centre in Newcastle. I was scared and alone, but I wouldn't dare show it or say I was lonely. I'd be seen as weak.

'The first time I stood up for myself, I won. I thought that I got respect after that. In fact, it wasn't respect at all – the other inmates feared me . . . As the years went by I went in and out of juvenile centres, where I embraced being feared.

'My suicide attempt was a good one, but it failed to kill me. So I made a decision to be a better person.'

The next day I had lunch with Amber Jones, and then Tyce and I trained together, using some workout equipment the council had built in the park.

When we arrived at his mum and dad's place afterwards, Mrs Carrington was in a jovial mood. 'Marnz is looking fresh as a daisy, and look at you,' she cheerfully taunted, pointing to Tyce's shirt, which was drenched in sweat.

Tyce's father had already made a head start on dinner by boiling the pasta. I whipped out my phone. A woman whose kids I used to babysit had texted me a recipe for the best tuna bake I'd ever tasted in my life.

'I thought it was your recipe,' Tyce's mum teased me. 'How are you going to impress the in-laws when it's not even your recipe?'

In the end, I did impress the 'in-laws', along with Tyce, who had started to worry when we couldn't get the consistency right when mixing the butter and breadcrumbs for the layer on top.

When we sat down to eat, Tyce told his parents he was going to get another tattoo. He already had quite a few tattoos, including a cross tatted on one arm, and a sleeve on the other.

'I don't like you getting tattoos,' his mum said. 'You've got enough. Just know that I don't like it.'

'I believe you've got a tattoo on your arm,' Tyce said.

'Yes, I got one when I was young and didn't know any better.'

'What about if I shave off both eyebrows and get your name tattooed on one and Dad's name on the other, so people know who I belong to?'

I started laughing.

Tyce's mum had seconds of the tuna bake. 'I never have seconds,' she said. 'This is seriously good.'

'So, did I redeem myself?' I asked.

'Yes,' she said.

After dinner, Tyce and I went to the pub for karaoke. We kissed in the car, and then we kissed some more. He was such a gentleman. He didn't try to sleep with me, even though he admitted he wanted to.

The next day, after church, Tyce and I went to Sunday lunch at his parents' place, which he said was a tradition. It was there that I met Tyce's eldest son – the one he'd had with Penny. He would have been about fifteen at the time. There was the awkward moment when we were introduced – we didn't know whether to shake hands or hug, so we went in for the hug-shake. Tyce told me later that when his son went home that night, he told his brother that his dad's new girlfriend was *really* Black. The things kids say . . .

Tyce had made up his mind that he was moving to Sydney to

be with me, so I rang one of my Koori friends to find out more about the Aboriginal hostels in Sydney.

'I didn't know you had a boyfriend,' she said. 'You've been keeping it a secret.'

'No, it's not a secret,' I replied.

Of course, Tyce's mum and sister were listening in. 'She wants to make sure he's a keeper,' Mrs Carrington said. I didn't tell her that, to me, Tyce was already a keeper.

We were all hanging out on the verandah later when I spotted the home screen on Tyce's phone. 'Why have you got a picture of Gabrielle Union?'

'Ay?' Tyce looked at me quizzically. 'Ain't that you?'

I laughed. 'Ah, no.'

'But I got that off your Facebook.'

'I had it on there during Doppelganger Week, where you change your profile picture to a famous person you've been told you look like. I mean, Tyce, I have thousands of photos of myself on Facebook . . . and you chose the one picture that *isn't* me? I'm kinda offended.'

Tyce immediately deleted the pic and chose another.

'You know,' I said to Mrs Carrington, 'Tyce's Facebook once said that he was "interested in men and women". I must say, I was a little confused when I saw it.'

'Have you had any offers?' Mrs Carrington asked him. We laughed.

'Here are the two women I love and respect more than any other women on earth,' Tyce said. 'And one of you is holding me to the ground while the other one is kicking me.'

We laughed and laughed.

♪♫

When I was back in Sydney, Tyce and I had our first fight. Little could I know that it was a sign of things to come. We were on the phone and Tyce started telling me in a laconic tone – as if it was the most normal thing in the world – how he once turned up to Penny's place with a sawn-off shotgun, fired a round at the wall and then grabbed his son, who he had plans to take interstate because Penny wanted to break up with him – and she wasn't the only ex he'd threatened to hurt.

'I don't want to be scared of the guy I'm with, Tyce. What if I do something to piss you off?'

He was really cut. 'You remind me of the type of person who sees me walking down the street and crosses over to the other side of the road, even though I've never done anything to you and don't even know you.'

It was my turn to be upset.

The reception started to go fuzzy, so I hung up and tried to call him back, but he wouldn't answer. He later told me he'd also deleted my text messages without reading them, after he'd sent me one saying he didn't want to talk or text. Later, he called a couple of times, sounding more and more sheepish. But I still had grave concerns after that conversation.

The next day I was really busy, so we didn't talk until that evening. He told me he'd smoked ten cigarettes that day. The day before he'd only had two.

When he came to visit me in Sydney a few days later, he didn't have any money. There were some things I was willing to pay for, and things I wasn't. I'd refuse to buy him cigarettes – but I did do things like pay for his licence renewal.

We were having lunch at Darling Harbour when he asked me a question I wasn't ready to answer: 'So, when are you going to sleep with me? No, really. Were you thinking of doing it next week, or the twenty-eighth of December?'

I laughed. It was April.

'I don't want to pressure you,' he added. 'But you know, if I could have got you pregnant back when we were in high school, I would have. That way, if another guy looks at you, I can go, "She's mine. Quit looking at her."'

'I always wanted to be the mother of your children.'

'True?'

'Yes, for real.' I started to share with him the story of the song I had written, inspired by him – the one I'd shared with Jimmy Little and had included on the mix CD.

'You know, I used to think songs had three verses – probably because I listen to so much rap. When I was in Tamworth, I wrote a song about how much I missed you. I had to cut the third verse, but it went something like this.' I began reciting the lyrics, pointing out that I had written them for a man to sing: *I always thought that you / would be the one to have my child / That she would look just like you with that same amazing smile / I always thought that you would / wear my ring and be my wife / But I guess nothing is certain / in this everchanging life.*

The look on Tyce's face was one of wonder and longing, like he was trying to will himself back in time. We walked to my car, where I presented him with a new guitar I had bought him.

He was speechless. His first instinct was to gesture that he couldn't accept it, but his demeanour changed almost immediately.

He spoke of how he needed to get accustomed to accepting acts of kindness.

'This is the first new guitar I've ever had,' he said. 'I've only ever had second-hand ones.'

I felt chuffed.

He later sent me a text saying he had named his guitar 'Missy' because 'she sounds so sweet'. He had been strumming away on it 24/7, honing his skills, and he'd even started to write a song about me. But that's when his past, he said, caught up with him. His parents had kicked him out over something he swore to me he didn't do. He said even though he was trying to do good now, he was labelled for life. I decided to go back to Muswellbrook to be with him and offer some support.

We stayed at a pub in Aberdeen. The pained look on Tyce's face as I paid for the room on my credit card failed to hide his embarrassment.

'Aww, Marnz,' he said. 'Thank you.' We had the choice of two dingy rooms, and I chose the one with two beds in it, even though I was pretty sure we would only be using one. The cement walls had cracks that reached from the ceiling and snaked their way down-wards like varicose veins. The paint was peeling off the ceiling.

'So, what happened with your parents? Why did they kick you out?'

'They accused me of going around to someone's place and roughing them up. I told them it wasn't true, and that I liked them better as drunks. At least they'd stand up for us then.' He said his mum still hadn't forgiven him for saying that – she had been sober for ten years.

Tyce sat on the single bed and looked at me. He was visibly nervous. Sweat was dripping down his forehead. He wiped his brow. 'You know, I hate it when you pay for everything. I've only ever been cashed up or stretched, like I am now. I've never just been comfortable. All it would take for me to set us up would be one armed robbery,' he said.

'You're not actually considering that, are you?'

'No,' he said. 'I promised you I wouldn't do that shit again, and I mean it. But you know, one robbery and I'd have enough money to pay for our wedding.'

He got out his guitar; he wanted to sing the song he had written for me. He was sitting on the bed in blue jeans, shirt off, revealing a muscly physique he hadn't had in high school, but which suited him now to a tee. He looked so hot. I decided to film him.

'Love ya, Marnz,' he said before launching into the most beautiful song I'd ever heard, his vulnerability shining through the lyrics. My hands shook at certain moments as I listened on intently. I was so touched by his words. He sang about our first kiss – he might have really liked me before, but 'like' became 'love' the moment our lips touched. He sang about how nervous he felt around me, how my smile made his heart flutter. He sang about how much he wanted me to be his, how he would do anything for me – anything to make me smile. My recording was interrupted by a phone call from Amber. I told Tyce we'd try again later. But that never happened.

I had made Tyce wait three weeks, which was a big deal for me. It had been about sixteen years since we had last made love, so it was a very significant moment for me. Afterwards, we lay there and talked. There was something I'd always wondered – something I had to ask him from our teenage years about the guy I'd lost my virginity to.

'Did you tell Dots not to call me?' I asked him. 'April said you told him not to call me.'

'Yeah, I did,' he said.

'Why?'

'He was talking shit about you in the boy's toilets. It took me a minute to work out who he was talking about, but when I did, I froze. I slammed him up against the mirror, but I didn't say anything. My look said it all.'

'What did he say?'

'I'm not going to repeat it,' he said. 'He was talking about you like you were one of "those" girls. That's all I'll say. A couple of his friends came up to me afterwards and asked me, "What did you do that to Dots for?" They got the beating that Dots missed out on. If it had been anyone other than Dots, I would have fucked him up real bad. I tolerated him for the rest of his life after that. I hate to talk bad about the Indigenous dead, but our friendship ended.'

Dots had died by suicide years earlier. Despite the fact I hadn't seen him for years, I'd been profoundly saddened by the news of his death. It had floored me, and I'd shed tears for him and his family. According to his sister, April, he had thought the world of me. She also called bullshit on the whole scenario, saying Dots never said a bad word about anyone, least of all me. If there's something I've learned, it's that people are complicated, multifaceted. The whole situation was tragic.

'Was he Indigenous?'

'Yeah. His mum is a Blackfulla. I was really cut. If you really had been one of "those" girls, I probably would have let it slide, but I knew you weren't.'

'I lost my virginity to him,' I said.

'I know. I used to worry about you so much. I thought if you could associate with a scumbag like him . . . I was worried about other guys feeding you drinks at the bar and trying to take advantage of you.'

It finally made sense to me why Tyce said he used to worry about me so much. The way he delivered this story, with such raw emotion – as if it had just happened yesterday – mixed with an element of detachment . . . It broke my heart. He was holding me as we lay in bed. I pulled him tighter.

Tyce got up in the middle of the night and disappeared for a couple of hours to, as he explained, get rid of his guns. He had been keeping the .410 shotgun in case anyone ever hurt his children. He was determined to change. He wanted to rid himself of anything that was tying him to his life of crime because, as he always said, 'You can't be a little bit pregnant.' If you're going to do something, you have to go all the way.

♪♫

In the morning, we drove to his mate Chase's house.

'Do you have any other music?' Tyce asked, scrolling through my iPod. 'Dr. Dre? Snoop? Ice Cube?'

'I did in the '90s,' I said. 'I thought you liked hip hop.'

'I do, as long as it was made between '92 and '96. My love for hip hop only extends to those years.' He had a smile on his face.

Chase lived in that area of South Muswellbrook known as 'The Bronx'. Having been to the *actual* Bronx, I thought naming this slice of the town after such a vibrant, dynamic borough was a bit rich. Sure, there was a dangerous edge to each, but the comparisons ended there.

Chase was really friendly when Tyce introduced us. He was a good friend to my baby.

CHAPTER 32

Inspired by Love and Anger

How can I expect God to listen to me when I pray,
when I'm not listening to Him?

'People don't change,' Tyce told me.

'Of course they do. I've changed a lot. I'm a completely different person to who I was.'

'People don't change,' he repeated. 'People adapt, evolve, readjust. They don't *change*. If you've changed, then who am I in love with?'

That was a good question.

We walked towards the Aboriginal hostel in Leichhardt, in Sydney's Inner West. Tyce had earlier presented me with a gift – an incredible piece of artwork he'd painted. It was gorgeous – a landscape in the colours of the Aboriginal flag: a sky fading from brilliant red to burnt ochre, the yellow sun setting on the black outline of mallee scrubland, a lithe man with a spear, hunting. Along with the song he'd written, it was one of the nicest gifts I'd ever received. I cherished them both.

We walked to the office, where Tyce registered his name. I lent Tyce money so he could pay the upfront costs of staying at the hostel. I wasn't aware at that stage that I would never get it back.

We went upstairs. 'Wow,' he said, surveying the room. 'This place is smaller than my cell at Long Bay. I guess it's slightly larger than the one at Silverwater though.'

I laughed. 'How come you've been to so many jails anyway?'

''Cos every time I play up, they move me. It's not like there's any incentive to be good in there. It's not like there are women at some jails, and if you behave you get to go to one of them. You know, it's not right that I get locked up so often. I'm just an Aussie larrikin. Australians love an Aussie larrikin. Look at the way they go on about Ned Kelly. People should love me too. I'm a good bloke. I'm just cheeky.'

We cuddled together on the single bed, lying side by side. I was so in love. I told him so.

'Marnz, I love you too. That big, big love.'

'Hi, Victoria.' I had left Tyce for a moment to look for a coffee shop in the area when Victoria Richards called.

'I'm so happy for you,' she gushed. On a weekend away with the girls from school, Victoria had expressed sympathy for me, saying I was unlucky in love. She'd said she couldn't understand why that was the case and how sad she was for me. It'd brought tears to my eyes. As we talked, I remembered that moment. Now, my story was different.

When I rejoined Tyce, he was downstairs with the Aboriginal

woman who ran the hostel. She was laying out the rules of the place.

'You're not allowed to take anyone upstairs to your room,' she said, not knowing that I'd already been up there. Tyce and I looked at each other, then at her.

'Okay,' we said in unison.

We went to the TV room to hang out, where a young woman who looked as if she'd had a hard life was watching a Tupac documentary. I later burned copies of every Tupac album Sedudzi had: *2Pacalypse Now, Me Against the World, All Eyez on Me, Strictly For My N.I.G.G.A.Z.* – except I annoyingly forgot to burn *Makaveli*, because it wasn't labelled as a Tupac album on iTunes.

A couple of days later, the woman tried to hand me 10 dollars for the CDs.

'No,' I said. 'Keep the money. It's a gift.'

'No,' she insisted. 'Take it.' She was no charity case.

Tyce reached his hand out and took the note. 'Thank you, sis,' he said with a smile. And when she left: 'Don't ever say no when someone offers you money.'

♪♫

When we made love in my car later that day, followed by one of our increasingly explosive fights, I had no idea that it would be the last time. Our fights were usually centred around a perceived lack of respect or a misunderstanding. He would misread me or think I was judging him, when I wasn't. I would often object to his tone, feeling as if he was belittling me. This particular fight was prompted by the fact he was high and talking shit. I drove off and left him not far from the hostel.

On the way back from church one Sunday morning, I confided in Tyce that I felt guilty about the fact we were Christians but still having sex out of wedlock.

'Well, that's it,' he said. 'No more sex.' I wasn't aware at that stage that he meant it. 'I don't want to be responsible for you sinning, so we're not going to have sex anymore. I've been to jail – I know how to entertain myself sufficiently.'

That's how it started, but his 'no sex' rule soon turned into a method of control. It was his way of keeping me in my place, punishing me for daring to love him.

Eventually, we moved into a rental apartment in Lilyfield in the Inner West together. We slept in the same bed – and yet he refused to sleep with me. Even though I was conflicted about sex, it had still been a powerful expression of our love for one another, a kind of communion in its own right. That he could resist me in this way made me feel neglected – not to mention unsexy.

When we applied for the apartment we lived in, I told the real estate agent I planned to live there with my boyfriend, and I was told the owner wanted everyone who was going to live there to be listed on the application form, with proof of income and previous residences listed.

'What am I going to put there?' Tyce asked, 'Silverwater Maximum Security?' We decided it was best to leave him off, given that we really wanted the place.

Tyce asked the boss at the building site up the road whether they had any work going and received a positive response, which was great news. I knew finding work would make him feel more secure, that he could contribute to the household, and it would also take the pressure off me. I was still on long service leave for six months on half pay and had been giving my credit card a workout.

When Tyce placed 20 cents into the offering plate in church one morning with so much gusto and pride, I was speechless. The pastor had preached about the blessings an offering would unleash, so Tyce had given all he had. It came straight from his heart.

Tyce and I joined a Connect Group at the same church. I thought it was going to be more of a Bible study, and I was excited to learn more about Scripture and grow in my faith. Instead, it was more of a social gathering – we ate, we prayed, we chatted . . . and that was it. On the way back from our first Connect, Tyce turned to me in the car. 'You know, I've been locked up with murderers and rapists, but I have never been as nervous as when I walked into that Connect Group. I'm not used to people being that nice to me.'

As we drove home, Tyce opened up about what it was like in jail – how on his first day in a maximum-security prison he was given a shiv, and told there was a war on between the Koories and the Asians. He was told to stab them if something started, before they had a chance to stab him. Jail was a violent place. Jail was a lonely place. Jail was a place that fed off and reinforced his trauma.

When we got home, another argument ensued, except this one had none of the venom of previous disagreements we had got ourselves into. The topic: asylum seekers.

'How dare they come to our country and expect us to roll out the red carpet when they've broken the law,' he said as he spooned four teaspoons of sugar into his coffee.

'You've broken the law plenty of times yourself, Tyce.'

'Yeah, well, I've paid for everything I did.' That was true. I tried another tack.

'You know, I was an asylum seeker. My parents came here illegally on a boat,' I lied, trying to prove a point.

'Really?'

I nodded.

'Well, you already know there's a different rule for you than there is for anyone else. I don't care if you came on a boat.'

'That doesn't even make sense. And, actually, we came by plane – *legally*. What would you do if you'd grown up in a country where bombs were going off outside your window and you and your family were in constant danger of being killed? Wouldn't you pack your bags and hop on a leaky boat to save the lives of your children?'

'Why are you letting other people's problems tear us apart? Don't let what anyone else is up to affect our relationship. I love you. Even the stuff about you that drives me crazy I wouldn't change because it's a part of you.' He took a sip of his sugar-laden coffee. 'I don't think you love me that way. If you did, you'd be far meaner to me. You'd flog me across the head every now and then.' He laughed.

That's not love! I wanted to scream. 'You can tell I love you because I'm *not* doing those things! Nigga—'

'I ain't no nigga,' he said. 'I'm Aboriginal, a Dunghutti man, a Gomeroi man, a Blackfulla, Koori. Call me what you want, but I ain't no nigga.'

I looked at him in wonder and used every ounce of restraint I had to refrain from saying what I was thinking at the time: *Well, that's no better!* I was from a marginalised community, but I had it much better than he did in Australia – in his own country. While I was damn near invisible as an African Australian, he was maligned by people with real power, to the point where life wasn't just hard but it took an enormous amount of determination to get ahead. And even then – even if you did make it – people would try to cut you down because they don't like uppity Blacks in Australia; they don't like tall poppies. You better know your place.

Top of mind was rarely the injustices Aboriginal people had suffered and continue to contend with – dispossession, inter-generational trauma, general negativity and stereotypes. Top of mind was never the fact that white Australians today are still bene-fitting from structures their forefathers put in place, to the detriment of marginalised communities. Top of mind was never the systemic racism that disproportionately incarcerates Black people – where kids as young as ten are being locked up, their futures squandered.

Top of mind instead, for some, were racist attitudes that placed blame on the oppressed.

Despite policies designed to eradicate an entire population and their way of being, Aboriginal and Torres Strait Islander cultures remain rich and diverse. There are Indigenous Australians doing big things in business, politics, academia, sport, music, media, dance, art, literature and education.

But life was hard, the playing field was not even – and no one demonstrated that more than my baby.

'Anyway,' I said. 'I've never really felt at home in Australia. I don't really feel like I belong anywhere. When I was in Ghana, people treated me like I wasn't from there – because I'd spent so much time away from the continent – and here I get asked every day where I'm from. It's the most annoying thing in the world. I feel like an alien.'

'Yeah, so do I, and I've got nowhere else to call home. I feel like an alien in my own country. It ain't easy to get ahead here. If there's one thing I really want it's to leave a house to my children. Dad bought his own house. I wanna do that too – and be able to pass it on to my kids.'

'Well, you're going to need multiple houses since you're populating the world.'

Before he could reply, I quickly changed the topic.

'Let's go get lunch in Newtown, and after lunch, let's get dessert. I know a place that makes the best fried ice-cream.' I looked at him excitedly, my mouth watering at the idea. 'I'll just put the washing out and then we'll go.'

Tyce looked at me warily. 'Yeah . . . okay,' he said.

We had lunch at a Thai place and then walked up the road to the Chinese restaurant, where we ordered our fried ice-cream.

'This is sweet as,' Tyce said.

'I know, right? So you've never had fried ice-cream before?'

He looked at me and shook his head. 'Years ago, I was out at the Chinese restaurant in Mussy with a bunch of people. We had a really nice meal. We were all having a great time. It was mad. Then one of the guys looks me straight in the eye and says, "Tyce, do you want some fried ice-cream?" I got up out of my seat and told him to fuck off. I thought he was taking the piss. Men can't get pregnant, and there's no such thing as fried ice-cream – that's what I thought at the time. We were out having this nice meal and then this guy goes and fucks it up by offering me something that doesn't exist. I had no idea all this time that fried ice-cream is actually a thing.'

Wow, I thought, *you've spent your whole life being misunderstood by others, but you've also misconstrued genuine niceties.*

I ended up leaving the washing out for a day too long. When I went down to collect it, the line had been nearly picked clean. My gorgeous Chinese-character-print bedspread and pillow cases, the red blanket my mother had given me, even my Nike socks – gone. The only thing they'd left was my underwear. *So, this is what it feels like to have stuff you value taken from you*, I thought. *Bastards.*

♪♫

The next day, Tyce and I were hanging out near the Opera House when it started to rain. A woman walked past, pushing a pram. Tyce went in for the kill. 'What is that woman doing pushing a pram in the rain? That poor baby is going to get all wet. She's an idiot. Don't you think she's an idiot?' I shrugged my shoulders. He turned on me. 'You wouldn't walk around in the rain with a pram, would you?'

I avoided the question. It was a stupid hypothetical. He repeated himself. 'You wouldn't walk around in the rain pushing a pram with *our* baby in it, would you?'

'Tyce –'

'No, seriously, would you?'

What came out of my mouth next was admittedly the most stupid thing I could say – the equivalent of pouring petrol on a simmering fire. 'What if we were homeless because you fucked up?' I asked.

That was it. I'd hit a raw nerve with an entirely probable scenario to his hypothetical question.

'What did you just say?' He squared his shoulders. He was mad. He sulked until we got home.

Tyce feigned a call with his sister, which I thought was real at the time, 'Yeah, I want you to come bash her for me. Yeah, sis. Sounds good. See you soon.' A full-blown argument ensued. 'I'm going to kill you, your whole family and half of Africa!' he spat.

'I'm leaving,' I said, and started to put my shoes on. He knew I was serious and quickly began to back-pedal.

'No, don't go,' he pleaded. 'If you go, I've got nothing to lose, and a man with nothing to lose is a very dangerous thing.'

I heaved a sigh. I was trapped in an apartment with a man who had just threatened to kill me, and I couldn't leave because God knows what he would do next. Equal parts distraught and terrified, I went to our room and shut the door while he slept in the lounge room.

In the morning, he came into the room. 'I'm so sorry,' he said. 'I didn't mean what I said. Sometimes I just get so wild and say things I don't mean, and people take me seriously. That's how come I've been in so much trouble.'

The phone call with Laura he'd feigned is what really upset me. Laura had always treated me with respect – she was a sister to me. I explained that to him. 'I'm not your enemy. I love you. I'm sorry about what I said, but you can't carry on like that. I should be able to make mistakes without that sort of reaction.'

'I know. I'm sorry. I love you too.'

He was so conciliatory. I forgave him, despite taking the threats against my family seriously. He'd said enough though to convince me that he didn't mean what he'd said. When I told a friend about the threats, she responded, 'You, your whole family and half of Africa? Well, he's ambitious.'

After we'd come to an uneasy truce over our differences, I offered to drive him to Hamilton, because there was heavy traffic on the way to the train station. He had an appointment at an Aboriginal medical centre and dental clinic, where he was going to have his missing teeth replaced. While we were there, he said he wanted to visit his friend's mother.

'You might as well,' I said. 'It's not my day today. I'm not going to get to do anything I want to do.' I said it in a matter-of-fact manner, simply pointing out that he might as well make the most of it – it was his day, not mine. But my words set him off again.

'How about you go back to Sydney and do what you want to do so I can stay here and do what I have to do?' he yelled. 'You're the type of person who does someone a favour so you can rub it in their face afterwards. Just fuck off back home.'

So, I left him. I drove off and left the bastard.

A week after moving in together, I decided it was time to call it quits. I'd resigned myself to the fact that this relationship was not going to work – it was becoming too toxic. But in the same way you're pulled back to the things you love, despite their capacity to destroy you, the break-up didn't last long.

John and I were visiting Dad in hospital after his knee replacement.

I wanted to be there for Dad, like I knew he would be there for me. (I would give him the opportunity a few years later when

I was hospitalised after an operation gone terribly wrong. I can still remember sitting up in my bed, looking at Dad, my heart full, my eyes smiling. He visited me almost every day, missing just one day because he was undergoing radiation treatment for prostate cancer. He had his own serious health issues but made sure he was there for me.)

John told me he wholeheartedly supported my decision to break up with Tyce. While John had been mostly AWOL during the relationship, he was now okay being in my life again, and I was grateful.

Shortly after the visit, though, Tyce sent me a text message saying he was sorry – he'd lost the only light in his life – and it touched me. I realised I had spent more than fifteen years trying to get over him, but I couldn't. In my heart of hearts I still loved him, for better or worse. I couldn't bear to be without him, and so I invited him back into my life.

We decided to take things slower this time, and to seek counselling. Our relationship was rocky. But there was hope.

John didn't hide his disappointment; he decided to go AWOL again.

CHAPTER 33

Because He Lives

Ignoring the warning signs can only end in pain.

Ping. I was lying on a massage table when my phone went off. I thought little of it. What *was* on my mind was the ferocity with which the massage therapist was working his 'magic'. It was anything but relaxing.

'Ouch. Too firm.'

The therapist eased up a little. It was as if he went from piercing my skin with a power drill to using that same drill to knead and prod me, after being generous enough to switch off the power.

I had dropped Dad off at rehab for his knee replacement that morning and thought I might as well get pampered while I waited. Some idea that was.

After an hour of torture, I sat up, got dressed and reached for my phone. I had a Facebook message from Tyce's brother, Xander: *Tyce got shot in the leg. He's in hospital. He's stable.*

What the fuck? I thought. *Tyce has been shot?*

I fired off an immediate response: *What the . . . Which hospital is he in?*

The replies came quickly, and it appeared that Tyce was in Muswellbrook Hospital, getting ready to be transferred to John Hunter in Newcastle. I called the hospital in Muswellbrook straightaway to see if I could talk to him. The nurse who answered the phone told me Tyce was downstairs having a cigarette. *Well, he must be alright if he's outside smoking*, I thought, and indeed hoped. Tyce rang me a little later. He said his friend Chase had inexplicably shot him when he went around to visit.

'I went in through the side door, like I always do. Chase shot me from another room, and then asked me if I wanted another one in the chest when I complained. It took me a minute to work out that I'd been shot. He had a silencer on the gun. It wasn't until I looked down at my leg that I saw the blood. The cops took the shoes you bought me as evidence.'

'*Evidence?*'

I had bought Tyce a pair of Nike sneakers for his birthday. We called them Sunrise Nikes, because they resembled the colours of the Aboriginal flag – black, red that faded to yellow but with orange in the middle.

'Yeah, evidence. They had blood on them.'

Tyce told me how Chase's mother, who lived next door, saw Tyce leaving the house after the shooting. He acted as if nothing was up. He had suitcases with him, and used them to cover his leg. He then got on his pushbike and rode to the nearest phone booth, where he rang his sister's ex, who came and took him to hospital. At first Tyce was telling people he'd been shot while riding his bike across Bowman Park, which of course was farcical.

Tyce was soon transferred to John Hunter Hospital. I raced over to be with him. He was his same old hilarious self. 'Hey, watch me tell this doctor to kiss my arse.' He winked at me.

'Ay, Doc.' Tyce motioned one of the doctors over. 'Doc, at the other hospital one of the doctors kissed my arse and said it tasted like chocolate. I want a second opinion.'

I didn't try to hide my laughter.

'Doc, are you familiar with CTG?' Tyce continued. 'I just asked the nurse here and she's never heard of it.'

'CTG?' The doctor asked, confused.

'Yeah,' Tyce said. 'Closing. The. Gap.' He was referring to the federal government's intention to address the disparity between Indigenous and non-Indigenous Australians when it came to inequality – including in health.

'CTG means something else in medical terms,' the doctor explained.

Tyce motioned for another doctor to come over and asked him the same question. That doctor wasn't familiar with the term CTG either.

'Well, I guess it's safe to say the gap isn't closing,' Tyce said.

I sat hovering over Tyce as I waited for him to wake up from surgery.

'Hi,' his surgeon said, walking into the room. 'Hey, you're from Muswellbrook, right?' he asked. It turned out he was from there as well. He was a friend of Tyce's who had grown up on Wollombi Road, proving it doesn't matter where you're from. Success can visit anybody.

Tyce would later tell me that Dr Fischer had read the job description for a surgeon and thought, *I can do that.* And indeed he did do that.

We sat and waited for Tyce to wake up. When he came to, Dr Fischer tried to lighten the mood: 'Hey, mate. I saw your dick when we were in surgery. Just saying . . .'

I laughed, and so did Tyce – a sure sign he was on the road to recovery.

Once Tyce was settled into his ward, I visited him regularly. Sometimes I'd walk in and find him with Dr Fischer.

'Cigarettes are the worst,' I overheard Dr Fischer telling Tyce. 'They kill the blood cells behind your eyes, which can lead to blindness. The smoke goes through your lungs and enters your bloodstream, affecting every part of your body.'

He turned to face me and said hello. When he left the room, Tyce said, 'That guy is a walking, talking anti-smoking commercial. He even told me what ward I would end up in if I don't quit – F1, where the dementia patients are.' We cracked up.

Back at the cottage that afternoon, I got a message from Xander: *I appreciate you being there, Marnz. Tell Tyce that Chase was shot dead last night by police.*

Whoa, I thought. *What the hell?* Tyce had told me to pray for Chase, and I hadn't – now this. I felt guilty, dumbfounded that this could have happened. I walked over to the hospital, not knowing how I was going to break the news.

When I did tell Tyce, he was shocked too. 'Oh, good God,' he said, tears welling up in his eyes. 'Chase . . . *Chase*,' Tyce repeated over and over again. Then he said, 'Wait a minute. This story sounds suss.' He rang his brother, who only had scant details before he said he had to go cook dinner.

'*Really?*' Tyce said to me. 'He had to go and cook dinner?' It was laughable. 'I just refuse to believe Chase was killed by gunfire in a showdown with police. I'm gonna call some others.' He phoned around. No one else had heard the news. After a while, Tyce decided it was false information – which it was. Our nervous laughter conveyed our relief.

Eventually, Tyce was discharged from the hospital and released into my care. Things should have been easier for us. He'd survived a shooting. We were building a home together. But our life together was never going to get easier. The construction job hadn't eventuated, and he was still without work – something I linked to his jail record. He was a statistic. Locked up at such a young age, he stood little chance – especially with recidivism such a key issue. The rate of Indigenous imprisonment was more than thirteen times higher than the imprisonment rate for non-Indigenous Australians. According to the 2017 Uluru Statement from the Heart, 'Proportionally, [First Nations people] are the most incarcerated people on the planet.'

Tyce's father had a great job when Tyce was growing up, but his mother was for many years afflicted by alcoholism, no doubt brought on by the trauma she'd experienced having had two siblings stolen. Tyce had a lot to deal with on top of whatever hardships everybody else deals with generally. We were living in different worlds, and so we were doomed. But I had to learn the hard way.

CHAPTER 34

My Beliefs

Love is never enough. Not when there are so many other things missing – like understanding and respect.

I honestly thought he might buy me a bunch of flowers because he had some money coming in that day: for being a good girlfriend to him. For loving him. For being faithful. For nursing him back to health.

Instead, when Tyce got his dole payment, he went to the pub. We had had a fight the previous night. He'd asked me what was wrong (twice apparently), and according to him I ignored him. So he got really angry.

'If you're going to show me that type of disrespect, you'll get the same from me,' he said. I got really upset. It had never been my intention to disrespect him.

'I can't talk to you,' I said. 'That's what's wrong.' I had always wanted to be in a relationship with someone I could talk to about anything and everything, the sour and the sweet.

I was genuinely sad. I felt trapped. *Is this all there is?* I asked myself.

Tyce was still refusing to sleep with me. The pain from the devastating fights we continuously had may have been alleviated if we'd truly made up. If he held me, caressed me, made love to me. But no.

'Your eyes are dilated,' Tyce said. 'You need to get them to jack up your medication.'

The comment cut me deeply. I yelled at him. He flung another insult my way. And then, calmly, he said, 'The thing is, with my record, I'm going to be the one who'll get taken away.'

I retreated behind the closed bedroom door again. I was scared of his anger, I was scared about what our future held. *Is this what life with him is always going to be like?*

He slept in the lounge room again that night, coming into the room briefly to say he loved me – all he wanted to do was talk. But there was nothing I could say that wouldn't fuel his anger. Like Drake, he could go from zero to a hundred in a matter of seconds. One minute he was telling me there was no one who could love me as much as he did, the next he wasn't loving me at all.

The next day he grabbed my car keys and was about to drive to the bank to withdraw his Centrelink payment, after I had already told him I was leaving in ten minutes.

I had an appointment with my psychologist, who I'd been seeing for about a year. She was really good – nothing like the counsellor I'd seen back in high school. I had already postponed this appointment for Tyce, so he could make it to a doctor's appointment and then a Centrelink appointment the previous week.

He yelled at me. 'I was going so I could give you money. I would have been back before you left.'

I got a call from him during my appointment. When I called him back, he had calmed down. 'Listen, Marnz, I don't want to fight with you,' he said. 'I love you.'

'I love you too,' I said. 'Is it okay if I get back around two this afternoon?' He had a Joblink appointment at three o'clock. He hesitated but said okay, so I went to get my hair done. I did something for myself for a change. I called him at around two and asked him if he wanted me to meet him somewhere, so I could take him to his Joblink appointment.

'Yeah, I'm at the pub,' he said.

'Which one?'

'I don't know. It's on Darling Street.'

I went to the pub I thought he would be at, but it turned out to be the wrong one. I called him again. He asked someone next to him where he was, and they said the Red Lion Hotel and gave him the address. Tyce was animated when we spoke, excited. I could hear the noises of the poker machine he was playing in the background – it made a sound indicating a win.

'I've just won about four hundred bucks,' he said.

'How much did you put in?' I asked.

'About ten dollars.'

When I arrived he was still playing the pokies, drinking from a glass of beer that was filled almost to the top.

'Do you want a bourbon or something?' he asked.

'You know I don't drink,' I said, and walked off to the ladies. He said something disparaging as I left.

When I returned he faced me. 'Do you want to go on a date

329

sometime? You know, a real one – where I pay for our meals?' It truly broke my heart. It was obvious our living arrangement – where I paid for everything – got to him even more than it got to me. I smiled and said yes. He started feeding another 20-dollar note into the machine.

'I'm going to wait in the car,' I said.

'Well, fuck off back home then.'

I went and waited in the car for a while. Dominos was close by and I was starving, so I ordered a pizza. Tyce had already eaten a pub steak and veggies, he'd told me, for 10 dollars, which he said was nice.

After a while, I went back inside the pub and asked for the keys to the house. 'Are you coming with me?' I asked.

'Yeah, but you won't wait for me.'

I told him I would and went back to the car. Fifteen minutes or so later, he showed up, wobbly on his feet. He took his shirt off and got in the car. I drove home, which was just around the corner.

As I was parking the car, my hand brushed up against his leg.

'Oh . . . you just touched me. Do you want to make love?'

I felt the electricity shoot through my groin at the mention of it. 'I thought I was banned,' I said.

'Are we going to have babies?'

He was desperate to have kids with me. When I asked him the other day how we would support them, he'd said with a child pension. A child pension! 'You're going to miss out on one of life's most beautiful gifts because you're worried about money,' he'd said.

His question hung in the air. *Are we going to have babies?*

'No,' I said.

'Why?'

'So many reasons, Tyce.'

When I reflect on this moment, I realise that comment would have hurt him deeply. While we were watching TV days earlier, a commercial came on urging men to buy their partners a diamond ring: 'That's how you show your love.'

Tyce had scoffed. 'That's not how you show your love! You show your love by having a baby.'

I parked the car and we got out.

'Did you see your psychologist today?' he asked.

'Yes,' I said.

'Tell 'em I said I'm gonna fuck 'em up.' I started crying. 'You're weak. Tell them to jack up your medication.' By then he was yelling. I was conscious of the neighbours tuning in to our argument.

'Drop me off at the train station,' he said.

'No.'

'Drop me off at the fucking train station!'

'No.'

His voice got louder and more aggressive. I hopped back in the car and went to start the engine to drop him off.

'I hate you,' I said. 'Don't bother coming back.'

'Don't worry about it,' he said, suddenly abandoning the idea of me driving him to the train station. 'Give me the money I just gave you.' He had given me a hundred dollars rent in the car after Centrelink (and the pokies) had come through, and he'd left two hundred on the dressing room table.

'No,' I said. 'You owe me that money. You actually owe me *double* that amount.' He'd made one rent payment since we'd moved in together, and I had returned it to him when we briefly split.

'Give me the money,' he repeated.

'No.' I got out of the car again.

'I'm going to burn out your fucking car,' he said.

I quickly shut the car door and locked it before starting to make my way inside.

He grabbed my arm. 'I'm going to smash you.'

I could see one of our neighbours looking at us from across the road.

'Well, let's get some witnesses up in this motherfucker.' Emboldened, I moved away from the doors of the apartment and towards the street. The neighbour got up and went inside.

Tyce pulled on my hoodie, which choked against my neck as I tried to move away. I screamed.

One of the residents in our apartment block called out to him. I didn't hear what they said, but I could hear Tyce's response.

'I'm not a grub. Don't call me a grub. Come down here so I can fuck you up.'

With his attention off me for a moment, I quickly swiped the keycard, went inside and waited till the glass doors slid shut. I started walking towards the elevator.

A curly haired woman was getting out as I got in.

'Don't go out there,' I said. 'My boyfriend is trying to get in.'

'Is that your boyfriend? I was going to go out there and stab him,' she said. If she had a weapon, it was concealed, but could this situation get any more shocking? 'Do you want to come back to our apartment? We're on level four.'

'No, I just want to go home.' I was clearly upset, and I wasn't keen to hang out with someone who had just admitted wanting to stab my partner.

Tyce was still yelling at the neighbours when I got upstairs. He hit the intercom button a few times, but I wouldn't let him in. I tried to talk to him through the speakers, but it was obvious he wasn't listening.

The police showed up shortly afterwards. One of the neighbours must have called them. About seven police officers showed up in three cars, which seemed like a ridiculous number. I could see Tyce getting handcuffed from the balcony. My heart broke all over again. I called out to the police officers and raced downstairs.

'I'm his partner,' I said.

'Stand back,' an officer responded. 'He might see you, and that can only aggravate the situation.' The comment was too much to bear. Is this what we'd come to?

They put him in the back of the paddy wagon. He was still yelling at the neighbours. 'I'm going to get you,' he said. 'You watch.'

An Aboriginal Liaison Officer was brought in to try to calm things down, but his presence did not have a calming influence on Tyce. A police officer must have leaned a little too heavily on his leg at one point, because Tyce called out in pain, telling them he'd recently been shot.

A few of the police officers came over one by one to question me. I was worried Tyce might think I was the one who'd called the police. I didn't want them there. I didn't want him put away. He'd been in enough trouble. I didn't want to inadvertently lead him into deeper waters. It hurt to see him hurting.

'I don't want to press charges,' I said.

'It's not up to you,' one of the cops replied. 'It's taken out of your hands in domestic violence cases 'cos the women often say exactly what you just said.'

This is a domestic violence case? I thought. *What the fuck?*

It took a while for that idea to sink in. Later, I realised that domestic violence isn't just about being hit by your partner – it's having your partner threaten to kill you; it's having your partner use sex as a control mechanism; it's having a partner gaslight you, making you feel like you're crazy and using your mental illness as proof that you are indeed crazy. There were so many signs I was in a domestic violence situation, but it was also very difficult to accept because I loved him. He loved me.

One of the police officers asked me if I could give a statement. I didn't want to in case it landed Tyce in even more trouble.

'What happens if I don't?' I asked.

'We'll charge him,' the officer said.

'Okay, I'll give a statement.'

Little did I know the cops were going to charge him anyway. One of the officers asked if they could come upstairs to take the statement. I was so embarrassed when they walked into the flat. It looked as if a tornado had hit it – unwashed dishes piled up in the kitchen sink, clothes scattered across the floor, empty bottles on the coffee table.

A couple of the officers introduced themselves briefly and then started asking questions, including whether Tyce and I had been intimate when we were teenagers. They told me they were asking because that's how they can establish whether someone is in a domestic relationship or not. It sounded more like they were being nosy to me.

After I had given my statement, they told me they would keep Tyce overnight and call me to pick him up in the morning. I went down to the station briefly to drop off the medication he'd been taking for his gunshot wound, his bag and his Bible.

The cops didn't call me in the morning. They let him go after a few hours and placed an AVO on him that stated he couldn't come near our apartment within seventy-two hours of drinking. This made me angry. It meant he couldn't come home – even if he wanted to.

I didn't know where he was. He was just gone. All this happened on a Monday. Come Thursday, I still hadn't heard from him. As far as I was concerned, it was over.

And so I responded by reaching out to Bravo, who had contacted me out of the blue a couple of weeks earlier, wanting to hook up. He had moved into music marketing, and was married with a daughter, one who I was shocked to see in a photo he had on his desk in the office he snuck me into: she was Black. I had mistakenly thought he fetishised Black women but would marry within his own race – I had seen that happen a lot with men from London, but it was much deeper than that. I didn't allow myself to think about the fact he was married. I didn't dwell on it. I was numb to reality. Technically, since I hadn't spoken with Tyce, I was still in a relationship too. This truism was reinforced when I later received a text message from Tyce via a payphone: JUST SAYIN LOVE YA ALWAYS.

But I just couldn't. The comedy had worn thin. He made me cry more often than he made me laugh. I broke up with him via text, telling him I deserved better and I wasn't going to stay in a relationship where I wasn't appreciated. I needed to be treated right.

Sometimes love isn't enough. Sometimes love doesn't conquer all. I just couldn't walk around on eggshells anymore – his temper was too much. The threats of harm, and the constant ridicule and put-downs were too much.

When a cop dropped by to serve Tyce with some papers, I told him we were no longer living together.

'You love him?' the cop asked.

'Of course I do.'

'A guy like that will always be in trouble. Always. You're best to stay away.'

I felt like saying, *Well, if you guys would just stop arresting him, he'd be in a little less trouble.* For fuck's sake, how did he stand a chance? He'd been marked since he was a kid.

I called Victoria Richards and told her it was over, explaining what had happened.

'I'm so sorry,' she said. 'I thought if anyone could get through to him it would be you. I thought the two of you were meant to be together. You loved each other so much. I thought you were exactly what he needed, that you'd be able to help him change.'

People don't change. Those were Tyce's words to me not so long ago. *People don't change.*

I ended up driving to Muswellbrook with Mum weeks later to drop Tyce's belongings off at Laura's house.

'Thank you for doing this,' Laura said. 'A lot of women in your position wouldn't have bothered.'

'That's not a problem,' I said.

'Tyce was going to come and see you. He was moping around, singing the blues. I guess he decided it was all too much for him.'

When Mum and I arrived back in Sydney, the gravity of it all hit me. My mind flashed back to the two of us as teenagers and then fast-forwarded to where we found ourselves now, our relationship damaged beyond repair. Once I stopped crying, a couple of days later, I wrote Tyce a letter and sent it via snail mail to his parents' house:

Dearest Tyce,

Never in my life did I imagine we'd get a chance at love. That after all these years we'd reunite. That you would be my man. That I would be your girl. These past few months have meant everything to me, and I'm so heartbroken that things didn't turn out. I've never loved any man but you. That was the case when we were teenagers, and that's the case to this very day. I'll always love and adore you. We never got to be Bonnie and Clyde when we were young and mischievous, nor were we ever Clair and Cliff Huxtable when we finally became a couple. We were Tyce and Marnz – whatever that means, whatever it's worth. Two country kids who had a thing for each other. You were everything I wanted in a man – smart, hilarious, talented, creative, fun and so much more. Once we reconnected, I truly believed we'd be together forever, but God has other plans for us. I ask this favour of you – that you get the help you need so that your overwhelming positives outshine the negatives. You have such a warm heart, and I admire you so much for wanting to help others. But please help yourself first. You've got such a bright future ahead of you. I believe in you and always will.

Look after yourself, babe. Whether I hear back from you or you feel you'll heal better without me in your life, know that my thoughts are with you and you'll forever stay in my prayers. There'll always be a part of my heart that belongs to you.

Marnz

CHAPTER 35

Just As I Am

*I prefer to think of an ending as a new beginning,
where hope and endless possibilities converge.*

Muswellbrook. June, 2021. I was sitting on the Carringtons' verandah, as I had done so many times before, except there were two people missing, two people who would usually have joined us. Alongside me was Tyce's father, but Mrs Carrington had succumbed to terminal lung cancer a few years earlier. And Tyce? Well, at that moment he wasn't doing too well.

I'd returned to Muswellbrook with my mother – it was the first time we'd been back together since my break-up with Tyce. The town had changed. Serhan's and Pearly Shell were long gone. Best & Less was now on the other side of town. The Commonwealth Bank had swapped one side of the road for the other, and Matthews Jewellers had moved, replaced by yet another bank – Newcastle Permanent. There were now a few families of African descent in town. But so many other people I had grown up with had moved away. Few of Mum's old crew or mine remained. Amber Jones was one of the only people from school left to catch up with. Only ever a phone call away, it was great to see her in the flesh and reminisce on old times. The population had grown to about 15,000 by the time we left town in the early 2000s. It was now back down to 12,000. Things change, things stay the same.

Mum and I were staying at a hotel, and as an homage to home-comings, I went to a local liquor store and picked up a bottle of 19 Crimes Cali Red, from Snoop Dogg's own label. Described as 'defiant by nature, bold in character, and always uncompromising', I quietly hoped some of that had rubbed off on me over the years. And if not, it never hurt to have a drink with mum, now that I was comfortable with having one or two drinks every now and again, after thirteen years as a teetotaller.

Mum wasn't a big drinker, of course – just the occasional splash, but I looked forward to going back to the hotel later that afternoon for a glass of Snoop's finest. Mum had a funny quirk when it came to some rappers. She often referred to Jay-Z as 'my son'. She had a soft spot for Kanye. And, whether it was intentional or not, she had developed the cutest nickname for the Doggfather: 'Snoopy Doggy Doggy'.

'Tyce has been sleeping in my car,' Mr Carrington said. 'I told him he can't stay here while he's on drugs. He comes in for a shower, has a feed, but I won't let him stay here unless he's clean. I mean, he's over forty. People say I'm being cruel, but I'm actually being kind.'

I looked straight ahead. An awning had been put up where none had been before, shade from the sun and privacy from prying eyes.

'Tyce had so much going for him at school,' I said. 'He was so smart, funny, good-looking, talented. I mean, those are just some of the reasons I fell in love with him. He showed so much promise. So, how does he end up in and out of jail, while I end up at the ABC? Yes, he needs to take personal responsibility for his decisions, but this country isn't fair. I've had to deal with racism and injustice, but nowhere near what Tyce has had to face.'

Mr Carrington nodded in agreement. I went on. 'He was put away when he was so young. And once you're in the system, it's very hard to get out. What are the cops doing arresting kids anyway?'

'I know,' Mr Carrington said. 'Sometimes he says he thinks he's better off in jail – he's got a bed there, and food.'

I shook my head in sadness and disbelief. Jail had not been kind to Tyce – he had made that very clear to me. But there was still hope for his future, and I hadn't stopped praying for him. I believe God has his back. All it took was the faith of a mustard seed. And I knew I wasn't the only one who was on their knees. As my mother would say, 'Never say die till the bones are rotten.'

When I rejoined Mum back at the hotel, she'd made quite a dent in the 19 Crimes Snoop Dogg Cali Red, her Bible right beside her: 'This Snoopy Doggy Doggy wine is so good!' It was a moment that seemed to embody everything I'd been through: the same lips that danced with Scripture and hymns, now warm with wine. Songs of worship and praise sung with the same voice that occasionally spoke of life's hardships. Hip hop and hymns: the two would always go hand in hand for me. My life would always straddle both. The sacred and the profane, all living on the same block, all divine in the end.

Being back in Muswellbrook for a few days, there were so many memories left to sort through; the weight of the past and present hung heavy on me. But I had time: things move at a different pace in the country.

We drank our 19 Crimes from the disposable wine glasses I'd picked up at Woolies, and I was about to rise and head off to bed – if I needed anything at that moment it was to rest, and be rested – but Mum put out a hand, telling me to sit still. There was understanding in her eyes, her hard-earned wisdom.

'Mawunyo,' she said. 'Let's pray.'

Resources

If *Hip Hop & Hymns* has raised any issues for you, there is help at hand. If you want to learn more, get help, take action or donate, there are many Indigenous-led organisations at the forefront of social justice campaigns, some aimed at changing the age of criminal responsibility in Australia.

GET HELP
Australia

Lifeline

Lifeline is a non-profit organisation that provides free, 24-hour telephone crisis support service in Australia.

Phone: 13 11 14

Text: 0477 131 114

Headspace and Headspace Yarn Safe

Headspace is the National Youth Mental Health Foundation providing early-intervention mental health services to 12–25-year-olds. There is also mental health help available to Aboriginal and Torres Strait Islander people via Headspace Yarn Safe.
Phone: 1800 650 890

Kids Helpline
Available anytime, for any reason, to people aged 5–25 years of age
Phone: 1800 55 1800

Brother to Brother (men only)
Brother to Brother is a 24-hour hotline assisting Aboriginal men. The crisis number is 1800 435 799

NEW ZEALAND
Lifeline Aotearoa 24/7 Helpline: 0800 543 354

Lifeline Aotearoa Free Text
HELP (4357)

Suicide Crisis Helpline: 0508 828 865 (0508 TAUTOKO)

LEARN MORE, TAKE ACTION & DONATE
Incarceration Nation: Prisoners On Our Own Land
You can learn more by watching the documentary *Incarceration Nation* on SBS On Demand. *Incarceration Nation* gives voice to the strength of those who have been harmed by racism in the justice system. Visit the Incarceration Nation website: www.incarcerationnation.com.au

You can also make a tax deductible donation to the Documentary Australia Foundation to support the *Incarceration Nation* film impact campaign.

Change the Record
Take action or donate through Change the Record – Australia's only national Aboriginal led justice coalition of legal, health and family violence prevention experts.
https://www.changetherecord.org.au/

More Cultural Rehabs Less Jails: healing places for Indigenous peoples to start their healing journeys

Follow the Facebook page Jeff Amatto 'More Cultural Rehabs Less Jails' and connect with founder Jeffery Amatto on LinkedIn to find out more.
https://www.facebook.com/JeffAmatto
https://www.linkedin.com/in/jeffery-amatto-7110b9154

You can support the **Uluru Statement from the Heart** by visiting https://ulurustatement.org/

You can advocate for Indigenous rights by joining the campaigns of the following groups:

Amnesty International
ANTaR
Aust Human Rights Commission
Change the Record
Democracy in Colour

Justice Action
Justice Reform Initiative
National Justice Project

You can donate to the following Indigenous-led organisations by visiting their websites.

Aboriginal Legal Service NSW
Blackfella Way
CASSE
Deadly Connections
The Dhadjowa Foundation
Homes Not Prisons
Incarcerated Trans & Gender Diverse Community Fund
Just Reinvest programs in Moree and Mount Druitt
Murri Watch
NAAJA Northern Australian Aboriginal Justice Agency

There are so many First Nations frontline organisations doing incredible work in their local communities. Find and support one near you by going online and searching First Nations Community Organisations, and entering your State or Territory.

These resources were compiled with the help of Incarceration Nation filmmaker Dean Gibson and Clara Williams Roldan from Documentary Australia. My thanks for your assistance and the work that you do.

Acknowledgements

When I said I was writing a book called *Hip Hop & Hymns*, one of my friends asked me, 'Is that *hymns* or *hims*?' Okay, fine. It was more than one friend.

There are plenty of hims who've been influential in my life – the number one Him being God. Without Him, I wouldn't be here today. I thank God for His love, mercy and forgiveness.

My earthly father: love you, Dad. My brother Sedudzi, thank you for so generously sharing your music, even during those periods when we weren't on good terms. I love you with all my heart. My brother John – you've always been in my corner. Thanks for the laughs, and your affection. My 'twin' brother, Selassie. I can't wait till the day we finally meet in person. Your joyful soul makes my heart sing.

My publisher/editor at Penguin Random House, Brandon VanOver. You get me and this story in a way that's made writing it such an enjoyable experience. I already miss our weekly one-hour chats about *Hip Hop & Hymns* – and the correspondence in between. I could not have asked for a better editor. This book wouldn't be what it is without you.

My agent, Benython Oldfield, at Zeitgeist Agency, thank you for backing me from day one and for being a loud and consistent cheerleader for my work.

Tracy Williams – I'm so blessed to call you a friend. Your encouragement and Godly wisdom have kept me going at times when it would have been so much easier to give up. Thank you for the spiritual and emotional support you continue to provide, and for constantly reminding me why this book matters.

Joshua Yasserie – your cover illustration is next level, an incredible work of art. Thank you for agreeing to be part of this project. And thank you for delivering. Thanks also to Luke Causby for your cover design.

There are many, many hers in my corner too.

Mum, you are my sunshine. Thank you for giving me the greatest gift anyone could ever give to a human being – the gift of knowing God. Thank you for your love and support, and for being my biggest cheerleader.

And I have a lot of cheerleaders! Maia Christine Anu, you're my sister from another mister. Thank you for your support for *Hip Hop & Hymns* – you've been there since the beginning! Thanks for being in my corner and for being a loving, caring and fun friend. I love being around you. Your infectious warmth brings me great joy. Raquel Nieto Veiga, thank you for reading so many drafts! Your feedback meant so much to me. You encouraged me, helped wipe away my tears and shared in my elation. And what a great idea of yours to name each chapter after a hip hop song or hymn! Can't wait to return the favour with your books. I love you so much, my dear friend. My sister, Sophia, well obviously I didn't take your 'don't write the book' advice, but the constructive feedback you gave me on an early draft made all the difference and I really appreciate it. Thank you for making my manuscript the ninety-seventh book you read that year! Love you, sis.

Laura Carrington – sista, thank you so much for your love and support, for taking the time to read my manuscript, and for championing my work. Love you and the fam with all my heart.

April Clarkson, I'm so grateful to you for challenging me to dig deep when it came to providing a fair and accurate portrait of your brother.

My former bosses at ABC Radio Sydney who so generously let me have so much time off so I could write, and have been supportive and excited about this project from day one – Melanie Withnall, Jen Oldershaw and Elizabeth Green.

My gratitude to the Australia Council for the Arts for seeing the merit in this book and backing it. I couldn't have taken all that time off to write without the grant I was awarded, and I'm most grateful.

Special thanks also to Justin Ractliffe, and the team at Penguin Random House Australia, and those who read my work and cheered me on, gave their time to be interviewed, jogged my memory or kindly gave me their blessing: Chloe Bayliss, Richard Glover, Tracey Kirkland, Pamela Freeman, Lauren McWhirter, Philippa McDonald, Philippa Paull, Nicola Harrison, P. Frank Williams, Kymberlee Norsworthy, Fonda Jackson, Sherene Loh, Malik Dixon, George Green and Rod Quinn.

My sincere thanks also to Stan Grant, Brooke Boney, A.D. Carson, Rodney O and Janice Petersen.

To the people who make the music I love – thank you.

To you, the reader – thank you for going on this journey with me. I'm so grateful. It means more to me than you could imagine.

And to anyone else who has helped bring *Hip Hop & Hymns* to life – thank you so, so much.

Much love to my 'Day Ones': 'How Can I Keep From Singing?'

About the author

Mawunyo Gbogbo is a music and pop culture reporter for Double J and ABC News, and the author of *Hip Hop & Hymns*.

She has worked as a journalist for ABC NewsRadio; a features reporter and producer for ABC Radio Sydney; a segment producer for the *Today* show on the Nine Network; and an associate producer for *Insight* on SBS TV, where she won a United Nations Association of Australia Media Peace Award for Increasing Awareness and Understanding of Children's Rights and Issues.

Mawunyo has a Master of Arts in Creative Writing from the University of Technology Sydney, and a Bachelor of Arts (Communication – Journalism) from Charles Sturt University in Bathurst.

She was born in Ghana, raised in Muswellbrook in the NSW Hunter Valley, and now calls Sydney home.